The Mission and Ministry
of
Jesus

A THEOLOGY OF JESUS

Volume 1

The Mission and Ministry of Jesus

✝

Donald Goergen, O.P.

Michael Glazier
Wilmington, Delaware

First published in 1986 by Michael Glazier, Inc. 1935 West
Fourth Street, Wilmington, Delaware, 19805. ©1986 by Michael
Glazier, Inc. All rights reserved.
Library of Congress Catalog Card Number: 86-45321
International Standard Book Number: 0-89453-603-6
Typography by Dick Smith.
Printed in the United States of America.

To Mom and Dad

Table of Contents

Preface

Someone may well ask: another book on Jesus? Whether it be the needs of our times, or the needs of the Church, or my own needs I do not know. Perhaps it only shows how enigmatic a person Jesus truly is. He is someone by whom we have been grasped but whom we are not able to grasp in a definitive way once and for all.

"Who do you say that I am?" (Mk 8:29) is one of the most pointed theological questions ever asked, and it remains with us still. This series of five volumes is my own tentative response after fifteen years of thinking about it. Nor can I make any pretense of the project being final. I am quite aware that every section of this book could be a book in itself. Indeed, most of the topics discussed have already been the subject of many specialized studies. But at some point integration and synthesis are in order. We need to pause and say: This is how far we've come. Where do we go from here?

I see this theology of Jesus not unlike the description given by a philosophy professor of mine of a circus clown he had seen as a child. The clown was standing on his head, juggling. My professor's response was that he had seen better clowns, better acrobats, and better jugglers — but he had never seen all of them done together. For there are far better biblical scholars than I; indeed, professionally, I am not an exegete at all. There are also better Church historians; once again, I am not professionally a historian. And, likewise, there are better philosophers.

Yet the time comes when we must move beyond the securities of our specializations and risk putting the picture together. As a theologian, with a constructive bent, this is what I have tried to do. In doing so, if my picture brings some closer to faith, or closer to Christ Jesus, or makes some of our preaching of Christ more effective and substantive, then I will see this project as having been more than worthwhile. It is written for students, but also for preachers who are called upon both to know Christ and to proclaim him.

The first two of the five volumes in this series pertain to the first christological task as outlined in the following reflection on methodology. The first two volumes are an interpretation of the earthly Jesus. This volume concerns his life and mission, the next his death and resurrection.

In a project such as this, one is deeply indebted to more people than one can name. I shall mention only a few. For their critical reading of part or all of the manuscript of volume one and their suggestions, Frank Benz, Raymond Martin, Boyd Mather, and particularly Jerome Murphy-O'Connor. For their assistance in editing the manuscript, Jon Alexander, Diana Culbertson, Stanley Drongowski, Michael Mascari, Michael Monshau, Patrick Norris, Richard Peddicord and Priscilla Wood. For their assistance with typing, Margaret Bunkers, Mary Fitzgerald, Ruth Mary Gendrich and Frances Plass. For their consistent encouragement and support, in addition to many of the above, and in addition to many others, Jim Barnett, Linda Hansen, Carmelita Murphy, Jerry Stookey, Pat Walter and Ann Willits.

With respect to inclusive language, I have found particularly helpful suggestions in *The Handbook of Nonsexist Writing* by Casey Miller and Kate Swift (New York: Harper and Row, 1980); and in Gail Ramshaw Schmidt's "De Divinis Nominibus: The Gender of God," *Worship* 56 (1982), 117-31. Biblical quotations are ordinarily taken from the Revised Standard Version, unless otherwise indicated, and sometimes adjusted in favor of inclusive language as justified by the Greek text.

Introduction

A Reflection on Methodology

Reflections on methodology properly belong both at the beginning and at the end of a theological task. One must be methodologically conscious from the beginning. Yet method alone cannot be one's only guiding concern, lest understanding be restricted by a too pre-determined approach. Theology is both art and science; it draws upon both precise technical concepts and creative intuitions. In so far as an awareness of method may be of help in the beginning, my method in doing this Christology comprises four steps or "moments": (1) Jesus research, (2) historical retrieval, (3) hermeneutical re-construction, and (4) socio-ethical evaluation. Christology comprises all four tasks, although the third may be considered Christology proper.

The first task of any christologist is Jesus research.[1] The primary concern of Christology is Jesus as the one remembered by the Church and proclaimed as the Christ. During the past two centuries, we have become increasingly aware of the contribution of scientific historiography and literary

---

[1]This does not mean that the norm or basis for Christology is the Jesus of modern historical-critical exegesis (cf. David Tracy, *The Analogical Imagination, Christian Theology and the Culture of Pluralism* [New York: Crossroad, 1981], 233-41; 242, n 5; 300, n 97; 334, n 15). I am more in agreement with Tracy than I am in disagreement with him. I will reserve a more detailed discussion of this question until volume two, in which I discuss the Jesus of historiography and the Jesus of faith. Although Tracy's point is valid, my disagreement is in his continuing to identify terminologically the Jesus of history with the Jesus of historiography.

criticism to the study of Jesus. Thus Jesus research has taken a new and vital turn. Jesus research is not so much Christology proper as it is a prolegomenon to Christology — a necessary even if only preliminary moment in constructing a Christology. Nor is Jesus research to be conceived only in positivistic terms, for it involves hermeneutics and methodological decisions of its own. Jesus research itself manifests varied interpretations of Jesus and relies upon varied approaches to Jesus.

Jesus research need not require Christian faith on the part of the researcher; nor does it require the bracketing of that faith. What is required is a coherent interpretation of Jesus of Nazareth and a considered reflection on the historiographical data pertinent to Jesus. Even though valuing objectivity, Jesus research is not purely objective knowledge. The Judaism, Catholicism, or Protestantism of researchers like

Tracy's point is valid if one accepts his clear definition of the historical Jesus as the actual Jesus who lived *in so far as he is known or knowable today by way of empirical-historical methods*; namely, the Jesus of historiography (Tracy, *The Analogical Imagination*, 245, n 20). The Jesus who lies at the basis of Christology is the Jesus remembered by the Church (in this I am in agreement with Tracy), *but* the Jesus remembered by the Church *may* be the Jesus of history (if one does not reduce the Jesus of history to being the Jesus of historiography). One cannot predetermine the outcome of one's Jesus research. Nor is the relevance of the historiographical search for Jesus only that of keeping alive the dangerous and subversive memory of Jesus (Tracy, *The Analogical Imagination*, 239; 334, n 15). The historiographical search makes a real contribution to our understanding of the Jesus of faith (see volume two) and can also be seen as a part of the contemporary Church's process of remembering Jesus (see Elizabeth Johnson, "The Theological Relevance of the Historical Jesus: A Debate and a Thesis," *The Thomist* [January, 1984], 1-43). Tracy identifies Schillebeeckx as claiming to ground Christology in the historical Jesus. Yet Schillebeeckx's own "experiment" is presented as an effort to retrieve the Jesus of the early Christian movement; namely, the remembered Jesus, or the Jesus of faith. Schillebeeckx writes, "The truth is that no reconstruction of historical data about Jesus can show that he is the Christ" (*Interim Report on the Books Jesus and Christ* [New York: Crossroad, 1982], 27), and, "I am not, however, saying in any way that the picture of Jesus as reconstructed by historians becomes the norm and criterion of Christian faith. . . It is not the historical picture of Jesus but the living Jesus of history who stands at the beginning and is the source, norm and criterion of the interpretative experience which the first Christians had of him" (ibid., 33). One's interpretation of Jesus *in faith* cannot be divorced from the knowledge which comes *from historiography*, even though the Jesus of faith cannot be reduced to the Jesus of historiography. Jesus research remains a necessary prolegomenon to Christology even if it is not the norm or ground for Christology by itself alone.

Geza Vermes, Edward Schillebeeckx, and Joachim Jeremias are bound to contribute to their interpretative horizons.[2] Yet Jesus research and a coherent interpretation of Jesus of Nazareth remain necessary to doing Christology today.

Since the primary sources for a study of Jesus are biblical, the first task of Christology involves biblical exegesis and hermeneutics. I am professionally a systematic theologian and not an exegete, yet systematic theology cannot be separated from biblical research even if it is distinct from it. Christology can hardly avoid the Scriptures. This first task of Christology sets in relief Jesus in his historicality and in his humanity. Among Catholic authors, Edward Schillebeeckx stands out as one who has done extensive Jesus research before attempting further reflections on Christology as such.

The second task in constructing a Christology is historical retrieval. Before re-constructing Christology for our period of history, we must seek to understand the history of the interpretation of Jesus, the history of Christology itself. One searches Christian tradition,[3] as well as Hebrew and Christian Scriptures, to understand Jesus Christ more deeply, appropriately and adequately. One does Christology in the light of historical Christianity's understanding of Jesus Christ, no matter what one's evaluation, appropriation, or rejection of a particular historical expression of the Christian faith may be. David Tracy expresses it thus:

> Tradition is inevitably present through the language we use: a recognition of that presence can also occasion a recognition that every tradition is both pluralistic and ambiguous (i.e., enriching, liberating, and distorting).

[2]See Geza Vermes, *Jesus the Jew* (Philadelphia: Fortress Press, 1973); Edward Schillebeeckx, *Jesus, An Experiment in Christology*, trans. Hubert Hoskins (New York: Seabury, 1979); Joachim Jeremias, *New Testament Theology, the Proclamation of Jesus*, trans. John Bowden (New York: Charles Scribner's, 1971).

[3]The modern classic on the theology of tradition is Yves Congar's *Tradition and Traditions, An Historical and a Theological Essay*, trans. Michael Naseby and Thomas Rainborough (New York: The Macmillan Co, 1967).

The fact that every tradition is ambiguous need not become the occasion to reject the reality of tradition as enriching. Rather the need is to find modes of interpretation that can retrieve the genuine meaning and truth of the tradition ("hermeneutics of retrieval") as well as modes of interpretation that can uncover the errors and distortions in the tradition ("hermeneutics of critique and suspicion").[4]

The re-appropriation of the meaning and truth within Christian tradition constitutes a second moment and second prolegomenon in constructing a Christology. The first task is primarily biblical, exegetical, and hermeneutical; the second task is primarily historical, namely, research into the history of Christian traditions. This historical research cannot be separated from hermeneutics either, for historical analysis is a hermeneutics of the christological tradition. To move from a biblical interpretation of Jesus to a contemporary re-interpretation of Jesus without a conscious dialogue with "the Jesus of Christian history" is to ignore the full implications of our modern historical consciousness, which necessitates an awareness not only of the historicality of Jesus but also of a history to Christology itself — Christology in search of its roots, the Jesus of Christian history as well as the Jesus of the New Testament. This second task of Christology sets in relief Jesus in his divinity and perduring significance. Aloys Grillmeier stands out as one among many who has done extensive historical research for the

[4]David Tracy, *The Analogical Imagination,* 146 n.80. Also see his *Blessed Rage for Order* (New York: Seabury Press, 1975), 3-21, 49-52, 72-79, 237-40 for further reflections on hermeneutics, retrieval, and tradition. Tracy's discussion of "criteria of appropriateness" is particularly relevant to the task of historical retrieval; see *Blessed Rage,* 28-29, 72-79. Bernard Lonergan's reflections on method are also apropos here; *Method in Theology* (New York: Herder and Herder, 1972), esp. 125-45 on the eight functional specialties, 153-73 on interpretation and hermeneutics, and 175-234 on history. Lonergan's first two functional specialties (research and interpretation) are both clearly involved in what I have called the first task of Christology — Jesus research. The first four functional specialties (research, interpretation, history and dialectic) are involved in the second task — historical retrieval.

sake of retrieving the meaning and truth in the Christian tradition.[5]

Our third task is a hermeneutical re-construction, or the construction of a Christology proper, an interpretation of the Christ-event in the light of contemporary consciousness. After encountering the historical and biblical Jesus as well as historical Christianity's continuing re-interpretations of Jesus, Christology seeks to construct an appropriate, coherent, and relatively adequate theology of Jesus Christ for our period of history, a theology which allows the Christ-event to be salvific for us, able to be experienced once again.[6] Christology must be both rooted (Jesus research and historical retrieval) and communicative (establishing a relationship to its world, our world). Christology proper, as a hermeneutical re-construction, seeks to bridge the gap between Christian history (Scripture and Tradition) and our contemporary, post-modern horizon.

Hermeneutics is involved in all of the first three christological tasks. Granted that there are different hermeneutical or interpretative principles involved depending upon whether one is talking about the hermeneutics of biblical statements, or the hermeneutics of conciliar, dogmatic, and historical statements, or the hermeneutics of constructing theology in the light of contemporary consciousness and experience. In all of these, however, hermeneutics involves an inquiry into how we understand historical materials and theological statements as well as an inquiry into their epistemological presuppositions.

Whereas exegesis and historical research are specific steps in the first two christological tasks, the results of these first

---

[5]Aloys Grillmeier, *Christ in Christian Tradition*, vol. 1, *From the Apostolic Age to Chalcedon (451)*, trans. John Bowden, second, revised edition (London: Mowbrys, 1975).

[6]Note David Tracy's criteria of adequacy, appropriateness, and intelligibility; *Blessed Rage for Order*, 28-29, 64-87; *The Analogical Imagination*, 238. Appropriateness refers to one's hermeneutics of the tradition; intelligibility refers to the coherence of the tradition's present self-understanding; adequacy refers to the horizon of common human experience. See also Schubert M. Ogden, "What is Theology?" *Journal of Religion* 52 (1972), 22-40.

two tasks along with philosophical reflection[7] and critical
reflection on one's own human experience are the primary
resources in the task of re-construction. The systematic
theologian, of course, cannot professionally be exegete,
historian, and philosopher all at once; yet, to some degree,
he or she must feel somewhat at home in those worlds to
perform his or her systematic theological task of re-
construction. A systematic theologian is concerned with the
historical Christian past (consider David Tracy's criteria of
appropriateness), with the inner coherence of his or her
re-construction (Tracy's criteria of intelligibility), and with
common human experience and the contemporary consciousness (Tracy's criteria of adequacy). Systematic theology seeks to be both intelligent (a philosophical, reflective,
and critical moment) and relevant (a creative, imaginative,
intuitive moment).[8] One is reminded of Alfred North Whitehead's description of speculative philosophy: "The true
method of discovery is like the flight of an aeroplane. It
starts from the ground of particular observation; it makes a
flight in the thin air of imaginative generalization; and it
again lands for renewed observation rendered acute by
rational interpretation."[9]

The first two tasks of Christology must be held in balance
with the third, and yet all three tasks are distinguishable.
There can be no radical break between biblical/historical
and constructive/systematic theological efforts. Bernard
Lonergan exemplifies such a balance when indicating two
inter-connected moments or levels in the critical study of
history: "In the first instance one is coming to understand
one's sources. In the second instance one is using one's
understood sources intelligently to come to understand the

[7]An illuminating article on this point is Fergus Kerr's "The Need for Philosophy
in Theology Today," *New Blackfriars* (June, 1984), 248-60.

[8]The word *relevant* has its advantages and disadvantages. See Tracy, *Blessed
Rage for Order*, 16, n 12; and 177.

[9]Alfred North Whitehead, *Process and Reality*, ed. David Ray Griffin and
Donald W. Sherburne, corrected edition (New York: Macmillan Co., 1978), 5, also
pp. 3-17; *The Function of Reason* (Boston: Beacon Press, 1958); and *Modes of
Thought* (New York: Macmillan Co., 1938).

object to which they are relevant."[10] The first two tasks of Christology have primarily to do with Scripture and Tradition as sources. In the third task one is using those sources in the light of a contemporary horizon to construct an intelligent and relatively adequate Christology for our day. There is both a "given" moment (the first two tasks of Christology done in the light of biblical hermeneutics and the hermeneutics of the traditions) and a "constructive" moment (the third task done in the light of critical philosophy and the hermeneutics of experience). Lonergan, defining systematics, argues that "the aim of systematics is not to increase certitude but to promote understanding," and also that "the understanding to be reached is to be on the level of one's times."[11]

At the same time that the more historical moments (the first two tasks) and the constructive moment (task three) must be held together as interdependent, they can still be distinguished. It is as if we are looking at the Christ-event with two eyes, with one eye on the past — Jesus research and historical retrieval, and a second eye on the present which seeks to re-present this selfsame Jesus in the light of a contemporary conceptual and experiential framework — hermeneutical re-construction. This third task of Christology, re-construction, constitutes Christology properly speaking. The constructive theologian seeks an interpretation of Jesus Christ which is biblically and historically appropriate, philosophically and rationally coherent, as well as experientially and socially relevant. "Systematic theologians cannot simply repeat; they must critically interpret the tradition mediating the event."[12]

---

[10]Lonergan, *Method in Theology*, 189.

[11]Ibid., 336 for the first part of the quotation, 350 for the second part; see 335-53 for his discussion of systematics.

[12]Tracy, *The Analogical Imagination*, 405. For David Tracy's suggestions for a revisionist model of theology, see *Blessed Rage for Order*, 32-34, 43-63. Tracy's revisionist suggestions recognize the value of complementarity, of thinking in terms of both/and. The first two models of theology which he explicates tend toward *either* tradition (orthodox theology) *or* modernity (liberal theology). The next two models affirm radically *either* God (neo-orthodoxy) *or* the world (radical

The third task of Christology attempts to relate two poles
of Jesus' existence, his humanity and divinity; as well as the
events of Jesus' life, death and resurrection; along with an
attempt to understand the pre-historical, historical, and
post-historical or eschatological stages of his existence. Just
as Schillebeeckx and Grillmeier among contemporary
Catholic theologians exemplify the first two tasks of Christology, so Piet Schoonenberg has provided a masterful
effort at re-construction.[13]

The fourth task in constructing a Christology is socio-
ethical reflection. One must evaluate his or her reconstruction in the light of its socio-political and ethical
implications. This is the moment of searching for the implications, of explicitly relating theology to praxis. It can be

secularism). Revisionism, rooted in correlation, is a critical reformulation of both
sides of the polarity. For thinking in terms of both/and, see Donald Goergen, *The
Power of Love, Christian Spirituality and Theology* (Chicago: Thomas More
Press, 1979), 268-80.

My major disagreement with Tracy in *Blessed Rage for Order* is over whether
the Christian systematic theologian need be in principle a believer (see 7; 18, n 35;
36, n 16; 57, n 3; 80). I maintain that the theologian qua theologian is in principle as
well as in fact a believer. This is especially true of the systematic theologian,
perhaps less so for the fundamental theologian, although in that case I would speak
of a philosopher or historian of religion. In *Analogical Imagination* Tracy modifies or nuances his opinion significantly, yet still maintains that "in principle" the
theologian need not be a believer (183 n 26; 398-99, n 7).

My major disagreement with *The Analogical Imagination* is with Tracy's understanding of systematic (or constructive) theology, specifically his suggestion that
the public "church" is the primary public of systematics, with academy and society
as secondary. Tracy's emphasis on the public character of theology and his
delineation of the three publics is significant and helpful (3-46); so is his delineating
of the three theological disciplines, fundamental, systematic, and practical theology. My disagreement is in his attempt to relate the three disciplines to the three
publics (54-79). To me, it doesn't seem to work; it is forced. It seems to work better
for fundamental theology than it does for systematic theology.

Tracy suggests that a theologian "will ordinarily be related to one primary public
and secondarily to the other two" (52). This is perhaps true in fact, but not in
principle, perhaps true for the theologian as a human and individual being, but not
for the systematic theologian qua theologian. Systematic theology, and Christology as systematic or constructive theology, is concerned with all three publics; it
must be professionally, confessionally, and socially responsible. It also articulates
a *personal* faith (see p. 6) but not a private one.

[13]See especially Piet Schoonenberg, *The Christ*, trans. Della Couling (New
York: Seabury Press, 1971).

argued that this task should come earlier in the process of theological re-construction, or by others that it is not an essential christological task at all. Yet socio-ethical reflection is necessary to Christology, and it need not necessarily precede the task of hermeneutical re-construction.

An evaluation of the hermeneutical re-construction in the light of its social and moral implications is as necessary to Christology as it is for theology in general, in order to prevent Christology from being ideology.[14] How does one know that one's Christology is truly *theology* and not simply *ideology*? Christology must be socially and morally responsible. Our choice is not between reflecting on the socio-ethical implications of Christology or not, but between a conscious explicitation of those implications or allowing the operative implications to remain unconscious or unarticulated. The consequences of a theology are part of the theology itself. Any Christology which makes claims to objectivity, or relies on biblical and/or historical sources, must still accept its social implications. No theology can be apolitical unless one consciously desires to make it socially irrelevant in the practical sphere — but even then it has its consequences. All theology supports some kind of praxis.[15]

David Tracy has made us aware of both the social character of a theologian and the public character of theology.[16]

---

[14]See Johann Baptist Metz, *Faith in History and Society: Toward a Practical Fundamental Theology* (New York: Crossroad, 1979); Juan Luis Segundo, *The Liberation of Theology*, trans. John Drury (Maryknoll: Orbis Books, 1976); Martin Seliger, *The Marxist Conception of Ideology: A Critical Essay* (New York: Cambridge University Press, 1977).

[15]Orthopraxis is a major theme in the recent writings of Schillebeeckx. Also see David Tracy, *Blessed Rage for Order*, 237-58; *The Analogical Imagination*, 69-82, 390-98, for his early reflections on praxis and theology; as well as his forthcoming third volume in his trilogy which intends to deal with practical theology. Also, of course, the liberation theologians, e.g., *Frontiers of Theology in Latin America*, ed. Rosina Gibellini, trans. John Drury (Maryknoll: Orbis Books, 1979); and Alfred T. Hennelly, *Theologies in Conflict, The Challenge of Juan Luis Segundo* (Maryknoll: Orbis Books, 1979). Also see the *Proceedings of the Catholic Theological Society of America*, vol. 30 (1975), 1-29 (Baum), 49-61 (O'Meara), 63-110 (Fiorenza); and vol. 32 (1977), 1-16 (Lonergan), 125-41 (Shea), and 142-77 (Fiorenza).

[16]Tracy, *The Analogical Imagination*, esp. 3-46.

Theology is and ought to be public discourse, conscious of three publics that form the social matrix of theology: academy, Church, and society. Indeed, theology must be professionally, confessionally, and socially responsible. The fourth christological task is primarily concerned with this social responsibility.

The social context of a contemporary theologian in the United States is a particular social, political, economic, and religious reality. These provide social facts from which one's social analysis begins in order to draw out the implications of one's Christology and thus in turn evaluate it. For example, no christologist in the United States can read the parable of the rich person and Lazarus (Lk 15:19-31) with any social and global awareness without realizing that the majority of people (God's people) in our world understandably and easily identify North Americans as the rich person. What are the implications of our Christology for this social reality — whether we see ourselves as individually responsible or not?

The relationship between Christology and social analysis involves *mutual* critique and something of a hermeneutical circle. Social awareness may cause us to revise our Christology, and vice-versa. Every social fact has the potential of raising questions. For example, American religious pluralism asks us how our Christology interprets non-Christian religious experience. What are the implications of our Christology for other religious traditions? I repeat that there is a dialectical movement between the first three tasks and this fourth task, which suggests that Christology is an ongoing process, never a definitive and closed system, but rather always in search of a more adequate way of expressing itself. This is partly why it is not essential that this fourth task come first, as long as it is taken seriously. The fourth task not only evaluates the prior re-construction but also provides the horizon for further re-construction.[17]

[17]I am aware of criticism of my position coming from two different perspectives. There are those who deny that theology and social analysis belong together. With these I am in complete disagreement. Others give the social analysis a position of

Christology itself benefits from a pluralism of approaches. An explicitly feminist or liberation Christology may insist that the task of social analysis come earlier in the christological process, that Christology be done in the light of a prior social analysis. There is no denying that the christologist or theologian as a human and social being has social and political views. It is in this sense that one is involved in a hermeneutical circle. One's socio-ethical values are with one from the beginning. The question is when in the christological process to reflect explicitly on the social dimension of Christology. One can do theology from the perspective of an explicit socio-political stance, in which case this fourth task would come earlier, probably first in the process; but one can also do Christology as focused first on Scripture, tradition, re-construction, and then clarify what one has done thus far in the light of a social analysis —leaving one's earlier work open for revision. In other words, what is demanded is not that a particular theologian opt for a particular social stance from the beginning, but that a particular theologian be held socially and morally accountable for his or her theology. A theologian is required to reflect socially as well as biblically, historically, and philosophically.

priority in theology. Here I simply argue that social analysis need not necessarily come first among the tasks a theologian is called upon to perform, that there is a dialectic that does give the social analysis a central and essential role, and that a plurality of approaches is to the benefit of Christology rather than a disservice. I am sympathetic to the caution of Joe Holland and Peter Henriot, *Social Analysis, Linking Faith and Justice*, revised edition (Maryknoll, New York: Orbis Books, 1983, in collaboration with the Center for Concern, Washington, D.C.), 93, "To be frank, the theological reflection we need is difficult to find in North America. Or perhaps it is more correct to say that theologians who are reflecting in this way are not yet numerous or prominent. Most theologians who are concerned with social justice practice theological methods that do not begin with social analysis." Two helpful and succinct essays on social analysis by a South African theologian are those by Albert Nolan, in *Justice and Truth Shall Meet*, Conference Proceedings (Oak Park, Illinois: Parable Conference for Dominican Life and Mission, 1984), 38-44, 62-73. Also important to the continuing reflection on the task of theology is Vincent Cosmao, *Changing the World, an Agenda for the Churches*, trans. John Drury (Maryknoll, New York: Orbis Books, 1984), esp. the concluding thesis, 107-9, "The role of theology is to render an account of the praxis of the faith."

Third world christologists like Leonardo Boff, Albert Nolan, and Jon Sobrino exemplify this social responsibility and task. The difference between my approach and that of an explicitly liberation Christology is over where one situates this task of explicit social conscientisation vis-a-vis our world. To do social reflection first has the disadvantage of limiting one's theology to those who have already undergone a particular social conversion rather than bringing one to a social consciousness on the basis of an interpretation of the Gospel and the Christian tradition. Both approaches are valid, and the two contrasting approaches can provide a mutual and desirable critique of each other. They can complement each other.

Not all the implications of a particular Christology are socio-ethical; some are explicitly religious in other ways. Christology must articulate these soteriological, anthropological, pneumatological, ecclesiological, and eschatological implications as well. My major point is that there are four moments in the christological process, four tasks: Jesus research, historical retrieval, hermeneutical reconstruction, and explicating the implications. In this particular series, volumes one and two are concerned with the first christological task, volume three with the second, volume four with the third, and volume five with the fourth. Christology is systematic theology done by a believer; who seeks to articulate a personal faith through public discourse; who seeks to be professionally, confessionally, and socially responsible; who does not ground the theology of Jesus on the Jesus of historiography alone; and who attempts a hermeneutical re-construction of who Jesus Christ is for us today.

Part One
One of Us

1

Christology: An Invitation To An Encounter

In every generation the good news of God's salvation needs to be proclaimed. It also needs to be reshaped for different periods of history, different cultures, and different generations. It includes the story of Jesus of Nazareth.

We can tell Jesus' story by beginning with the Eternal Word; or by beginning with Jesus of Nazareth, this same Word enfleshed in the history of Judaism, this Word as Incarnate; or by telling our own stories and how we have come to follow Jesus and be his disciples. Many ways of telling the story are possible, as long as they effectively proclaim the message of God's salvation. In taking up the task of proclaiming that message once again, in my own fashion, I begin with Jesus of Nazareth, the man Jesus who was one of us. Perhaps it is difficult for us at times to believe in Jesus' humanity and it takes faith to affirm it. Sometimes it is easier to focus solely on his divinity or not to believe in him at all. For many these appear to be the only choices: to picture him either as an Exalted One far removed from us or as one who has nothing to offer us. We must therefore first make some connection with him. This connection is our common humanity or common human condition.

An imaginative approach to Jesus as human is Nikos

Kazantzakis' *Last Temptation of Christ* (1951).[1] The book should not be read for accurate historical details; it is fiction. However, fiction has a great capacity to penetrate and present truth. While Kazantzakis' novel itself must be judged in terms of its art, its Christ must be evaluated in terms of the criterion Kazantazkis set for himself: "This book was written because I wanted to offer a supreme model to the person who struggles."[2] Who was Jesus of Nazareth for Kazantzakis? One who struggles. There may be more to Jesus' story than this, but this is essential to the story. Kazantzakis wrote, "We struggle, we see him struggle also, and we find strength. We see that we are not all alone in the world: he is fighting at our side."[3] A Jesus who struggles as we do is not far removed from the biblical presentation in the *Epistle to the Hebrews.*

The Compassionate One

The *Epistle to the Hebrews* presents a sophisticated Christology centered on the sacrifice of Christ. Jesus is presented as priest according to the order of Melchizedek

---

[1]Nikos Kazantzakis, *The Last Temptation of Christ*, trans. P. A. Bien (New York: Simon and Schuster, 1960), written 1950-51. The central continuing struggle for Jesus in Kazantzakis' *Last Temptation* is that with the flesh, embodied for Jesus in Mary Magdalene. It is not the accuracy or inaccuracy of this particular struggle, however, which is important, but the fact of Jesus' human struggle in general. There were many and varied influences in Kazantzakis' own life: Christianity, Buddhism, communism, Nietzsche, Bergson, the struggle for the liberation of Crete, to name only a few. Kazantzakis was born in Herakleion, Crete, in 1883, at which time Crete was struggling for freedom from the Turks. He was later taught by Franciscans, studied law in Athens, and studied philosophy in Paris. He died of leukemia in 1957. For further reading on Kazantzakis, consider: Samuel C. Calian, "Kazantzakis: Prophet of Non-Hope," *Theology Today* 28 (1971), 37-49; Richard Chilson, "The Christ of Nikos Kazantzakis," *Thought* 47 *(1972),* 69-89; Helen Kazantzakis, *Nikos Kazantzakis, A Biography Based in His Letters* (New York: Simon and Schuster, 1968); James Lea, *Kazantzakis — The Politics of Salvation* (University, Alabama: The University of Alabama Press, 1979), which also provides an up-to-date bibliography; Pandelis Prevelakis, *Nikos Kazantzakis and His Odyssey* (New York: Simon and Schuster, 1961).

[2]*The Last Temptation of Christ*, 4.

[3]Ibid., 3.

(Ps 110), superseding the Levitical priesthood. The author prepares the way for Jesus' priesthood by showing that Jesus, as mediator, is higher than the angels and superior to Moses. The literary form of *Hebrews* is not so much that of a letter as it is that of a homily.[4] We do not know to whom this homiletic exhortation is being given, but there is evidence to suggest a Jewish Christian community familiar with Jewish institutions and traditions. Although the present title, "To the Hebrews," was not included until the third or fourth centuries, it does reflect the content and context of the homily.

We do not know who the author is either. It is generally agreed today that it is not Paul. The attribution of authorship to Paul goes back to Clement of Alexandria, yet Origen later described the author as "only God knows." The date of *Hebrews* is also a problem. Although many have favored a post — 70 C. E. dating, there are more and more who argue convincingly for a date prior to 70 C.E.[5] There is no reference in the homily to the destruction of the Temple in 70 C.E., and this silence may suggest that it had not yet taken place.

We find our christological starting point in Hebrews 4:15 which points us to Jesus' compassion and mercy.

> [14]Since then we have a great high priest who has passed through the heavens, Jesus, the Son of God, let us hold fast our confession. [15]For we have not a high priest who is unable to sympathize with our weaknesses, but one who in every respect has been tempted as we are, yet without sin.[16] Let us then with confidence draw near to the throne of grace, that we may receive mercy and find grace to help in time of need.
>
> [1]For every high priest chosen from among us is appointed to act on our behalf in relation to God, to offer

[4]See George Wesley Buchanan, *To the Hebrews*, The Anchor Bible, vol. 36 (Garden City, New York: Doubleday and Co. 1972), esp. 246-68.

[5]See George Wesley Buchanan, H. W. Montefiore, J. A. T. Robinson, and C. Spicq.

gifts and sacrifices for sin. [2]He can deal gently with the
ignorant and wayward, since he himself is beset with
weakness. [3]Because of this he is bound to offer sacrifice
for his own sins as well as for those of the people. [4]And
one does not take the honor upon himself, but he is called
by God, just as Aaron was.

[5]So also Christ did not exalt himself to be made a high
priest, but was appointed by him who said to him,
"Thou art my Son.
today I have begotten thee";
[6]as he says also in another place,
"Thou art a priest for ever,
after the order of Melchizedek."

[7]In the days of his flesh, Jesus offered up prayers and
supplications, with loud cries and tears, to him who was
able to save him from death, and he was heard for his
godly fear. [8]Although he was a Son, he learned obedience
through what he suffered; [9]and being made perfect he
became the source of eternal salvation to all who obey
him, [10]being designated by God a high priest after the
order of Melchizedek. (Heb 4:14-5:10)

The theology of *Hebrews* presents Jesus as a priest. What
must be kept in mind, however, is that as priest Jesus feels
sympathy with our weaknesses because he too was tempted,
struggled, searched in every way that we do. The human
condition and its struggle was not foreign to him. Yet in
pointing to this full participation in our humanness, he still
cannot be called a sinner in the way that we are sinners.
Nevertheless, his identity with us is complete and we can be
assured of his understanding.

While the assertion that Jesus is our high priest may seem
to remove Jesus from our midst, the text attempts to prevent
the implication that his priesthood separates him from us.
The first verses of chapter five make this clear. What the
author of *Hebrews* means by this declaration of Jesus as
priest must be clarified. The theology of the homily quickly

points out that a priest is no different from the rest of us except by function. Every priest is "from among the people," "weak in many ways," and offers sacrifice "also for his own sins." Thus there is a solidarity between the priest and other human beings.

The priest is one of us, but one of us who acts on our behalf in our relations with God. One does not choose this function of one's own accord but is called by God. There are two emphases in the text: identity or sympathy with others and a divine calling. But the call does not make the one called any less one of us. *Hebrews* describes Jesus as supreme high priest, and also as Son of God. However, this does not remove Jesus from the world of human suffering. The author makes it quite clear: "Although he was a Son, he learned obedience through what he suffered" (5:8).

One can also make this point by reference to the priesthood of all believers from the *First Epistle of Peter*, 2:9-10.

> But you are a chosen race, a royal priesthood, a holy nation, God's own people, that you may declare the wonderful deeds of him who called you out of darkness into his marvelous light. Once you were no people but now you are God's people; once you had not received mercy but now you have received mercy.

We are all priests. What is affirmed of Jesus is also affirmed in some way of all of us. The priesthood of Jesus does not make him different from us. Jesus is the supreme high priest, but we are all priests. Jesus is the supreme exemplification of a kind of priesthood which is manifest elsewhere as well.

The complete and utter humanness of Jesus is central to the message of *Hebrews* because it guarantees the mercy which will be shown us. How can we be sure, as we face judgment, that "there is grace," or that in time of need "we will receive mercy"? Because Jesus, God's own Son, knows what it is like, knows the human drama from the inside out, knows the immense difficulty of the human life and struggle.

Hence, he cannot but sympathize with us when we stand before him. As H. W. Montefiore says, "He sympathizes because he has, through common experience, a real kinship with those who suffer."[6]

The point can be well made if we stay close to the Greek text of 4:15. "For we do not have a high priest (*ou gar ekhomen arkhierea*) who is not able to feel sympathy (*mē dunamenon sumpathēsai*) with our weaknesses (*tais astheneiais hēmōn*), but rather one who has been put to the test (*pepeirasmenon de*) in all ways (*kata panta*), in a fashion similar to us except for sin (*kath homoiotēta khōris hamartias*)." How can the heavenly priest, Jesus, sitting in the presence of God, be interested in our trials and sorrows? Because he has experienced them himself. "Well is he able to sympathize, just as a doctor who many times has been sick (*Bene potest compati, sicut medicus qui pluries fuit infirmus*)" (Hugh of St. Cher). *Pepeirasmenon* is in the perfect tense and thus indicates not simply a single event (Mt 4:1-11) but something continuing throughout Jesus' life (Lk 22:28). *Peirazō* means to tempt or test. But its meaning can best be brought out by a "put to the test" translation.[7] This calls to mind the context of the Israelite experience of being put to the test in the wilderness. The author makes the identity between the struggle of Jesus and ours so strong, Ceslaus Spicq observes, that he quickly includes a qualification, namely the area of sin.[8]

Our discussion thus far helps us to delineate an important christological and methodological principle. A proper understanding of priesthood and of Jesus does not remove

---

[6]H. W. Montefiore, *The Epistle to the Hebrews,* Black's New Testament Commentaries (London: A. and C. Black, 1964), 91.

[7]Cf., Joachim Jeremias, *New Testament Theology, the Proclamation of Jesus,* trans. John Bowden (New York: Charles Scribner's Sons, 1971), 74-75.

[8]Ceslaus Spicq, *L'Epitre aux Hebreux,* Etudes bibliques, vol. 2 (Paris: J. Gabalda et Cie, 1953), 93. The "sinlessness" of Jesus is something to be discussed in volume four of this series.

either of them from human experience. But how do we come to a proper understanding of priesthood? The answer is —through a reflection on the life and death of Jesus and through an encounter with him. We come to a knowledge of priesthood by understanding Jesus, and not vice-versa. A pre-conceived theology or pre-understanding of priesthood does not help us to elucidate the mystery of Jesus. Rather Jesus helps us to elaborate a true understanding of priest-hood. Jesus is our starting point, not any previous even if highly sophisticated prior conceptions. The failure to realize this methodological principle has grave consequences. It prevents Jesus from challenging our preconceived universe.

This then is how the author of *Hebrews* proceeds. We have a high priest who is in the very presence of God, namely Jesus. Hence, in the very presence of God, we have one who sympathizes with our weaknesses and who has been tried in every way that we are. Thus we can be confident that mercy will be ours. Yet, lest there be any confusion in speaking of Jesus as priest as if this might remove him in some way from an identity with us, the author quickly clarifies what an authentic understanding of priesthood is. A priest is from among the people, weak in many ways, gentle, one whose function is to serve God on behalf of the people and offer sacrifice for sin. This function does not make a priest less than one of us, but rather a mediator for us. So Jesus is like us in every way, yet one chosen from among us to act on our behalf in our relations with God, but still one of us. Hebrews 4:14-5:10 is simply an elaboration of the same point made earlier in 2:17-18 — "Therefore he had to be made like his brothers and sisters in every respect, so that he might become a merciful and faithful high priest in the service of God, to make expiation for the sins of the people. For because he himself has suffered and been tempted, he is able to help those who are tempted." This theology of Jesus as compassionate seems to re-present accurately the historical Jesus of Nazareth whose life was full of compassion (Mt 11:28-30; 14:14; 15:32; Lk 6:36).

A Strong "No" to Docetism

If our starting point in Christology includes the conscious affirmation of Jesus' real humanity and compassion, as so clearly stated in *Hebrews*, then we must also in the beginning clearly resist docetism, the tendency to deny full reality to the humanness of Jesus. Although heretical, docetism was never a specific heresy associated only with one individual, movement, or era in the life of the Church. Rather it manifested itself in various forms and in varied heresies and was especially prominent among Christian Gnostics of the second and third centuries. The docetic tendency seriously impairs any doctrine of Incarnation and denies the reality of Jesus' bodiliness as well as the reality of his sufferings. Jesus did not fully participate but only seemed to enter into the fleshly, historical and material realm. The word relates to the Greek *dokein*, which means "to appear" or "to seem." The docetists or "seemists" maintained that Jesus only appeared to have or seemed to have a bodily and earthly existence but was essentially a divine being. Some denied only the reality of his death which they say he miraculously escaped, Judas Iscariot or Simon of Cyrene having taken his place. One cannot determine with certitude the roots of this view. Some point to the tendency in the Hellenistic world to view the material world itself as evil, as in Manicheism for example.

Serapion, the eighth bishop of Antioch (died c. 211 C.E.), was the first to use the word *docetists* to describe Christians of this perspective. Its early presence was manifest by the need to refute it on the part of an even earlier bishop of Antioch, Ignatius (c. 35-110 C.E.).

> And so, be deaf when anyone speaks to you apart from Jesus Christ, who was of the race of David, the Son of Mary, who was truly born and ate and drank, who was truly persecuted under Pontius Pilate and was really crucified and died in the sight of those 'in heaven and on earth and under the earth' (Phil 1:10). Moreover he was truly raised from the dead by the power of His Father; in

like manner His Father, through Jesus Christ, will raise up those of us who believe in Him. Apart from Him we have no true life.

If, as some say who are godless in the sense that they are without faith, He merely seemed to suffer — it is they themselves who merely seem to exist — why am I in chains? And why do I pray that I may be thrown to the wild beasts? I die then, to no purpose. I do but bear false witness against the Lord.[9]

One of the more challenging and complex docetic threats to early Christianity was Gnosticism. The major sources for our knowledge of the Gnostics are patristic writings which refute them, such as those of Irenaeus,[10] and in the nineteenth and twentieth centuries Coptic versions of some of the Gnostic writings themselves. In 1945 the discovery of the Nag Hammadi Library in Egypt gave us fifty-two Gnostic treatises, forty new ones if we subtract duplications and those which were previously extant.[11] This discovery has affected Gnostic studies to the same extent that the discovery of the Qumran scrolls affected Jewish studies.

The word *gnosis* itself means knowledge and refers to saving knowledge. As such there is a completely orthodox sense in which one can speak of Christian gnosis.[12] That such a distinction can be made is obvious from the title of Irenaeus' major work, usually called *Adversus Haereses*, but which bears the actual title, "The Detection and Over-

[9]Ignatius of Antioch, "To the Trallians," trans. G. Walsh, *The Fathers of the Church*, vol. 1 (New York: Christian Heritage, 1947), 104-5 (par. 9-10).

[10]Irenaeus, "Against Heresies," *The Ante-Nicene Fathers*, vol. 1 (Grand Rapids: Wm. B. Eerdmans Co., 1885), 309-578. Also see John Lawson, *The Biblical Theology of Saint Irenaeus* (London: Epworth Press, 1948).

[11]For further reference to the Nag Hammadi materials, see James M. Robinson, "The Jung Codex: The Rise and Fall of a Monopoly," *Religious Studies Review* 3 (1977), 17-30; and James M. Robinson, editor, *The Nag Hammadi Library* (New York: Harper and Row, 1977).

[12]See Louis Bouyer, *The Spirituality of the New Testament and the Fathers*, trans. Mary Ryan, History of Christian Spirituality, vol. 1 (New York: Desclee Co., 1963), 211-75.

throw of the So-Called False Knowledge." Gnosticism, in
the strictest sense, refers to a heretical Christian movement
of the second century. Yet, as a movement, it is difficult to
confine. Although many attempts have been made to pinpoint the origins of Gnosticism, it is best to remain open to a
variety of ingredients: apocalypticism, mystical and sectarian Judaism, late Hellenistic philosophy, heterodox Christianity, Zoroastrian and perhaps even Indian religion.

The simplest approach to understanding this milieu in
which Christianity developed during the second and third
centuries is to mention characteristics which many or most
of the so-called Gnostics had in common.

> The basic elements common to them all are (1) a distinc-
> tion between the unknown and transcendent true God on
> the one hand and the Demiurge or creator of the world on
> the other, the latter being commonly identified with the
> God of the Old Testament; (2) the belief that man in his
> true nature is essentially akin to the divine, a spark of
> their heavenly light imprisoned in a material body and
> subjected in this world to the dominance of the Demiurge
> and his powers; (3) a myth narrating some kind of pre-
> mundane fall, to account for man's present state and his
> yearning for deliverance; and (4) the means, the saving
> *gnosis,* by which that deliverance is effected and man
> awakened to the consciousness of his own true nature and
> heavenly origin.[13]

Gnosticism incorporates a belief in a saving knowledge,
often secret knowledge, or knowledge incomprehensible to
those insufficiently spiritual. Many Gnostic systems speak
of three classes of people: the spiritual people who are "by
nature" or "by origin" saved; the "psychics" who have a
latent capacity for gnosis and need to have the Gnostic
gospel set before them; and the "earthly" or "material"

---

[13]R. McL. Wilson, *Gnosis and the New Testament* (Oxford: Basil Blackwell, 1968), 4.

people who will never be saved.[14] Gnosticism as a movement was one of the carriers of docetism. Material creation was evaluated negatively and thus Jesus would not have fully partaken of it. Even though Gnosticism is understood as a Christian heresy and even though docetism has been explicitly rejected by the Church, neither tendency is easily uprooted from Christian life itself. Theologies of the Incarnation can manifest a docetic tendency, though rarely explicitly docetic.

The Christian faith eventually rejected, explicitly and definitively, any effort to compromise the humanity of Jesus. The Council of Chalcedon in 451 C.E. referred to Hebrews 4:15 in order to make its own assertion concerning Jesus' humanity and our own, that Jesus' humanity is essentially the same as ours, con-substantial with ours.

The rejection of docetism in Christology has been echoed strongly in recent times. One major characteristic of most twentieth century Christology is a renewed emphasis on the humanity of Christ. No doubt that modern humanism has contributed to this as well as all the motives which lay behind a return to the "Jesus of history." But a significant aspect of recent systematic Christology remains an explicit rejection of docetism.[15] Two twentieth century theological representatives can suffice: Donald Baillie and Wolfhart Pannenberg.

Donald Baillie was a Scottish Presbyterian, an experienced parish minister as well as professor of systematic theology. In *God Was in Christ* (1948) he wrote:

> It may be safely said that practically all schools of theological thought today take the full humanity of our Lord more seriously than has ever been done before by Christian theologians. It has always, indeed, been of the essence of Christian orthodoxy to make Jesus wholly

[14]Robert M. Grant, *Gnosticism* (New York: Harper and Brothers, 1961), 16.

[15]See D. M. Baillie, *God Was in Christ* (New York: Charles Scribner's Sons, 1948), 11-20.

human as well as wholly divine, and in the story of the
controversies which issued in the decisions of the first
four General Councils it is impressive to see the Church
contending as resolutely for His full humanity as for His
full deity . But the Church was building better than it
knew, and its ecumenical decisions were wiser than its
individual theologians in this matter. Or should we rather
say that it did not fully realize the implications of declar-
ing that in respect of His human nature Christ is consub-
stantial with ourselves? At any rate it was continually
haunted by a docetism which made His human nature
very different from ours and indeed largely explained it
away as a matter of simulation or "seeming" rather than
reality. Theologians shrank from admitting human
growth, human ignorance, human mutability, human
struggle and temptation, into their conception of the
Incarnate Life, and treated it as simply a divine life lived
in a human body (and sometimes even this was conceived
as essentially different from our bodies) rather than a
truly human life lived under the psychical conditions of
humanity. The cruder forms of docetism were fairly soon
left behind, but in its more subtle forms the danger continued in varying degrees to dog the steps of theology
right through the ages until modern times.[16]

Wolfhart Pannenberg has been another major figure in
recent christological inquiry. A German Lutheran, his
Jesus-God and Man (1964) explicitly delineated two
methods: a Christology "from above" and a Christology
"from below."[17] Since the publication of his Christology,
theologians have addressed themselves to one or other of
these two methods. Pannenberg's rejection of Christology
from above reflects the same need to do justice to the
humanity of Jesus. For a Christology from above begins
"from the divinity of Jesus," whereas a Christology from

[16]Ibid., 11.

[17]Wolfhart Pannenberg, *Jesus—God and Man*, trans. Lewis Wilkins and Duane
Priebe (Philadelphia: Westminster Press, 1964), 33-37.

below goes "from the historical man Jesus to the recognition of his divinity."[18] A Christology from above "presupposes the divinity of Jesus" and "takes the divinity of the Logos as its point of departure."[19] A Christology from below begins with the humanity and the history of Jesus in contrast to the Eternal Word.

I, too, begin with the humanity of Jesus for several reasons. First, this is where the Church itself began. Disciples in the time of Jesus as well as the first believers after the resurrection knew the human Jesus. The story of the earthly Jesus was the point of continuity between the preresurrection and post-resurrection followers. Both had come to follow this Jesus whom they now professed to be still alive, raised from among the dead. Second, to begin where the first of our brothers and sisters in the faith began is to enable us to come to the faith from within, to reexperience their experience, to recognize (re-cognize) Jesus and encounter him again. Third, we need to avoid docetism. The humanity of Jesus is of ultimate significance for us. If Jesus is not "like me," of "one nature with us," then he has much less to say to me. Redemption is a different matter if he is not fully one of us — for then we have not yet been redeemed! Thus we cannot let go of Jesus' humanity. Later, in volumes three and four, we will speak of the divinity of Jesus more explicitly. To begin there, however, opens us to the possible danger of that divinity overshadowing the fact that Jesus was one of us.

The Humanness of Jesus

Both the testimony of the Scriptures and the historical effort to remain faithful to them point toward Jesus as human like us, even if the "like us" has to be nuanced. Yet this qualification presents a problem. In so far as it is

[18]Ibid., 33.
[19]Ibid., 34.

qualified at all, how can we come to know or interpret the humanity *of Jesus*? For we must be methodologically careful. I point out that we bring pre-conceptions to our understanding of Jesus and we "use" him to confirm these rather than allow him to challenge them. The same applies to his humanity. We cannot assume that our preunderstanding of humanity is correct.

Althouth we all have a great deal of experience with what it means to be human, our experience is still wrapped up in what it means to be less than human as well. The word *human* itself admits a variety of connotations. Sometimes it means "fragile" or "weak"; something is only human; to err is human. Sometimes it conveys a degradation to which a human being can sink; Ivan Albright's painting "Into the World Came a Soul Named Ida," is a portrait of a pathetic human being. So is Oscar Wilde's "Dorian Gray." Sometimes the negative experience of the human becomes so intense that we judge an action to be inhuman although human beings were capable of it. The Holocaust affects us in this way. Contrasted with this, "human" can also connote dignity. Dorothy Day and Albert Schweitzer were outstanding examples of humanity. Given the variety of meanings of the word *human*, how are we using this word when we approach Jesus? Indeed, can we really use it at all?

This very problem is the reason we must be careful. Our prior conceptions of what it means to be human have been primarily learned. When we come to Jesus, perhaps they will have to be re-learned. We cannot force our previous conceptions, no matter how well founded in personal and collective human experience, to be applied to Jesus; otherwise, we "use" him and learn nothing from him, we use him to confirm what we already do.

Rather, when we approach Jesus we need to allow him to disclose or reveal to us what being human means. We must allow him to lead us to a deeper or newer understanding. Christology is not a deduction from prior conceptions as is the popular concept: Jesus is God; God knows all things; therefore, Jesus knows all things. Or: Jesus is human; to be human is to suffer; therefore, Jesus suffers. Christology is not a deduction but an invitation to an encounter. Jesus does indeed suffer. We know that, however, not because we have deduced it from some concept of human nature, but because Jesus has revealed it to us. We can see the difficulty in finding an appropriate starting point for entry into the quest for Jesus. He is human, but we have to allow him to tell us what his humanity means.

Karl Barth's *Christ and Adam* and Jerome Murphy-O'Connor's *Becoming Human Together* exemplify this methodological awareness.[20] Barth's essay on Romans 5 (1952) shows Barth moving closer to the "humanity of God," but still quite conscious that there is a dilemma concerning the relationship between Christology and theological anthropology. Barth's christocentric theology makes him acutely aware when he comes to anthropology that one cannot simply begin with "phenomena of the human," or our experience, or an abstract human nature. We must rather, begin with Christ.

For Barth, Paul does not leave it an open question "whether Adam or Christ tells us more about the true nature of man."[21] For Barth, "Adam can therefore be interpreted only in the light of Christ and not the other way around."[22] Methodologically, we must take Barth quite seriously on this point: "The *special* anthropology of Jesus Christ...is the *norm* of *all* anthropology."[23] Christology is normative for anthropology and not the other way around.

Murphy-O'Connor contrasts with Barth. Barth's speciality is dogmatics, Murphy-O'Connor's is exegesis.

---

[20]Karl Barth, *Christ and Adam, Man and Humanity in Romans 5*, trans. T. A. Smail (New York: The Macmillan Co., 1968). Jerome Murphy-O'Connor, *Becoming Human Together, The Pastoral Anthropology of St. Paul*, revised edition (Wilmington, Delaware: Michael Glazier, Inc., 1982). For an awareness of this same methodological point, also see Wolfhart Pannenberg, "The Christological Foundation of Christian Anthropology," *Humanism and Christianity*, Concilium, vol. 86 (New York: Herder and Herder, 1973), 86-100; Jon Sobrino, *Christology at the Crossroads, A Latin American Approach*, trans. John Drury (Maryknoll, N.Y.: Orbis Books, 1978), 82.

[21]*Christ and Adam*, 44.

[22]Ibid., 40.

[23]Ibid., 36.

Murphy-O'Connor stresses historical critical scholarship while Barth remains skeptical. On the present question, however, they share a common insight. According to Murphy-O'Connor, "we are conditioned to think of Christ in terms of ourselves. He is human and we are human, and it is natural to move from the known (ourselves) to the unknown (Christ)."[24] Yet this is false methodology. The "known" provides "data" derived from what we recognize as fallen or sinful humanity. But it is exactly here that qualifications start to be made. We cannot assume that our fallen, sinful human lives can be the basis for coming to a clearer understanding of what it means to be human in such a way that it helps us shed light on the humanity of Jesus. "Objective observation of contemporary humanity can never result in a portrait of humanity as such. The best it can produce is a portrait of fallen humanity which is inapplicable to Christ."[25] Once again, Christology leads to anthropology and not the other way around. "We cannot have an authentic understanding of humanity unless we first know Christ."[26]

Thus, we must set aside for the moment what being human really means. We must first look more closely at the humanity of Jesus. This does not mean, however, that we have no basis whatsoever with which to begin our study of the humanity of Jesus. There are in fact two bases upon which we can presently build. The first is Scripture; the second is a clarification of our pre-understanding which we leave vulnerable to challenge, and which may find confirmation in Scripture.

Thus, first, although we are not yet ready to say in a final way what the humanity of Jesus consists in (and thus our own humanity), we can say something in a preliminary way based upon Scripture. We have already explored the text of

[24] *Becoming Human Together*, 33.
[25] Ibid., 40.
[26] Ibid., 36.

Hebrews 4:15. *Hebrews* speaks of Jesus being tempted in every way that we are. Thus the humanity of Jesus includes struggle, trial, being put to the test. Second, we can make clear our own pre-understanding. What is meant by humanness? I mean that Jesus participated in the physical, emotional, intellectual-moral, spiritual, and historico-socio-cultural dimensions of our lives.[27] This statement contains five assertions which need to be refined. Yet, for the present, our experiences, intuitions, reflections, philosophical anthropology, and Scripture seem to support such an understanding.

Jesus' humanness means that he had a human body. The details of this body we do not know — height, weight, presence or absence of certain "defects" — but Jesus was a physically embodied human being.

Jesus also felt the kinds of feelings you and I feel.[28] We need not overstate the implications of this. But his feelings certainly included, given biblical testimony, *pain* (the passion narratives), *anger* (the cleansing of the Temple, Mk 11:15-19), *grief* (the death of Lazarus, Jn 11:32-38), *sadness* (weeping for Jerusalem, Lk 19:41-44; Gethsemane, Mt 26:37-39), *compassion* (the little children, Mt 19:13-14; healing two blind men, Mt 20:19-34), *affection* (e.g., for Lazarus, Jn 11:3,5,11,33,35-36, 38), and *joy* (Lk 10:21). In all he possessed a capacity to love and to suffer. Jesus' humanity was emotional as well as physical.

[27]There are other ways in which one might speak in a general fashion about "humanness." Cf., Russell F. Aldwinckle, *More Than Man, A Study in Christology* (Grand Rapids: William B. Eerdmans Pub. Co., 1976), 112-14; John Macquarrie, *In Search of Humanity, A Theological and Philosophical Approach* (New York: Crossroad, 1983), esp. chap. 1; Edward Schillebeeckx, *Christ, The Experience of Jesus as Lord*, trans. John Bowden (New York: Seabury Press, 1980), 731-43.

[28]Cf., Joseph Blenkinsopp, *Sexuality and the Christian Tradition*, (Dayton: Pflaum Press, 1969). Tom Driver, "Sexuality and Jesus," *New Theology*, no. 3 (New York: Macmillan Co., 1966), 118-32. William Phipps, *The Sexuality of Jesus* (New York: Harper and Row, 1973). John A. T. Robinson, *The Human Face of God* (Philadelphia: Westminster Press, 1973), esp. 36-98.

One of the more difficult questions is that of the human knowledge of Jesus.[29] To be human is to be finite and to develop within limits. One's capacity often exceeds one's actual knowledge, but even our capacity is limited. I shall never know all there is to know. Likewise, Jesus' participation in human modes of knowing and human intellectual activity indicated that he too needed to learn what he knew, that he learned from experience and reflection.

This is also true in the area of self-knowledge. He grew in an understanding of his mission or vocation. He had to trust in God and live at times by faith. His future was not always clear. This does not mean that he did not have a profound knowledge and understanding of the Hebrew Scriptures, nor that he was not extremely sensitive and perceptive in human situations. He did speak with authority. We need not determine the limits or extent of Jesus' knowledge here. We only need affirm that in his intellectual life, as in his physical and emotional life, Jesus was like us.

The question of Jesus' self-understanding is an important topic in New Testament Christology.[30] Did Jesus know that he was God? Did he think of himself as the Messiah? How did he understand his mission? We shall return to such questions in future chapters. Raymond Brown has spoken of Jesus' knowledge as a combination of normal ignorance and more than ordinary knowledge and perception.[31] We cannot psychoanalyze Jesus, yet some things can be deter-

[29]Piet Schoonenberg, *The Christ*, trans. Della Couling (New York: The Seabury Press, 1971), 123-35, discusses contemporary developments in theology concerning Jesus' earthly knowledge in relationship to the Scholastic view in which Jesus possessed the beatific vision while on earth. Raymond Brown's *Jesus, God and Man* (Milwaukee: Bruce Publishing Co., 1967) is a biblical, although on some points dated, presentation devoted to different aspects of the knowledge of Jesus. Also see the bibliographical essay by Engelbert Gutwenger, "The Problem of Christ's Knowledge," *Who Is Jesus of Nazareth?*, Concilium, vol. 11 (New York: Paulist Press, 1965), 91-105.

[30]E.g., the early study of Oscar Cullmann, *The Christology of the New Testament*, revised edition, trans. Shirley Guthrie and Charles Hall (Philadelphia: The Westminster Press, 1959). Also Reginald Fuller, *The Foundations of New Testament Christology* (New York: Charles Scribner's Sons, 1965).

[31]Raymond Brown, *Jesus, God and Man*, 45-49.

mined on the basis of the records available to us. For example, he saw himself as a prophet to Israel.

We simply affirm here that Jesus' human knowledge was not without limits, even in areas of vital interest to him. If he did foretell the fall of Jerusalem, this would have been no more than Jeremiah had done and was a perceptive analysis of the times.[32] Although he sensed the betrayal of Judas, this may have been acute perception. Although he knew that death was in store for him, the destinies of the prophets of old as well as of John the baptizer would have been clues. Like us, Jesus had to study, grow in understanding, make moral decisions, and put the puzzle of life together for himself without all the pieces being in place.

Jesus was also like us in his need for faith and prayer.[33] We may at times lack faith or are even without it. Or perhaps we are not willing or able to persevere in prayer. Faith and prayer are still capacities of the human spirit. The same is true of the spiritual life of Jesus. For many of us it is difficult to affirm that there is more to our interior lives than psychic life alone, that spirit cannot be reduced to psychism, *pneuma* to *psyche*. Yet there is more to us than our biological and psychological (emotional and intellectual) dimensions alone. We also are "embodied spirits." Jesus manifests this human spirit, this capacity for self-transcendence, this capacity for contact with the Spirit of God, in his faith, prayer and preaching. Jesus participated in the spiritual and intellectual as well as emotional and physical aspects of human existence. Jon Sobrino, a contemporary Latin American theologian, writes that faith is "the key Old Testa-

---

[32]Ibid., 68-70.

[33]Schoonenberg writes, "Jesus does not speak to us primarily on the basis of a distinct foreknowledge, but on that of a trusting certainty concerning the victory of God and of God's Kingdom" (*The Christ*, 130). This shows the close tie between Jesus' knowledge and spiritual life. Often what is interpreted as infused knowledge may indeed be his extraordinary trust in God. See *The Christ*, 136-52. Also see G. E. Howard, "Notes and Observations on the 'Faith of Christ'," *Harvard Theological Review* 60 (1967), 459-65. Also Martin Buber, *Two Types of Faith*, trans. Norman P. Goldhawk (New York: Harper and Row, 1951).

ment concept in terms of which Jesus understood himself."[34]

The Scriptures confirm Jesus' embodiment, feelings, perceptiveness, lack of complete knowledge, and reliance on faith and prayer. We must now consider the meaning of the historico-socio-cultural dimension of Jesus' life. Each of us has a history and an environment of which we are a part and which is a part of us. This does not mean that we cannot transcend cultural and historical realities. However, they are never left completely behind. They exert a determinative influence on us even as we do on them. To know someone is to know something of that history and social milieu, something of the past and present situation of the person. In reference to Jesus this means that we must have some knowledge of Palestinian and especially Galilean Judaism in the first century C.E., of early Judaism, the Judaism of the times of Jesus.[35] To know it requires some understanding of Israelite and Judean history, the Hebrew Scriptures and post-biblical Jewish literature. We must know something of the development within Judaism in the first century, the world into which Jesus was born and in which he was raised. For, from a historical and cultural perspective, Jesus was a Jew.

There was also a proximate temporal and social milieu; his family, Mary, Joseph, and Nazareth. They raised him. Even in setting oneself over against aspects of one's familial background one is being formed by its influence. As a relational being, Jesus was the center of a network of varied

[34]Sobrino, *Christology at the Crossroads*, 85, also 79-145.

[35]The Judaism of the New Testament world, the Judaism between 200 B. C. E. and 100 C. E., was a very formative period for the Jewish religion. It is difficult to describe the Judaism of this period in a concise expression. It comprises both Palestine and Diaspora. For many years the expression "Late Judaism" was used. If we take into consideration the whole history of Judaism, however, the Judaism in the time of Jesus was not late. "Late" reflects a Christian perspective which is often uninterested in the history of Judaism after 70 C. E. Today, realizing that Judaism itself is a post-exilic development, and that Judaism as we know it had its roots in the rabbinic Judaism of the Tannaitic age, the expression "Early Judaism" seems to describe more accurately the period of the New Testament world. It is the time of late Second Temple Judaism, but early Judaism nevertheless.

relationships who were formative in his earthly life and from whom he cannot be abstracted. To uproot Jesus from his context is to approach him docetically.

In the end, the humanity of Jesus must speak for itself. Our statements about the various dimensions of this man remain open to being challenged. We can feel comfortable with our general observations, however. They are confirmed by Scripture and not simply derived from our experience of sin. Yet all of these statements are open to revision. They are pre-conceptions open to question.

The issues of the humanity of Jesus and his identity with us really come down to one question. We want to know whether it was really as tough for him as for us, whether his search and struggle were real, whether he really knew what it is like to be one of us. To paraphrase a statement from Jeremy Bentham, "The question is not, Can he *reason*? nor Can he *talk*? but, Can he *suffer*?"[36] To this question Scripture and Tradition give an unequivocal answer (Heb 5:8). The question is not whether his core human nature was like ours, but whether his existential condition was. And it is his identity with this condition, our condition, to which the Scriptures give witness.

[36]Jeremy Bentham was speaking here of ethics and the rights of animals. His text reads, "The question is not, Can they *reason* nor Can they *talk*? but, Can they *suffer*? See *An Introduction to the Principles of Morals and Legislation* (Oxford: Clarendon Press, 1892), 311 (chap. 17, par. 1, sect. 4, n.1).

2

Jesus' Roots in Palestinian Judaism

Being human, Jesus was of necessity a person in history. To find the Jesus of history we must first face the scandal of particularity. Jesus did not exist in the abstract but was situated historically and geographically. The human Jesus was a Palestinian Jew from Galilee in the first century of the Common Era.

Judean History

Crisis and Exile (587-539 B.C.E.). In 597 B.C.E., the kingdom of Judah and the city of Jerusalem fell before the power of King Nebuchadnezzar (605/4-562) and the Babylonians; as was Babylonian custom following Assyrian practice, many of the conquered were transported and resettled. Because of ongoing agitation and rebellion in Jerusalem, however, an even greater blow was inflicted ten years later in 587. The city itself, including the Temple, was leveled to the ground and burned, and a second deportation took place. The impact of this sixth century B.C.E. experience on the Judean people was captured in Psalm 137.

> By the waters of Babylon
> there we sat down and wept,
> when we remembered Zion . . . .

Judea was not completely depopulated with the two deportations of 597 and 587. Many remained behind and some fled to Egypt. Those who were deported were not completely deprived. Some acquired property and many entered trade. Not all returned when it was later possible to do so. With the exile Judaism came to be lived not only in Palestine, but also in the Diaspora, in centers like Babylon and Egypt, and Diaspora and Palestinian Judaism continued to co-exist after the exile as well. The exile was later interpreted as God's judgment on the infidelity of God's people, and so distinctive duties such as circumcision, Sabbath observance, regulations concerning ritual purity, became increasingly significant for the people.

The Persian Period (539-332 B.C.E.). The period of the exile lasted almost sixty years. In 539, Cyrus, King of Persia from 550 to 530, defeated Nabonidus, King of Babylon, and the Persian Empire was founded.[1] One year later, 538, an edict of Cyrus (Ezra 6:3-5) allowed the Jewish people to return home and to rebuild the Temple. The project was placed under the direction of Sheshbazzar and later Zerubbabel, both of the line of David. Jerusalem and the surrounding area were subject to the Persian king; but Persian policy allowed subject peoples a cultural autonomy. Sheshbazzar proceeded with the reconstruction of the Temple, but progress was slow. Jerusalem was thinly populated even after the return of exiles; harvests were poor. Neighbors, especially the Samaritans, were hostile; morale declined. But in 515 the new Temple was completed. This Second Temple Period is the immediate background for the Palestinian Judaism of the time of Jesus. We know little about the period following the completion of the Temple. However, we do know that the hope and fervor of the people again declined. Nehemiah (c. 445), a Jew in the court of Artaxerxes in Persia, obtained permission to go to Jerusalem and help. He facilitated the rebuilding of the city walls and

---

[1]See *Oxford Bible Atlas*, ed. Herbert May and G. H. Hunt, second edition (London: Oxford University Press, 1974), 29 and 35, for the rulers of the Persian, Ptolemaic, and Seleucid empires.

provided administrative leadership. Ezra (c. 428)[2] provided spiritual leadership and came with permission to restore observance of the Law which he publicly read.

Aramaic was the language of western Persia. The Jews learned to speak it, and it gradually replaced Hebrew as the spoken language of most Jews. One of the significant effects of Persian administration was the political separation of Judea from Samaria. Cyrus had restored Jerusalem as a temple state, much to the dissatisfaction of the Samaritans. The returning exiles considered themselves the true Israel and thus also tended to separate themselves from the Samaritans. Political autonomy for Jerusalem increased under Nehemiah. When the Samaritans built their own temple on Mt. Gerizim later, estrangement was complete. The final blow came during the reign of Antiochus IV when Samaritans did not support Jewish opposition to his reforms.

The Hellenistic Period (332-63 B.C.E.): *The Ptolemies* (323-198 B.C.E.). In 336 Darius III (386-331) became the ruler of Persia and Alexander the Great (336-323) became the ruler of Greece and Macedonia. Alexander's conquest of Persia and of the East between 336 and his death in 323 B.C.E. at the age of 33 extended as far as India. His conquests began the era of Hellenization. By 332 he had taken Asia Minor, Phoenicia, Palestine, and Egypt. Jerusalem and Samaria gave little resistance. Later an uprising in Samaria led to the destruction of the city and the establishment of a Macedonian colony. Displaced Samaritans who survived centered their life around ancient Shechem.

Upon Alexander's death in 323, his generals attempted to parcel out his empire among them. Ptolemy I (323-285) took Egypt and established his capital at the newly built city of Alexandria, and Seleucus I took ancient Babylonia and Syria with capitals at Seleucia on the Tigris and Antioch in

---

[2]See John Bright, *A History of Israel*, third edition (Philadelphia: Westminster Press, 1981), 391-402. F. M. Cross, "A Reconstruction of the Judaean Restoration," *Journal of Biblical Literature* 94 (1975), 9-11, places Ezra c. 458 B.C.E., before Nehemiah.

Syria. Both claimed Palestine. By the end of the fourth century, however, with the battle of Ipsos (301 B.C.E.), Palestine fell under the rule of Ptolemy and remained under the Ptolemies for one century. During this period Alexandria grew and became a center for Judaism as well. Jews in Egypt soon became Greek speaking, and the Hebrew Scriptures were eventually translated into the famous Greek Septuagint translation, begun under Ptolemy II (285-246). The Ptolemaic administrative unit was smaller than that of Persia. In Palestine there were four such units: Galilee, Samaria, Judea and Idumea.[3] Other than this the Ptolemies did not attempt any major changes.

The Hellenistic Period (332-63 B.C.E.): *The Seleucids* (198-63 B.C.E.) and *Hasmoneans* (167-63 B.C.E.) When Antiochus II, the Great (223-187), became king of the Seleucid Empire, he won back what the Seleucids maintained was theirs, Coele-Syria or Palestine, after defeating Ptolemy V Epiphanes in 198.[4] Jews welcomed the change at the time, and Antiochus was considerate of the Jewish people. Greek culture in Palestine was on the move. In Palestine itself, there had developed a number of Greek cities since the time of Alexander's conquest: Sebaste (Samaria), Philadelphia (Amman), Ptolemais (Acco), Philoteria (south of the lake of Galilee), and Scythopolis (Bethshean). Antioch and Alexandria had also become Greek cities.

In 187 Antiochus III was killed, and was succeeded by his son Seleucus IV (187-175), who was assassinated and succeeded by his brother Antiochus IV Epiphanes (175-163), whose rule became critical. His policies led to Jewish revolt. The tension at first centered around the high priesthood. The legitimate high priest for centuries had been of Zado-

---

[3]Idumea, a Graecized form of Edom, was the southern portion of Palestine south of Judea and the Dead Sea. The Idumeans or Edomites supposedly descended from the older son of Isaac, Esau or Edom, and thus were kindred to the Hebrews. During the reign of John Hyrcanus (135-104), the Idumeans were conquered and forced to accept Judaism. Several centuries before Jesus the Idumean territory south and east of the Dead Sea became Nabatean and Idumea was strictly limited to southern Judea west of the Dead Sea.

[4]For the rulers of the Seleucid Empire, see n. 1 of this chapter.

kite lineage. When Antiochus Epiphanes became king, the high priest was Onias III. But rivalry developed between two families, the Oniads (who were a priestly family and pro-Ptolemaic) and the Tobiads (an aristocratic lay family, pro-Seleucid and hellenist). Onias III's brother, Jason (a Greek name he preferred to Hebrew), an Oniad, but Tobiad ally and member of the Jewish hellenist party, bribed his way into the office of high priest and had himself appointed by Antiochus Epiphanes in 175. This brought a pro-hellenist into the high priesthood itself, but still an Oniad and Zadokite. Jason carried out many hellenist reforms in Jerusalem, which virtually became a Greek city with a gymnasium.

Three years later, in 172, Menelaus (Greek for Menahem) bribed his way to the high priesthood and Antiochus appointed him to replace Jason. Menelaus was neither Oniad, nor Zadokite, but a Tobiad and extreme pro-hellenist. The Tobiads were an aristocratic Jewish family, originally based in Amman, who had compromised their Jewish religion with Greek life. Antiochus' finances were in bad shape and Menelaus' sympathies were hellenistic, so Menelaus did not stand in the way of Antiochus' confiscating funds from the Temple in Jerusalem to pay debts. During Antiochus' invasion of Egypt in 168, the situation became worse. Antiochus was irritated by a command from Rome to return home. Hearing about opposition in Jerusalem, he sent a commander in 167 to enforce his policies. Because of resistance, the city was partly destroyed, walls torn down, people enslaved, and a military Greek citadel called the Acra was established. The cult of Zeus was introduced into the Temple — the abomination of desolation (Dn 9:27, 11:31, 12:1).

Loyal and pious Jews, the Hasidim, organized resistance (1 Mc 1:42, 7:13; 2 Mc 16:6). In the village of Modein, northwest of Jerusalem, where Mattathias of the Hasmonean family and his five sons (John, Simon, Judas, Eleazar, and Jonathan) lived, Mattathias was asked by an officer to offer sacrifices to a pagan god. He refused, killed a fellow

Jew who was trying to do so, then killed the officer. He and his sons and some of the Hasidim fled to the Hills. The revolt had begun (1 Mc 2:19-28). Shortly thereafter Mattathias died, and his third son, Judas called Maccabeus (the hammer), continued the revolution. This became known as the Maccabean War.

Antiochus was preoccupied with other problems. Within a couple of years, Judas took control of Jerusalem, cleansed the Temple (1 Mc 4:36-59) and in 164 the Temple was rededicated. Since then the feast of Hanukkah or Dedication has commemorated the event (which Jesus observed in John 10:17). This was the beginning of the Hasmonean period, the dynasty following Mattathias, a period of Jewish independence.[5] Antiochus Epiphanes died in 163. The Jews, divided between the Hasidim and the hellenizers who sought Syrian Seleucid interventions, further aggravated the situation. But the Seleucid leaders were burdened with other problems and the Jews were granted religious liberty.

Conflict continued, now no longer simply for religious freedom but rather for political supremacy within Judaism. Practically speaking Judas was the leader of the Jewish people. Later, in opposition to the appointment of the helle-

---

[5]The word Hasmonean is derived from Asamoneus, the father of Mattathias, according to Josephus. The name Maccabees usually refers to Mattathias and his sons, and Hasmoneans to their descendants from 135-63 B.C.E., beginning with John Hyrcanus I, son of Simon. The Maccabean and Hasmonean rulers were:

Judas Maccabeus	164-161
Jonathan	161-143/142
Simon	143/142-135/134
John Hyrcanus I	135/134-104
Aristobulus I	104-103
Alexander Jannaeus	103-76
Alexandra	76-67
Aristobulus II	67-63

In 63 B.C.E. Pompey took Jerusalem. Cf., Emil Schurer, *The History of the Jewish People in the Age of Jesus Christ*, revised by Geza Vermes, Fergus Millar, and Matthew Black, 2 vols. (Edinburgh: T. and T. Clark, [1885] 1973-79), 1:125-42, 613.

nist Alcimus to replace Menelaus as high priest, Judas once again defeated the Seleucids in a battle in which the Seleucid general was killed. The Seleucid response, however, led to a Jewish defeat and the death of Judas in 161 B.C.E.

With the death of Judas, the Maccabean party was defeated, and the hellenist Alcimus remained high priest. Jonathan, the brother of Judas, was now chosen as leader (161-143). Another brother, John, was attacked and killed while attempting to transport their personal belongings out of the country. Later, in 160, Alcimus died.   Jonathan consolidated his power. Hellenist Jews sought intervention but the Seleucid leadership made peace with Jonathan and the Maccabees remained in control. By 153 Jonathan was appointed high priest and so his party became *politically and religiously* supreme. Jonathan sought, however, complete liberation from the Seleucid empire and lay seige to the Syrian garrison, the Acra, still in Jerusalem. In a later battle with the Syrians, Jonathan was imprisoned and murdered. Simon, his brother, took over, the last left of the five. (Eleazar had been killed in an earlier battle while Judas was still in charge.) Under Simon the goal of Jonathan was completely accomplished, the Acra defeated, and the Jewish people became completely independent in 142. In the third year of his reign, Simon's ranks were made hereditary by the people, and a new hereditary high priesthood came into existence. Simon, however, died violently, murdered along with two of his sons by a plot on the part of a power-seeking son-in-law.

The royal and priestly offices had been declared hereditary for Simon, and so his third and surviving son succeeded him. With Simon, the rule of the Maccabees ended; and with his son John Hyrcanus I (135-104), the Hasmonean dynasty proper began. The Syrian empire became increasingly weak; Judea was able to maintain its independence. Hyrcanus I left five sons, and was succeeded by his eldest, Aristobulus, who ruled for a year (104-103), and who had put his mother in prison to prevent the rule from passing to her. Aristobulus' rule no longer reflected Maccabean spirit;

Greek culture became favored. When Aristobulus died, his brothers whom he had also imprisoned were released. The eldest was Alexander Jannaeus (103-76). His rule was marked by war, expansion, and alienation from a growing and popular party, the Pharisees. Upon his death, his wife, Alexandra Salome, ruled (76-67) with their eldest son, Hyrcanus, as high priest, years during which she overcame the Hasmonean estrangement from the Pharisees.

Upon her death her sons Hyrcanus II and Aristobulus II contended for the throne. The end result was the Roman occupation by Pompey in 63 B.C.E. Aristobulus II was taken prisoner. Hyrcanus II was recognized as high priest but not king. The seventy year interlude of Jewish independence had ended. From approximately 142 B.C.E. until 63 B.C.E. there had been a fairly independent Hasmonean Jewish state. Such independence would not exist again until the twentieth century.

The Roman Period (63 B.C.E.—324 C.E.)

63 B.C.E.	Capture of Jerusalem by Pompey
49 B.C.E.	Crossing of the Rubicon by Julius Caesar
48 B.C.E.	Death of Pompey
44 B.C.E.	Assassination of Julius Caesar
42 B.C.E.	Defeat of Brutus and Cassius by Antony and Octavian
37-4 B.C.E.	Reign of Herod the Great in Palestine
27 B.C.E.-14 C.E.	Reign of Augustus (Octavian) as Emperor of Rome
6 C.E.	Beginning of the Rule of Roman Procurators in Judea
70 C.E.	Destruction of Jerusalem and the Second Temple by Titus
132-135 C.E.	Second Jewish Revolt of Bar Cochba

The traditional date for the founding of the Roman Republic was 510 B.C.E., about the same time as the beginning of post-exilic and Second Temple Judaism. By the middle of the third century, while the Ptolemies were in control of Palestine, Rome was in control of all of Italy and emerging as a world power. In 146 B.C.E. Rome finally destroyed Carthage and thus controlled the western Mediterranean including Spain. Rome expanded toward the east. Macedonia had become a Roman province in the mid second century, c. 148 B.C.E. Greece became a Roman protectorate after 146, supervised from Macedonia.[6] In 133 Pergamum came under Roman control and Rome had a foothold in Asia. By 62 B.C.E. Pompey had helped to stabilize the eastern frontiers of Rome. In 63 he had taken control of Jerusalem.

Pompey in the East and Julius Caesar in the West were the rivals as Palestine came under Rome's dominion, and they were the contenders for power in Rome's First Civil War which brought the Republic to a close. In 49 B.C.E. Julius Caesar crossed the Rubicon and became dictator. Pompey was defeated. After Pompey's death in 48 B.C.E., Hyrcanus II and an old friend, Antipater, (who was half Jewish and from Idumea or southern Palestine) befriended Julius Caesar, who in turn treated them well, establishing Hyrcanus II as ethnarch with some political authority and Antipater as procurator of Judea. Antipater had two of his Idumean sons, Phasael and Herod, appointed to positions, the former over Jerusalem and the latter over Galilee, c. 47 B.C.E.[7] In 43 B.C.E. Antipater was poisoned. On March 15, 44 B.C.E., Caesar had been assassinated. Mark Antony moved against the conspirators and Brutus fled to Macedonia and Cassius to Syria. Both were defeated in 42 B.C.E. at Philippi by Antony and Octavian, and Antony became ruler in the East and Octavian, Caesar's adoptive nephew, in the West. Antony was won over by Herod, Phasael, and Hyrcanus. A Parthian invasion led to Phasael's and Hyrcanus' imprisonment. Herod escaped, made his way to Rome, won

---

[6]Regarding these dates, see W. W. Tarn, *Hellenistic Civilization*, third edition (New York: New American Library, 1975), 37-39.

[7]Antipater had four sons and a daughter: Phasael, Herod, Joseph, Pheroras, Salome. Herod was born in 74 or 73 B.C.E. He died in 4 B.C.E. Josephus says he was seventy when he died.

the favor of Octavian, and was declared by the Roman senate to be king of Judea. With Rome's support, and within three years, he established himself in Palestine.

Herod sought the favor of Rome, first of Antony and then of Octavian, and knew enough to rely upon it. He began his rule with many enemies. The Pharisees and the people only tolerated him. He was only half Jewish and was a friend of the Romans. In 32 B.C.E. war broke out between Antony and Octavian, and in 31 B.C.E., Antony was defeated at Actium off the west coast of Greece. Having returned to Alexandria, both Antony and Cleopatra committed suicide.[8] Herod had consistently sought the approval of Antony, and now had to regain the confidence of Octavian.

Herod built palaces and fortresses, new cities with theatres and racetracks. In Jerusalem he had built for himself a lavish fortified palace (c. 24 B.C.E.) and a theatre, as well as having rebuilt the fortress north of the Temple which he named the Antonia in honor of Antony. The old site of Samaria was built up as a Roman city and named Sebaste. In 22 B.C.E. he began a new city on the coast which took twelve years to build and which he named Caesarea. He named two new fortresses after himself, the Herodia, and he restored and improved others, e.g., Machaerus east of the Dead Sea and Masada on the western shore, which he furnished with luxurious palaces. He also began to rebuild the Temple in Jerusalem since the Temple constructed under Zerubbabel no longer was in harmony with the new magnificent buildings of his Herodian Jerusalem. To support his projects and campaigns, Herod imposed heavy taxes.

Herod lacked any strong interest in Judaism itself. He tended to promote Graeco-Roman culture, and yet remained conscious of the popularity of the Pharisees and

---

[8]Ptolemy XI died in 51 B.C.E. and was followed by Ptolemy XII, Cleopatra's younger brother, who was also her husband. Cleopatra assembled her own troops in Syria, and in 49 with the help of Julius Caesar she overthrew her husband and brother, became the ruler of Egypt and the mistress of Caesar. After the assassination of Caesar in 44 B.C.E., Cleopatra returned to Egypt and began her liaison with Antony, c. 42 B.C.E.

other Jewish nationals. His many fortresses, new ones, restored ones, improved ones, were likely placed to protect him not only from foreign foe but also from domestic conspiracy and resentment over his increasing despotism. He decidedly had the favor of Rome and Augustus, who expanded his territory and allowed him the title of king, a title that no one within the Roman Empire could use without the approval of emperor and senate. The title was granted only to individuals and was not hereditary. Usually lesser titles, like tetrarch, were those given. The last years of Herod's rule were filled with family problems, jealousy, and plots. He changed his will several times, and in his final will named Archelaus king, Archelaus being the older son of a Samaritan wife, Malthace; and he named his son Antipas tetrarch of Galilee and Perea; and Philip, the son of a different wife, tetrarch of northeastern territories.[9]

Herod died, hated in his own home, in 4 B.C.E., of an illness which had plagued him the last few years of his life. During his reign Jesus of Nazareth had been born. This Herod, called the Great, must be distinguished from his son, Antipas, known as Herod Antipas, who ruled as tetrarch in Galilee, the Herod ruling during most of the lifetime of Jesus. Both Antipas and Archelaus plotted against each other and pleaded for their causes in Rome, but Augustus decided in favor of the final will of Herod, except that the title of king was not given. Archelaus was made ethnarch, the other two tetrarchs. Judea, Samaria, and Idumea fell under the rule of Archelaus; Galilee and Perea under Antipas; Batanea, Trachonitis, Auranitis, Gaulanitis, and Paneas under Philip. Jesus grew up and preached around Capernaum within the territory of Herod Antipas, but also passed to places like the Caesarea and Bethsaida in the tetrarchy of Philip, and when he went to Jerusalem was within still another political district.

[9]For a discussion of some of the issues connected with the will of Herod the Great, see Harold W. Hoehner, *Herod Antipas* (Cambridge: University Press, 1972), 269-76. Hoehner concludes to six such wills. Schurer, however, refers only to three wills, vol. 1, 324-26.

Philip was tetrarch from 4 B.C.E. until 34 C.E. The people in Philip's territory were predominantly non-Jewish. They were Syrian and Greek. Philip himself, unlike the others, seems to have been a respected ruler. He rebuilt Paneas (today Banyas) at the source of the Jordan, north of the Lake of Galilee, and named it Caesarea Philippi, not to be confused with Herod the Great's famous Caesarea on the Mediterranean. Philip also rebuilt Bethsaida.

Herod Antipas was tetrarch from 4 B.C.E. until 39 C.E. (frequently called simply Herod despite the resulting confusion with his father). His districts were broken into two, Perea and Galilee. Young Herod Antipas took after his father — ambitious and clever. Jesus called him "that fox" (Lk 13:32). Like his father and like the other Herods, Antipas was a builder. His most splendid project was a new capital at one of the more beautiful places in Galilee, on the western side of the lake, which he named Tiberias for it had been built during the reign of Tiberius.

Archelaus was ethnarch from 4 B.C.E. until 6 C.E. Of all Herod the Great's sons, Archelaus seems to have been the worst. His rule extended to Judea, Samaria, and Idumea. He too was a builder. His reign was so corrupt that a Jewish and Samaritan deputation to Rome accomplished his dismissal and banishment to Gaul in 6 C.E. Antipas and Philip may have been a part of the delegation.[10] After that, his territory was placed directly under Roman rule with a Roman governor of its own. Thus in the adult days of Jesus, Galilee was under Herod Antipas and Judea under more direct Roman governance.

The ordinary title for a Roman ruler of the equestrian rank was that of procurator, which also indicated one of his

---

[10]Hoehner, 103-9. Hoehner suggests that it was upon this occasion that Antipas began to be called Herod: "One of the probable results of Antipas' voyage to Rome in 6 C.E. is that he then acquired the dynastic title of Herod. It seems that the name *Herod* became a dynastic title after Herod the Great's death. The first clue to this is in the context of Archelaus' deposition where Josephus specifically states that Antipas was now called Herod. Up to this time he is always called Antipas, whereas after this time he is always designated Herod" (105-6).

major responsibilities — finances.[11] In extreme situations
the Roman procurators in Judea were subordinate to the
governor of Syria. The procurator of Judea did not reside at
Jerusalem but at Caesarea Maritima (Herod the Great's
Caesarea). On special occasions, such as the major Jewish
feasts when special surveillance was necessary, the procurator left Caesarea and resided at Herod's palace on the west
side in Jerusalem. From 26-36 C.E. the procurator was
Pontius Pilate. In addition to the financial administration,
the procurator also commanded the troops and had judicial
authority.

Within administrative, financial, military, and judicial
limits, the Jews were self-governing. After Archelaus, during the period of the procurators, the Jewish aristocratic
Sanhedrin was also a governing body. The procurator was
overseer, but in many affairs the Jews were left to themselves. The high priest was president of the Sanhedrin, but
the high priest was appointed by the Romans (at least until
41 C.E.). The Sanhedrin and the procurator both governed.
Jewish courts made decisions according to Jewish law, even
in criminal matters.

In 66 C.E. revolt broke out. By the end of 67 Vespasian
had subdued Galilee and within the next year much of
Judea. The death of Nero in 68 required Vespasian to return
to Rome. The actual siege of Jerusalem did not begin until
70 C.E. and was conducted by Titus over a five month
period. The city was taken, the Temple destroyed. Practically speaking it was the end of the Sadducees and Essenes.
The future of Judaism lay with the Pharisees and their
attempt to reconstruct Judaism which was now left with no

---

[11]A. N. Sherwin-White has shown, in *Roman Society and Roman Law in the
New Testament* (Oxford: Clarendon Press, 1963), 7-12, that the technical title for
the governors of Judea of equestrian rank prior to the reign of Claudius (41-54
C.E.) was that of "praefectus" rather than "procurator." Procurator came into use
under Claudius. Yet I have retained the more commonly accepted designation
here.

Temple. The year 70 C.E. ends the Second Temple period. The last stronghold was that of Masada which finally fell in 73 C.E.

The Political Situation

During the first century of the Common Era, under the Roman occupation, religion, politics and geography contributed to a division of Palestine into Judea (politically administered by Roman procurators, yet the religious center of Judaism), Samaria (also politically administered by the Roman procurator, yet religiously distinct from Judaism), and Galilee (under the administration of Herod Antipas, geographically separated from Judea, but religiously identified with Judaism).

Judea. Judea is a land of hills, many barren and stony. Its three chief towns were and are Beersheba, Hebron and Jerusalem. Hebron is the highest town in Judea and was David's first capital. Jerusalem also rises high, as one notices if one goes up to Jerusalem from Jericho.

In 6 C.E., with the banishment of Archelaus, Rome's presence in Judea became more evident. Coponius was appointed the first procurator. Quirinius became legate in Syria and took a census of the territory to determine taxes. Judas the Galilean led a resistance which was centered in Jerusalem and stirred the people to an unsuccessful rebellion.

The first procurators of Judea were: Coponius (6-9 C.E.), Marcus Ambivius (9-12 C.E.), Annius Rufus (12-15 C.E.), Valerius Gratus (25-26 C.E.), Pontius Pilate (26-36 C.E.), and Marcellus (36-37 C.E.). The Roman emperors during this time were: Octavian known as Augustus (died 14 C.E.), Tiberius (14-37), and Caligula (37-41). Because Pilate as procurator was not careful about respecting Jewish customs, his rule occasioned popular uprisings in Judea. During his rule as procurator Jesus of Nazareth was sentenced to death. The terms of both Valerius Gratus and Pontius Pilate were long: under Tiberius the procurators were allowed to remain for longer periods, in contrast to terms under Augustus. Valerius Gratus had appointed four high priests in his day: the last of these was Joseph Caiaphas (18-36 C.E.), son-in-law of Annas, who had been high priest when Valerius Gratus first came to Judea.

The procurators in Judea supervised financial, military and some juridical affairs; within limits the Jewish people were free to govern themselves. The highest Jewish governing body was the Sanhedrin, something of an upper class legislative and judicial body, presided over by the high priest. In the beginning the body was primarily Sadducean but gradually incorporated Pharisaic members as well. Its origin is difficult to determine. It was first mentioned around 200 B.C.E., and grew in importance under the Hasmoneans, but seems to have had little power under Herod the Great (who is said to have killed the majority of its members). After 6 C.E. it grew again in importance within Jewish and religious life. After the fall of Jerusalem in 70 C.E. and the consolidation of Judaism at Jamnia later, the Sanhedrin ceased to exist.

The Sanhedrin was composed of 71 members. There were the "elders," the lay aristocrats, heads of prominent Jewish families, "the principal men of the people" (Lk 19:47); then there were the scribes, the learned or those who had been taught (Jn 7:15), generally Pharisees first admitted around 75 B.C.E.; and finally the chief priests, mostly Sadducean. Thus the Sanhedrin was composed of both Sadducees and Pharisees, a lay and priestly aristocracy. The high priest was its head; it met in or near the Temple.

Samaria. To the north of the land of Judah is the land at one time occupied by the tribes of Ephraim and Manasseh, descendants of the two sons of Joseph. The territory extended north of Judea between the coastal plain on the west and the Jordan valley on the east. Its northern boundary is the important and fertile Plain of Esdraelon, also

called the Valley of Jezreel. In the time of Jesus, the central
section of this region had become the land of the Samaritans. A small group of Samaritans in Palestine today are
still centered around Nablus, worshipping on Mt. Gerizim
at Passover time.[12]

The religious division between Samaritans and Jews is
explained differently by each group.[13] Jews trace the origin
of the conflict to the Assyrian conquest of the northern
kingdom and the destruction and repopulation of Samaria
at that time, with its resulting syncretism. Antedating this,
however, there was already a north/south rivalry. Samaritans trace the origin of the conflict earlier, to the period of
Judges. Eli, desirous of the high priesthood, set up a sanctuary at Shiloh to rival an already existing one at Mt. Gerizim,
the sanctuary and priesthood associated with Shiloh being
rejected by the Samaritans. Samuel was affiliated with the
sanctuary at Shiloh thereby manifesting an unaccepted and
invalid lineage. Thus, even before the times of David and
Solomon, a division existed between the Samaritans with
their authentic worship at Mt. Gerizim and those who were
later loyal to Saul who had been anointed king by Samuel.

Developments in the post-exilic period only aggravated
and completed an already existing tension. After the return
from Babylon, under Persian administration, Judea and
Samaria were politically separated. Jews conscientious
about fidelity to their laws naturally emphasized a purity
and separatism. Zerubbabel's efforts to rebuild a Temple on
Mt. Zion pushed another wedge between the worshippers at
Mt. Gerizim and the Jewish community. A century later,
Nehemiah rebuilt the walls of Jerusalem, reinforcing the
separation. The Samaritan governor Sanballat tried to pre-

[12]A fairly recent discussion of the contemporary Samaritans is that by Shemar-
yahu Talmon, "The Samaritans," *Scientific American* 236 (January, 1977), 100-
108.

[13]A thorough exploration of Samaritan thought is that of John MacDonald,
The Theology of the Samaritans, The New Testament Library (Philadelphia: The
Westminster Press, 1964). For the two versions of the split between the Samaritans
and Judaists, see 14-29.

vent the walls from being rebuilt. Such events deepened animosity on both sides. By this time there were also two versions of the Torah, the Samaritan and the Jewish. The Samaritans built a Temple on Mt. Gerizim to rival the Second Temple in Jerusalem sometime in the fifth or fourth centuries. Relations were probably at their worst during the Hasmonean and Herodian periods. Although the Samaritans were likewise struggling against hellenization, they did not support Jewish efforts to resist Antioches Epiphanes and his desecration of the Jewish Temple. John Hyrcanus detroyed the Samaritan temple after capturing Shechem in 129 B.C.E. The Roman era during the time of Augustus liberated the Samaritans from Hasmonean and Herodian oppression, and, as in Judea, they were allowed under Rome their own internal administration. During the time of Jesus an intense hatred existed beteen the Samaritans and the Jews.

Galilee had been a part of the northern kingdom of Israel but had never been a part of the rejection of Mt. Zion and Jerusalem's cultic leadership. Thus Samaria was also separated religiously from Galilee. This separation became political and was aggravated by the Assyrian conquest of the north which had taken place in two phases: (1) a setting up of the province of Megiddo (of which Galilee had been a part) and (2) the destruction of Samaria.[14] The treatment accorded the provinces of Megiddo and Samaria differed radically. Samaria was leveled to the ground when defeated and organized as a separate province: people were deported, and foreigners from other parts of Assyria replanted. Thus Galilee and Samaria were administratively separated and treated differently. Samaria, a greater center of resistance, was treated more harshly and estrangement between Galilee and Samaria developed further.

Galilee. North of Samaria is Galilee, divided into Upper and Lower Galilee, the elevations of Upper Galilee reaching

---

[14]Sean Freyne, *Galilee from Alexander the Great to Hadrian, 323 B.C.E. to 135 C.E., A Study of Second Temple Judaism* (Wilmington, Del. and Notre Dame, Ind.: Michael Glazier and University of Notre Dame, 1980), 23-26.

over three thousand feet whereas the hills of southern Galilee do not reach higher than two thousand feet. In northern Galilee rain is heavier, land more forested, and villages are smaller. It is the beginning of the Lebanon. Rain is a distinctive feature of all of Galilee. Lower Galilee was the land of Jesus. Today, Nazareth is the largest town in the area. In the time of Jesus it was only a small village, and the city of Sepphoris (Saffuriyeh) was the center. The ministry of Jesus primarily took place around the shores of the lake in the region of Capernaum.

At the time of Jesus Galilee was a region with an independent consciousness of its own. Stricter Jews in Judea regarded Galileans with some disdain (Jn 1:46; 7:41, 52). Interiorly, it is a hill country which contrasts with the plains on both sides as Galilee moves toward the sea or the lake. The majority of the settlements in lower Galilee are on the slopes of the hills and not the valley floors and this secludes them from neighbors. Life in the valley along the Jordan and around the lake was more cosmopolitan than in the inner hill country. Galilee is the most fertile, productive and agricultural region of Palestine. The central hill country was inhabited more by Israelites, whereas the older Canaanite population persisted on the coast and along the plain of Esdraelon which outer region then became the home of newcomers during the Hellenistic period.

Sean Freyne has raised questions concerning the common and mistaken assumption that Galilee was more revolutionary and nationalistic than Judea.[15] In fact, the more direct Roman presence in Judea as well as the presence of the Temple made it the locus of greater resentment and resistance. Galilee comprised a significant Jewish and also Hellenistic population on the periphery of the major disturbances within Judaism. It seems to have suffered less from the Roman occupation. Hellenization and urbanization had set in, but the Jewish population was still primarily rural and peasant.

[15]Ibid., 208-55.

Prior to the foundation of Tiberias by Antipas, Sepphoris was certainly the most important city in Galilee. It was a strong fortress and also the seat of one of the five councils into which the Jewish nation had been divided in 57 B.C.E. It was the only such seat in Galilee. It was a Jewish city, and yet was pro-Roman during the Jewish Revolt of 66-70 C.E., probably indicating a cautious political stance within the city after a previous rebellion in 4 B.C.E. upon the death of Herod the Great in which the governor of Syria had destroyed the city. It was subsequently rebuilt by Antipas. Despite its importance, Sepphoris maintained a limited sphere of influence within Galilee. It was hated by the Galileans, but not because the Jewish population of Sepphoris was lax. It was, rather, the aristocratic seat of wealthy landowners.

Tiberias, ideally located in a fertile region on the lake with hot springs nearby, was the rival of Sepphoris during the thirty year period when it was Antipas' capital. It had been founded sometime between 18 and 23 C.E. and dedicated by Antipas to the Roman Emperor. It had a mixed population, a Greek minority, a Jewish majority, despite its location above tombs which was a violation of Jewish law. Galilean Jews had to be forced to live there. After Antipas the capital once again became Sepphoris, probably during the reign of Nero. Like Sepphoris, Tiberias had limited influence on the Galilean population and was also a hated city. It too was aristocratic and reflected the economic situation of the widening gap between the rich, aristocratic landowners living in Tiberias and Sepphoris, and the rural peasant population which was becoming more poor.

The Socio-Cultural Situation

In the encounter with Hellenism, which began prior to the conquests of Alexander the Great, Judaism became both hellenized and also intensely centered on Torah (the Law). By the time of Jesus, Palestine had been under hellenistic cultural influences for over three centuries. The distinction beween Palestinian and Diaspora Judaism cannot be equated with the distinction between non-Hellenistic and Hellenistic. Martin Hengel writes, "From about the middle of the third century B.C. *all Judaism* must really be designated '*Hellenistic Judaism*' in the strict sense."[16]

During the post-exilic and especially Persian period, the classical pre-exilic Hebrew gradually gave way to Aramaic, the common language of the western Persian Empire. Both languages continued to exist, but by the first century Aramaic was the spoken language of the Jewish people. With the conquest of Alexander, however, and the surge of hellenization, Greek also became prominent and many Palestinian Jews began to speak or read Greek. The Jews who wanted to advance socially needed to know Greek. With the coming of the Romans, Latin was also introduced into Palestine. According to the Fourth Gospel, Pilate had the inscription on the cross of Jesus written in Latin, Greek and Hebrew (Jn 19:20). Latin was used by the Romans for official purposes and did not become a spoken language among the Jews. Greek had been a spoken language among the Romans and thus was a common language for communication in the Near East as a whole during the first century.[17]

It is difficult to determine the extent to which Greek was used in Palestine prior to Alexander the Great. In the first century, however, Greek was widely used and may well have been the primary language of even some Palestinian Jews. Joseph Fitzmyer follows C.F.D. Moule in interpreting the Hellenists and Hebraists of Acts 6:1 as two groups of Pales-

[16]Martin Hengel, *Judaism and Hellenism, Studies in Their Encounter in Palestine During the Early Hellenistic Period*, trans. John Bowden, 2 vols. (Philadelphia: Fortress Press, 1974), 1:104.

[17]A good summary of the linguistic situation is provided by Joseph Fitzmyer, "The Languages of Palestine in the First Century A.D.," *Catholic Biblical Quarterly* 32 (1970), 501-31; also in *A Wandering Aramean, Collected Aramaic Essays* (Missoula, Montana: Scholars Press, 1979), 29-56. Also see Robert Gundry, "The Language Milieu of First Century Palestine," *Journal of Biblical Literature* 83 (1964), 404-8; Martin Hengel, *Judaism and Hellenism*, vol. 1, 58-65; Harold Hoehner, *Herod Antipas*, 61-64.

tinian Jewish Christians.[18] The Hellenists were Jews or
Jewish Christians who habitually spoke Greek. Koine
Greek was the bond that held the Hellenistic world together
and its influence eventually surpassed that of Aramaic.
According to Hengel, "We have to count on the possibility
that even in Jewish Palestine, individual groups grew up
bilingual and thus stood right on the boundary of two
cultures."[19] Most probably some of the immediate disciples
of Jesus were bilingual. Andrew and Philip had Greek
names. Simon Peter, Andrew's brother, later took missionary journeys into the Western Diaspora where only Greek
was spoken. Evidence suggests that Jesus spoke Greek but
this suggestion must be seen only as probable. He was from
Nazareth which was rural and less hellenized, yet Greek was
spoken quite extensively in Galilee as a whole and especially
in the cities. Aramaic remained the primary language but
Greek was widespread as a second language. The name by
which we know Jesus himself is Greek (*Iēsous*), a hellenized
form of the Semitic Jeshua (*yēshûaʿ*).

Although Aramaic became the common language of Palestine during the post-exilic period, it never completely
replaced Hebrew. Opinions vary as to the extent of its use,
but Hebrew did not die out completely. There was probably
a vernacular Hebrew of the first century which later became
Mishnaic Hebrew. It is difficult to know whether Jesus
actually used Hebrew or not. J. A. Emerton concludes that
Jesus ordinarily spoke Aramaic, but perhaps also spoke
some Hebrew.[20] He maintains the high probability that
Hebrew was still used as a vernacular by some Jews in the
first century C.E. and continued to be used well into the
second century — in contrast to some who have maintained
that it was simply a dead language at this time. Yet Aramaic

[18]Fitzmyer, "Languages," *CBQ*, 515. C. F. D. Moule, "Once More, Who Were
the Hellenists?" *Expository Times* 70 (1958-59), 100-102.

[19]Hengel, *Judaism and Hellenism*, vol. 1, 105.

[20]J. A. Emerton, "The Problem of Vernacular Hebrew in the First Century A.D.
and the Language of Jesus," *Journal of Theological Studies* 24 (1973), 1-23; also
the earlier "Did Jesus Speak Hebrew?" *Journal of Theological Studies* 12 (1961),
189-202.

was the vernacular of most Jews. The cultural situation was bilingual and trilingual. The use of Aramaic was predominant; there was a widespread use of Greek and possibly a continued use of Hebrew among some. With respect to Jesus our conclusions remain tentative. He ordinarily spoke Aramaic in its Galilean dialect, which was different in pronunciation from the southern dialect spoken around Jerusalem. He probably spoke some Greek and at least read Hebrew.

The urban as well as the linguistic situation was much affected by hellenization, and the urban centers were an important part of first century Palestine, providing a vehicle for hellenization. More and more cities had become hellenized. The Cisjordan coastal plain comprised eleven Greek city states as they were organized under the Ptolemies, old Phoenician or Philistine cities or ports organized into Greek states, most falling under Hasmonean dominion during the period of Jewish independence but regaining some autonomy under Rome.[21] In addition to the coastal cities there were the Transjordan Greek cities as well; a league of these in Roman times was called the Decapolis, but they existed as states in the earlier Hellenistic period as well.

In addition to the Decapolis and the coastal cities, there were Greek cities in Galilee and Samaria. Philoteria was probably at the south end of the sea of Galilee, and probably dated from Ptolemaic times. In the far north, at the foot of Mt. Hermon, was Paneas, modern Banyas, the Caesarea Philippi of the tetrarchy of Philip. The city of Samaria had been settled with Greeks or Macedonians in Alexander's time, and was re-established under Herod the Great as Sebaste.

Thirty such Hellenistic or Graeco-Roman cities can be named, yet the heart of Palestine, especially Judah, remained Jewish, as one can see in the efforts of the pious Jews to resist the overwhelming hellenization around them during the Seleucid and Maccabean periods. Yet a Greek

---

[21]See Freyne, *Galilee*, 101-54; *Zondervan Bible Atlas*, ed. E. M. Blaiklock (Grand Rapids: Zondervan, 1969), 250-55, 293-94, 360-86.

fortress and a gymnasium were even established in Jerusalem under Antiochus Epiphanes and a theatre and an amphitheatre under Herod the Great. At the same time that Greek civilization was penetrating Palestinian Judaism, especially in more urban areas and among the upper classes, Judaism was resisting it lest it lead to a loss of identity. It was the forced hellenization under the stubborn Antiochus Epiphanes which precipitated the Maccabean revolt. The encounter with Hellenism had precipitated an internal crisis over how inclusive Judaism could be. The religious perspective was influenced by the socio-economic reality, the small but wealthy upper urban class increasingly favorable to Hellenism and a larger group who resisted the tendency to compromise.

After the Maccabean success, hellenization met with a defeat. The Hasidim had been ready to throw their lot in with Mattathias and his sons. These Hasidim may have been an ancestor of the later Pharisees and Essenes. They were rigorous with respect to the Law and the antagonism between hellenists and Hasidim was focused on the Law.[22] The encounter of Judaism with Hellenism became an encounter within Judaism itself, an encounter representing religious views, but also socio-economic ones, which views also had political implications. The success of the Maccabean and Hasidic revolt meant a continued sensitivity of Palestinian Judaism toward criticism of the Law, the tendency toward segregation from non-Jews, and a heightened national consciousness.

Hope and Eschatology in Judaism

Hope in pre-exilic Israel. Strictly speaking, the word "eschatological" refers to an end to history as we know it. Religious consciousness in Israelite and Judean history became eschatological; it was not that way in the beginning.

---

[22]Hengel, *Judaism and Hellenism*, vol. 1, 175-254, 303-14.

The eschatological perspective was a post-exilic phenomenon.

Throughout much of its history, Israel's consciousness was historical. Israelites were aware that the Lord had acted on their behalf in the days of old. Supreme among these acts, of course, was the exodus from Egypt with its promise from the Lord for a land of their own. The time of David (1000-961 B.C.E.) and Solomon (961-922 B.C.E.), the early monarchy, was also a time when the Lord seemed to favor the people. As the people looked back to these days and events, they saw the Lord close to them. Their history was a religious history, and this religious history was the basis for their identity. "The people" implied "the history," the major events of which were recalled and commemorated. The Moses-Sinai-Exodus tradition (especially in the north) and the David-Jerusalem-Zion tradition (primarily for the south) were essential to the self-understanding of the people.

The ideal of kingship which Judah set for itself was a religious ideal.[23] The king was the Lord's anointed one. The anointing signified his being chosen by the Lord and his function as an agent of the Lord. The king also acted as a priest during the great religious festivals. Thus great demands and expectations were placed upon the king. He was only human, "one chosen from the people" (Ps 89:20), dependent on the Lord, yet the Lord's own son by adoption (Ps 2:7). The king was expected to manifest the Lord's justice; he was to be an advocate for the oppressed, helpless, and unprotected; he had an obligation to provide for the poor (Ps 72). It was important that the king be faithful to this ideal so that the people would prosper and the Lord's favor remain with them. The king was anointed by another of the Lord's representatives, the priest.

The history of the kings of Israel and Judah, however, show that they fell short of the ideal. The kingship came to

[23]See Sigmund Mowinckel, *He That Cometh*, trans. G. W. Anderson (Nashville: Abingdon Press, 1954), 56-93.

be associated with unfulfilled expectations which gave rise to a hope for their fulfillment with the next or a future king.[24] This hope for the future was not in the pre-exilic period an eschatological hope, but it was rather an imminent and historical hope. This future but still historical consciousness emerged in the southern kingdom along with and within the prophetic movement. Two important texts indicative of this hope for a future king are those of Isaiah 7:10-14 and 9:1-6. Both passages are pre-exilic and, in their original setting, not eschatological in the strict sense. Both are important christologically because of a messianic interpretation later given them.

> Again the Lord spoke to Ahaz, "Ask a sign of the Lord your God; let it be deep as Sheol or high as heaven." But Ahaz said, "I will not ask, and I will not put the Lord to the test." And he said, "Hear then, O house of David! Is it too little for you to weary men, that you weary my God also? Therefore the Lord himself will give you a sign. Behold, a young woman shall conceive and bear a son, and shall call his name Immanuel." (Is 7:10-14)

The more probable interpretation of the original prophecy is that it referred to a future king of Israel soon to be born and in whom the hope and expectation of the people would be fulfilled. It was not looking forward to a far distant or final time. Indeed the young woman may have already been with child. The fact that the prophecy remained unfulfilled opened it to later re-interpretation, but originally it indicated a sign soon to be given to King Ahaz by the Lord. The woman would bear a son and give him the name Immanuel, and this would be a sign from the Lord to Ahaz. The sign would only be given, however, if the king showed trust in the Lord by refusing to negotiate with Assyria. If Ahaz was willing to trust in the Lord, a sign would be given him. Isaiah was thinking of an actual woman, possibly even the wife of King Ahaz.

[24]Ibid., 96-102.

Isaiah becomes intuitively certain that the queen is with child, that she will bear a son, and that Yahweh intends this as a token that the promise stands secure, that the wicked designs of the enemy will come to nothing, and that all the good fortune and salvation which, in accordance with the covenant, are associated with the birth of a prince will again be realized. *If* the king dares to commit himself and the country to Yahweh's omnipotence, she will bear a boy whose birth is the fulfillment of all the thoughts and wishes which were associated with the king and the royal child. Then the new-born child will be the ideal king whose very existence is a guarantee that "with us is God."[25]

There are, of course, other interpretations of this text. Most reject it, however, as a messianic prophecy in the sense that messianism came to be understood later in Judaism. Rather the text gives an example of the birth of hope in Israel as Israel looked forward to one to come. But at this period the one to come was to be a king of the Davidic line soon to appear.

But there will be no gloom for her that was in anguish. In the former time he brought into contempt the land of Zebulun and the land of Naphtali, but in the latter time he will make glorious the way of the sea, the land beyond the Jordan, Galilee of the nations.
The people who walked in darkness
 have seen a great light;
those who dwelt in a land of deep darkness,
 on them has light shined.
Thou has multiplied the nation,
 thou hast increased its joy ;
they rejoice before thee as with joy at the harvest,
 as men rejoice when they divide the spoil.

[25]Ibid., 118. Also see Otto Kaiser, *Isaiah 1-12*, trans. John Bowden, second edition, Old Testament Library (Philadelphia: The Westminster Press, 1983), 151-72.

> For the yoke of his burden,
>> and the staff for his shoulder,
>> the rod of his oppressor,
>> thou hast broken as on the day of Midian.
> For every boot of the tramping warrior in battle tumult
>> and every garment rolled in blood
>> will be burned as fuel for the fire.
> For to us a child is born,
>> to us a son is given;
> and the government will be upon his shoulder,
>> and his name will be called
> "Wonderful Counselor, Mighty God,
>> Everlasting Father, Prince of Peace." (Is 9:1-6)

Here the awaited child was a king-to-be who would sit upon the throne of David and fulfill the expectations of the people: fidelity to the Lord and peace and justice in the land. The birth of the child itself would be cause for joy; the people look forward to his coming reign. Darkness has been turned to light. Again we cannot explicitly identify who the child or prince was. Nor can we be certain that this was a prophecy of Isaiah himself. It may well have come from the circle of his disciples. But this is not important. The text points to a hope within pre-exilic, eighth century B.C.E. Judah, not an eschatological hope, but simply a hope for the future. In addition to the gaze toward the historical past, the great days of old, the times of David and Solomon and the Exodus itself, there also emerged a gaze toward the imminent historical future when God's presence would again be felt by the people and God's anointed one would reign over a land with peace and justice.

Hope During the Exile. Judean hope was seriously challenged and transformed with the disasters of 597 and 587. Was there anything at all to hope for? The city of the cult and the Temple itself had been destroyed, the future of the royal house and Davidic line had become precarious, the people were exiled and scattered. Yet the hope of Israel was not destroyed. It developed and took the shape of a hope for

an eventual restoration.[26] The crisis helped to turn the eyes
of the people even more to the future when the Lord would
once again visit the people and restore them. This hope,
unlike pre-exilic hope attached to a future king and his
reign, was simply at first a hope for the defeat of Babylon
and a return to Jerusalem. Exilic hope was not eschatological either. It looked forward to a future time in history, not
to the end times as such. The future was still very much of
this world — a political, national, as well as religious future.

The pre-exilic hope had been both prophetic and kingly.
It was prophetic in that it arose within or was associated
with prophetic or Isaian circles. It was kingly or royal in that
the hope was fixed on a future king or royal figure. The fall
of the northern kingdom had already created one crisis.
Amos and Hosea had proclaimed it. In the south, Isaiah not
only announced impending disaster but introduced the
notion of a remnant who would be saved. The destruction in
the south, however, was beyond belief. Yet even Jeremiah,
who knew that disaster was coming, held up a hope for
some.

> For thus says the Lord of hosts, the God of Israel: Houses
> and fields and vineyards shall again be bought in this
> land. (Jer 32:15)

The hope for restoration ranged from a naive optimism
(Jeremiah 39) to the prophetic hope against hope (Jeremiah
32). The task of reconstruction involved not only a political
hope but a religious call to conversion, such as is found in
Ezekiel. After the needed purification, the future day of the
Lord would come. Although politics and religion can be
distinguished, they cannot be separated in Israelite and
Judean history. The religious convictions of the people gave
birth to a hope which was both political and nationalistic.
The basis for the hope was the promise of the Lord.

With Deutero-Isaiah the hope was sustained, the end of

[26]Mowinckel, *He That Cometh*, 133-54.

the exile foreseen, and the hope for the restoration was transformed into grandiose and cosmic proportions. Cyrus on the horizon and the imminent fall of Babylon were indeed good news.

> How beautiful upon the mountains
>   are the feet of him who brings good tidings,
> who publishes peace, who brings good tidings of good,
>   who publishes salvation,
> who says to Zion, "Your God reigns." (Is 52:7)

The late exilic and early post-exilic Deutero-Isaian message was that the Lord of Israel had called and used Cyrus for his own purposes — to overcome Babylon and set God's people free. The royal house and temple would be restored; the Lord would give the ruler true righteousness; peace and prosperity would reign once again in the land.

A central feature in the late exilic or early post-exilic hope was the victory of the Lord and the Lord's coming reign in Zion. The Lord would rule. Although the aspirations remained national, the reign of God became central to the Jewish hope. But this reign was to be neither other-worldly nor eschatological. The Lord would make a new covenant with the people, and all the nations of the world would bow before God (Is 48:9-11). The expression which summed up this hope for the coming reign was "the day of the Lord." This great and glorious day contained several features: the political liberation of Israel, the restoration of the dynasty of David, the reunion of the north and the south, the return of the Diaspora, the religious and moral purification of the people, fertility in the land, peace among the nations, the restoration of Jerusalem as political and religious center of the world to which all the nations of the earth would give homage. It was a universalism and yet a nationalism.

The Emergence of Eschatological Messianism and Post-Exilic Hope. After the exile, prophecy in Israel died out. But there developed a role for the sage and wisdom, for the scribe and Torah, and for the high priest and Temple. It was during this period that Jewish hope became eschatological

and there emerged a messianic consciousness.[27] Pre-exilic
and exilic hope had been prophetic, royal, and nationalistic.
This nationalism continued with the development of
messianism.

The Hebrew and Aramaic words for "messiah" mean "the
anointed one." The Greek equivalent is "christos." This
Messiah (or Christ), a post-exilic development, was an
eschatological king associated with the end times. One does
not find the concept of the eschatological Messiah as such in
the Hebrew Scriptures. There messiah simply means the
king. The concept of an ideal king as the Lord's anointed one
is early in Israelite history, but this anointed, earthly king
and representative of the Lord is not the same as the later
expected Messiah. Centuries of development led from the
concept of the ideal king to the expectation of an eschatological king or Messiah. The eschatological aspect arose out
of the disillusion of the post-exilic hope: the restoration was
in no way comparable to what was expected or hoped for.
Thus the hope fastened itself further into the future; the day
of the Lord may not be close at hand but will come. The
Messiah was not only an eschatological figure but was a
political and national figure as well, an expected king whose
reign would be final.

The source materials for developing the concept of Messiah were the Scriptures, in particular the prophetic literature, especially as it had come to be interpreted or
understood in the post-exilic period, not as it had been
understood in the eighth or sixth centuries B.C.E. In addition, many of the prophetic and messianic passages in the
Hebrew Scriptures were themselves of post-exilic origin.
Exceptions to this would be at least Isaiah 7:10-14 and 9:1-6,
but these came to be re-interpreted within a post-exilic
world of messianic eschatology. The Messiah is, as
Mowinckel indicates, "the ideal king entirely transferred to
the future, no longer identified with the specific historical
king, but with one who, one day, will come."[28]

[27]Ibid., 126-33.
[28]Ibid., 123.

It should be clear, if for no other reason than to bring
clarity into the complexity of eschatology, that not all hope
was eschatological. The history of Israel's hope was not
coterminus with the history of Jewish eschatology, although
the former includes the latter. One can distinguish between
prophetic hope (pre-exilic) and messianic hope or eschatology (post-exilic). There was a prophetic eschatology only in
the sense that the prophets are re-interpreted, but eschatology was not in the consciousness of the earlier classical
prophets themselves. One can well argue whether Deutero-
Isaiah has eschatological elements, although he probably
does not in the strict sense. His was a hope for restoration,
and it was only the disillusion accompanying the actual
restoration that produced eschatological hope. Israel's hope
developed amid continued disillusionment. It shifted from
the notion of the king as a national, political, historical
figure and an anointed representative of the Lord to a king
to come, to the king of the restored kingdom, to the final
eschatological king (a national, political and historical figure but *the* anointed one). The kingdom was always both of
this world and of God. The Messiah would be the future
eschatological fulfillment of the ideal king who would reign
on behalf of the Lord whose reign it truly was. This Messiah
was to be a historical king of David's line.[29] Other expressions also connoted this messianic figure, such as the Son of
David.

The messianic concept itself underwent development and
variation. In the earlier post-exilic stage the Messiah was in
the background; it was the Lord who would rule and gather
the peoples together. The Messiah at first would not actually establish the kingdom but would rule once God's reign
began. Gradually, however, varying and even inconsistent
expectations developed. The dominant messianic conception was that of a political, national, this-worldly, historical
figure of David's line.[30] Micah 5:1 led to the belief that he

[29]Ibid., 155-86.
[30]Ibid., 280-345.

would be born in Bethlehem. In addition to the royal Davidic Messiah, there developed a less prominent expectation of a "priestly, Levitical Messiah." During the Maccabean/Hasmonean times royal and priestly functions became united in one person. The *Book of Jubilees*, which was important to the Essenes, spoke not at all of a future for the house of Judah but only for the house of Levi. In the *Testament of the Twelve Patriarchs*, a Levitical Messiah existed along with the Davidic Messiah of the house of Judah. Thus some expectations included that of a new high priest as well as a new king. Yet the dominant notion remained that of the Son of David.

The coming of the Messiah was known to God alone. Due to Israel's sins, the Messiah's coming was delayed; Israel needed to be cleansed. A period of repentance would precede the coming of the Messiah, and there would be forerunners to prepare his way and call the people to conversion. Malachi, the last of the biblical prophets, spoke of the return of Elijah. His prophecy formed the basis for the widespread belief in a prophet like Elijah as the forerunner of the Messiah.

> Behold, I will send you Elijah the prophet before the great and terrible day of the Lord comes, And he will turn the hearts of fathers to their children and the hearts of children to their fathers, lest I come and smite the land with a curse. (Mal 4:5-6)

Initially this was not so much a hope for Elijah himself as for an eschatological prophet anointed with the spirit of Elijah. The concept of a translated Elijah coming from heaven is probably a post 70 C.E. development.[31]

In addition to the Elijah expectation, Moses or a prophet like Moses was expected.

---

[31]James D. G. Dunn, *Christology in the Making. A New Testament Inquiry into the Origins of the Doctrine of the Incarnation* (Philadelphia: The Westminster Press, 1980), 92-95.

> The Lord your God will raise up for you a prophet like me
> from among you, from your brethren — him you shall
> heed — just as you desired of the Lord your God at Horeb
> on the day of the assembly , when you said, "Let me not
> hear again the voice of the Lord my God, or see this great
> fire any more, lest I die." And the Lord said to me, "They
> have rightly said all that they have spoken. I will raise up
> for them a prophet like you from among their brethren;
> and I will put my words in his mouth, and he shall speak
> to them all that I command him." (Dt 18:15-18)

Enoch also gets mentioned as a forerunner, as does "the
Prophet of the end times." Sometimes several forerunners
were envisioned.

We can see the complexity and variety of messianic
expectations and these have not included the later apocalyptic influences. We already see kingly (the Davidic Messiah),
priestly (the Levitical Messiah), and prophetic (the forerunners) expectations with respect to the age to come, and
sometimes but not often these get combined into one. The
Messiah himself was to be endowed with the gift of God's
holy spirit. He was to free his people, and his dominion was
to include all the nations and he was to rule with justice. Not
only did messianic hopes vary but not all the Jewish people
were equally influenced by them. Messianism for some was
a minor aspect of their faith.

Apocalyptic Eschatology. Jewish hope for the future
eventually became an eschatological hope and a messianic
hope. In the post-exilic period eschatology developed in
other than strict messianic directions as well. Late in the
post-exilic period eschatology became apocalyptic.

One of the influences in late Second Temple Judaism was
a temporal and spatial dualism: the notion of two eras, "this
age" and "the age to come," with an abrupt transition from
one to the other. The present era was under the dominion of

the powers of evil, a "kingdom of Satan," and the age to come, a "kingdom of God." [32]

The apocalyptic kingdom of God, however, was not the same as the messianic kingdom. The messianic kingdom was of this world; the apocalyptic kingdom was otherworldly. The two kingdoms represented different expectations with regard to the eschatological future. An apocalyptic dualism developed within Judaism during the Hellenistic period and manifested Babylonian and Persian influence as well as the influence of the "new learning" or "wisdom." This apocalyptic dualism gave rise to an otherworldly, transcendent side to eschatology. The "day of the Lord" was understood to be an age completely different from what we experience here on earth and a divine intervention from outside of history would bring it about. The "new eschatology" was not only a temporal and dramatic dualism. It also tended to be cosmic and individualistic — involving cosmic forces and calamities, and the object of salvation was the individual rather than the nation.

The apocalyptic view of the two ages presented the present order as evil and transitory, and the coming age as supernatural, eternal, and blessed. Also, in the final days, the satanic power would appear as an "Antichrist," sometimes envisioned more historically, sometimes more supernaturally, but always the powerful enemy of God who would be crushed in the latter days. Then the Lord, "the Ancient of Days," would sit in judgment over the living and the dead. The doctrine of resurrection, taught by the Pharisees, had its own history, and was not simply the result of apocalyptic thought, but apocalyptic influenced its way of being conceptualized as well. We must not think, however, that this apocalyptic speculation simply replaced the earlier speculation or that the two were always easily distinguished. The

[32]Mowinckel, *He That Cometh*, 262-84.

apocalyptic and messianic perspective continued together and were often mixed.

Many of the earlier, political, nationalistic expectations continued to exist along with the new other-worldly expectations. They not only continued but often mingled with each other as worldly and other-worldly elements blended. One of the ways by which the two perspectives were reconciled was the notion of the millennium.[33] Typical of millennial thought was the idea that there would be an interim age between the present age and the age to come, the present being followed by a period of a thousand years. The length varied, during which millennium or messianic age an earthly messiah would rule, then die. Then the end would come with its new heaven and new earth and new supra-terrestrial order. We find this eschatology in the Ezra apocalypse. It involves a first judgment prior to the Messiah's kingdom on earth, and a second judgment prior to the new creation. There were variations on this millennial theme where the glorious millennium was the conclusion of the present age rather than an interim period. In this variation the resurrection of the dead did not precede but followed the reign of the Messiah. There also developed the distinction between the kingdom of the Messiah on this earth and the kingdom of God in the new world. These interpretations exemplify the efforts to unite the conflicting "this-worldly" and "otherworldly" perceptions of the future.

The this-worldly messianism and other-worldly apocalypticism, although distinguishable and co-existing within Judaism between 200 B.C.E. and 100 C.E., interpenetrated and influenced one another. As George Foot Moore writes,

> For orderliness we may distinguish between the national form of the expectation, a coming golden age for the Jewish people, and what for want of a better word may be called the eschatological form [what we have been calling apocalyptic form], the final catastrophe of the world as it is and the coming in its place of a new world, which in so

[33]Ibid., 168, 277, 324-27.

far as it lies beyond human experience of nature we may call supernatural. But it must be understood that in all the earlier part of our period the two are not sharply distinguished, but run into each other and blend like the overlapping edges of two clouds.[34]

Although the idea of Messiah varied, the prevailing expectation associated with him was that of a political and national savior for Israel. This form of the Jewish hope was popular with the people whereas apocalyptic eschatology was not. Apocalyptic was related to learned wisdom, priests, and oriental thought.

Apocalyptic eschatology emerged and spread within Israel between 200 B.C.E. and 100 C.E., a period of crisis and revolt, from the Maccabean wars to the Great War of 66-70 C.E. Between the two revolts there was the experience of political freedom gained (with the Hasmoneans) and of political freedom lost (with the Roman occupation) — a time of extensive religious self-reflection which was then formed into a new literature. The many roots of apocalypticism are difficult to pin down. H. H. Rowley's long accepted view was that apocalypticism was a development of ancient prophecy.[35]

We must be careful in our references to apocalyptic. As P.D. Hanson, and more recently J. J. Collins, have pointed out, we must distinguish the literary genre (apocalypse), an eschatological perspective (apocalyptic eschatology), and a socio-religious movement (apocalypticism).[36] The word apocalypse refers specifically to a literary genre adopted by

[34]George Foot Moore, *Judaism in the First Centuries of the Christian Era*, 2 vols. (New York: Schocken Books, [1927] 1971), 2:323. Material in brackets mine. Moore presents a good summary of messianic expectations and eschatology, vol. 2, 323-95. Also see Schurer, vol. 2, 488-554.

[35]H. H. Rowley, *The Relevance of Apocalyptic* (New York: Harper and Row, 1955).

[36]Paul D. Hanson, *The Dawn of Apocalyptic* (Philadelphia: Fortress Press, 1979), 428-44, esp. 429-34. Also, John J. Collins, *The Apocalyptic Imagination, An Introduction to the Jewish Matrix of Christianity* (New York: Crossroad, 1984), esp.1-32.

apocalyptic seers to communicate their messages. In addition to apocalyptic literature, there is apocalyptic eschatology, a particular type of eschatology that is often contrasted with prophetic eschatology and exemplifies the difference between a historical, this-worldly perspective and a dualistic, other-worldly perspective. But eschatology itself is not necessarily the most characteristic trait of the literary apocalypses or the apocalyptic socio-religious movement. Nor can the apocalyptic eschatological perspective be identified with any one group or party within Judaism. Nor is it uniform; there are different types or strands of apocalyptic eschatology.

Besides referring to a body of literature and a type of eschatology, apocalypticism was a social and religious movement in which the disappointment and frustration connected with historical hopes became resolved. Such movements can be recognized in the early post-exilic period, in the second century Maccabean period, in the first and second centuries C.E., in the Middle Ages, as well as today. Apocalypticism involves an extra-historical reversal of the course of history. In history the righteous suffer and the unrighteous prosper. This situation was to be reversed by a divine intervention.

Hanson has directed much of his research toward showing that apocalyptic movements arise out of identifiable sociological settings: for example, a group experience of alienation and oppression or a group reaction against foreign domination, as found in the Maccabean response to Antiochus IV; or a group reaction against a dominating party within one's own nation, such as Hanson describes the early post-exilic conflict surrounding the rebuilding of the Temple. For Hanson, the origins of apocalypticism lay within this inner community struggle. After the exile there were two distinctive and rival plans for the restoration — a visionary program (Deutero-Isaiah 60-62) and a Zadokite program (Ezekiel 40-48).[37] Conflict between the proponents

---

[37]Paul D. Hanson, 6-77, 89-100.

of these two programs was inevitable after the ascendancy and dominance of the Zadokite group returning from the exile and their disregard for the ideals of the Levitical group which had remained in Palestine during the exile. The Zadokite program of those returning left little or no room for the Levitical/Palestinian group within the cult itself. The social situation at the time of the construction of the Second Temple excluded one group from a significant role in the cult and alienated that group from its oppressor. The alienated group translated its own hopes into a more visionary and apocalyptic perspective. This situation of polarization and conflict provided the social matrix for the development of prophetic eschatology into apocalyptic eschatology.

A group response to oppression or powerlessness, as Hanson points out, can take many forms: (1) effort at reform (the alienated priests in the rebuilding of the Temple); (2) the withdrawal and the founding of a new, more utopian society (Qumran Essenes); (3) retreat into a subculture or subsociety (some hasidic movements); (4) violent revolution (the Zealots).[38] The less the oppressed group looks to history for resolution, the more its eschatological perspective becomes apocalyptic. Apocalypticism involves a particular religious response to the contradictions of history when the solution to the polarizing, historically-experienced alienation is seen to lie beyond history.

Although apocalyptic eschatology manifested a continuity with prophecy, it is clearly distinguishable from what we have called prophetic eschatology. Apocalyptic eschatology also manifested a relationship to wisdom.[39] The apocalyptic notion of a divine world order was based in the wisdom tradition.

---

[38]Ibid., 435.

[39]See Gerhard von Rad, *Old Testament Theology*, trans. D. M. G. Stalker, 2 vols. (New York: Harper and Row, 1962-65), 2:263-315; *Wisdom in Israel*, trans. James D. Martin (Nashville: Abingdon Press, 1972), 263-319.

3

Jesus and the People

With respect to Galilee, Sean Freyne has emphasized a distinction between city and country which endured despite hellenization.[1] In addition to this urban and rural social distinction, there was also the economic reality of class distinction. A. N. Sherwin-White notes the absence of a middle class in the socio-economic world of Galilee.[2] Freyne points out that the economic developments which did take place in Galilee in the second and first centuries B.C.E. were to the advantage of the few rather than the many.[3]

In Galilee, agriculture was the most important occupation and the basis of economic life. The fishing industry was confined to the region around the lakes. Even given the fact of increased urbanization, Galilee's population was largely rural. Sepphoris and Tiberias were the only two urban centers. Since Galilee remained so rural and agricultural, a key to the economic situation was the question of land ownership. The Galileans were for centuries a fairly stable

[1] Sean Freyne, *Galilee from Alexander the Great to Hadrian, 323 B.C.E. to 135 C.E., a Study of Second Temple Judaism* (Co-published by Michael Glazier and University of Notre Dame Press, 1980), 195.

[2] A. N. Sherwin-White, *Roman Society and Roman Law in the New Testament* (Oxford: Clarendon Press, 1963), 139-43. Also see Freyne, *Galilee from Alexander the Great to Hadrian*, 165, 176; Harold Hoehner, *Herod Antipas* (Cambridge: University Press, 1972), 70-73.

[3] Freyne, *Galilee from Alexander the Great to Hadrian*, 1976.

population. There was no great change in land ownership patterns in the Ptolemaic and Seleucid periods. This trend was altered during Herodian times as more and more land was confiscated by or distributed by Herod the Great and Herod Antipas. Herod the Great may have owned over half the land in his kingdom.[4] Thus there developed the two classes of wealthy landowners and impoverished peasants. By the time of Jesus this was the dominant picture.

The situation in Judea was not the same. Whereas Galilee remained influenced by agriculture, Judea was dominated by the city of Jerusalem. Jerusalem's sphere of influence as a "Hellenistic" city gave her a unique character and position. In Jerusalem there was not only a growing distinction between the rich and the poor, but also the semblance of a middle class.[5]

The rich of Jerusalem included not only large property owners, but also tax farmers, merchants, a priestly "aristocracy," and the royal family. Wealth manifested itself in one's homes, clothing, monuments, servants, banquets, and in the number of wives. Within the middle class in Jerusalem, many working with trades and crafts owned homes and shops in the bazaars. Some of the priests were middle class; others were very poor. Only the priestly aristocracy belonged to the wealthy class itself, for example, Ananias, Annas, Caiaphas. Many of the ordinary priests lived in poverty, as did the majority of the people.[6]

The economically poor included the domestic servants in the homes of the rich, an even larger number of day laborers, and an increasingly large number of beggars concentrated around the holy places — the blind, the lame, the lepers. Also among the poor were many scribes, teachers, and scholars of the Law who were forbidden to be paid for their services. Some of these had other trades, but most had to depend on subsidy.

[4]Hoehner, *Herod Antipas*, 70.

[5]Joachim Jeremias, *Jerusalem in the Time of Jesus* (London: SCM Press, 1969), 27-30, 51-57, 73-84, 100-108.

[6]Ibid., 96-119.

The Jewish Aristocracy

The Sanhedrin reflected both Jewish self-rule with respect to internal and judicial affairs but also a power elite within Judaism. Although by the time of Jesus it included representation from a larger, more popular, and Pharisaic base (after 76 B.C.E., the rule of Salome Alexandra), it was predominantly aristocratic. According to Joachim Jeremias, its seventy-one members fell into three groups: chief priests (the priestly aristocracy), elders (the lay aristocracy), and scribes (of the Sadduccees and of the Pharisees, an emerging power base of some of the scholars).[7]

The clergy or priesthood in Judaism manifested both higher and lower ranks, a priestly aristocracy in contrast to the majority of priests who were less powerful and often poor. All the priestly offices were hereditary. The aristocracy comprised both the reigning high priest and the chief priests; the others were simply known as the priests and Levites. According to tradition, the Zadokite family, named after Zadok, the chief priest under Solomon, held the high priesthood in unbroken succession since Aaron (actually probably only since Solomon). This uninterrupted succession lasted until the appointment of Menelaus (172-162) under Antiochus IV Epiphanes, an appointment which ended the Zadokite line of high priests in Jerusalem. In 152 Jonathan the Hasmonean took the high priesthood to himself, a descendant of a priestly but non-aristocratic, non-Zadokite priestly family. His assumption of the high priestly office met with criticism and resistance. The Hasmoneans retained the high priesthood until the time of Herod the Great who put to death all the males of the Hasmonean line. During the Herodian and later Roman period high priests (most of whom were considered illegitimate, not from high priestly families) had come to be appointed by will of the king or the procurator.

The reigning high priest was the head of the priesthood and president of the Sanhedrin. He was the only human

[7]Ibid., 197, 222; see 147-245.

being entitled to enter the Holy of Holies, once a year on the Day of Atonement. Even if no longer functioning as a high priest, he retained the title of high priest. In rank after the high priest were, in order: the captain of the Temple, the directors of the weekly course, the directors of the daily course, the overseers of the Temple, and the treasurers. The captain of the Temple was chosen from among the aristo-cratic priestly families and could well succeed to the high priesthood itself. The Palestinian Talmud indicates that the high priest would not be elected high priest if he had not first been captain of the Temple. The captain was, in general, in charge of the cult and the officiating priests. After him came the 24 directors of the weekly courses, then up to 156 directors of the daily courses. The director of the weekly course had a week of duty once every twenty-four weeks and during the three pilgrim festivals. He performed rites of purification. Each weekly course consisted of four or more daily courses. The directors of weekly and daily courses lived throughout Judea and Galilee and not necessarily in Jerusalem. The next officers, the overseers and treasurers, were permanent appointments. There were at least seven overseers and three treasurers who administered finances, revenues and expenses.

The chief priests who were permanent in the Temple formed an aristocratic elite with seats and votes in the Sanhedrin. Thus within the priesthood itself there existed a social gap between the chief priests and the others. The high priest and Jerusalem chief priests came from special priestly families. In the first century C.E. there were two groups of high priestly families, the legitimate descendants of the Zadokites serving in Leontopolis (in Egypt, where Onias III had founded a Temple), and the illegitimate Jerusalem group. The Jerusalem group exercised great power. Of the twenty-eight who were high priests between 37 B.C.E. and 70 C.E., two were legitimate, one was the last of the Hasmo-neans, and twenty-five were illegitimate or from non-high priestly families who rose quickly to power in the Herodian-Roman period. Twenty-two of these twenty-five came from four Jerusalem families, the two most powerful being the families of Boethus and Annas, with eight high priests each. Annas, his five sons, his son-in-law Caiaphas, and grandson, Matthias, were all high priests.

In contrast to the priestly aristocracy were the "ordinary priests" and "Levites." The "priests," all the priests of Judea and Galilee, were divided into twenty-four groups or classes by tradition. Each group was responsible for one week of duty every twenty-four weeks, and each group was further divided into four to nine families who took turns with daily duties during that week. These priests came to Jerusalem only for their duties which involved two weeks of the year and the three pilgrim festivals. Still lower on the social scale were those simply called Levites. They too were divided into twenty-four groups. They were singers and musicians in the Temple and performed other responsibilities including that of a police force for the Temple.

All of these offices were hereditary. All were descendants of the tribe of Levi. Some were also descendants of one Levite in particular, Aaron. Thus there was already a distinction among the descendants of Levi, the "Levites" so called, and the Aaronites or priests. Within the priesthood there was a further distinction among the descendants of Aaron. The high priests were descended from one prominent Aaronite, namely Zadok. The "Levites" (the non-Aaronite Levites) were a lower order than the "priests" (the non-Zadokite priests) who were lower than the high priests (the Zadokites). With the flight of the Zadokite family and the destruction of the Hasmoneans, the priestly aristocracy continued with the new wealthy Jerusalem families.

In addition to the priestly aristocracy, there had also developed a lay aristocracy. In post-exilic times, without a king, ancient ruling families had become the basis of social order. These heads of the prominent families began to play a new role in a new society. In the post-exilic world, the Sanhedrin, the supreme assembly, represented both the leading priestly and lay families of Judaism — the aristocracy. The lay aristocracy, heads of the leading Jerusalem families, were the "elders" of the people. They were large land-owning families and mainly Sadducees.

In addition to the chief priests and the elders, the scribes were represented on the Sanhedrin. Some of them were priests but most were not. They had given their lives to study and scholarship and usually began these studies at an early age. Scribes were also called rabbis, but this title had not become fixed in the time of Jesus nor was it limited to those who had undergone formal study. Apart from the chief priests and elders, only scribes were members of the Sanhedrin. This group represented a less aristocratic portion in the Sanhedrin, since theoretically any male could become a scribe if he gave himself to a life of study. There were Sadducean scribes, but a large number were the scribes of the Pharisees.[8] This was the only way the Pharisees were represented on the Sanhedrin. The aristocratic families were Sadducean.

Taxation

During the Ptolemaic and Seleucid periods tax collecting was taken away from a specific representative of the king (the practice in the Persian period) and given to the highest bidder, a practice known as tax farming.[9] Opening tax collection to a bidder opened the door to widespread abuse. Whatever revenue the collector could gather over and above what he owed became his own income. Hence most tax collectors were both wealthy and despised. During the Roman period the system of tax farming continued. The Roman officials in Palestine had responsibility for collecting taxes, but the taxes were frequently farmed out. These tax farmers were sometimes Roman, sometimes Jewish, and

---

[8]There is some dispute about who the scribes were. I have followed Jeremias here, *Jerusalem in the Time of Jesus*, 233-45. Yet it has also been argued that the scribes and Pharisees were co-terminus or synonymous. See Ellis Rivkin, "Scribes, Pharisees, Lawyers, Hypocrites: a Study in Synonymity," *Hebrew Union College Annual* 49 (1978), 135-42. Also, Ellis Rivkin, *A Hidden Revolution* (Nashville: Abingdon Press, 1978).

[9]For further background on taxation, see Marcus Borg, *Conflict, Holiness and Politics in the Teachings of Jesus* (New York: Edwin Mellen Press, 1984), 31-33; Freyne, *Galilee from Alexander the Great to Hadrian*, 183-194; F. C. Grant, *The Economic Background of the Gospels* (London: Oxford University Press, 1926), 87-110; Hoehner, *Herod Antipas*, 73-79.

they hired others, often Jews, to do the actual collecting. Zaccheus evidently was a Jewish tax farmer in the Jericho region. The Jewish tax collector was generally despised both for the wealth which he collected at the expense of others, his fellow Jews, and also for the service which he performed for the oppressive foreign power, an act of disloyalty for Jewish nationalists. From the Jewish perspective, the tax collector was a public sinner.

In addition to the method of collection, another major problem was the burden imposed by two sets of obligations. Both sets affected the farmers the most. There was a civil or political tax imposed by the foreign political power as well as the religious tax or tithes required of the Jews by the Law. F.C. Grant writes, "Under the Romans, therefore, there was a twofold taxation of the Jewish people, civil and religious; each of these had been designed without regard to the other, and therefore could not be modified in its favor." [10]

In addition to the Roman/ Herodian taxes, the Jews were taxed as part of their religious obligations, and varied tithes existed, such as on agricultural produce. These supported the priests, Levites, Temple treasury, and some went to the poor and to the scribes. F. C. Grant lists twelve such religious tax obligations which had accumulated and describes the sum total as "nothing short of enormous." [11] For example, the Law required every year an offering of "first fruits," which ranged from one to three percent of the produce. Also, every year, there was the tithe of ten percent for the support of the priests, Levites, and Temple. In the first, second, fourth and fifth years of the seven-year sabbatical cycle, there was a second tithe of an additional ten percent. In the third and sixth years, there was a tithe of ten percent for the poor. Thus the amount required by Law on agricultural produce alone was over twenty percent. There was also the annual Temple half shekel tax (about a day's wage).

To these religious (divinely revealed) taxes, the Romans had added their own crop, land and poll taxes. The taxes due

[10]F. C. Grant, *The Economic Background of the Gospels*, 89.
[11]Ibid., 94-97.

Rome were over and above the requirements of the Law. Grant estimates that "the total taxation of the Jewish people in the time of Jesus, civil and religious combined, must have approached the intolerable proportion of between 30 and 40 percent; it may have been higher still."[12]

The Religious Situation

It is a mistake to think of early Palestinian Judaism as a unified whole. The many cultural, economic, political, and religious factors at work between 200 B.C.E. and 70 C.E. manifested themselves in pluralism and sectarianism. There was the earlier split between the Hellenists and the Hasidim over how much of tradition could be compromised with the new Hellenistic civilization, and this was followed by pro- and anti-Hasmonean forces, as well as Herodian and anti-Herodian factions. By the first century C.E., there were at least three major "parties" — the Sadducees, Pharisees, and Essenes — as well as other varied ascetical, baptist, messianic and resistance movements.

Although we think of the *Sadducees* as a religious party, they were a social, economic, and political party as well.[13] Socially the Sadducees were the aristocratic members of society, the economically wealthy. Politically they were those who had sufficiently benefited from Roman presence to be politically favorable to the *status quo*. In 66-70 C.E., however, the uprising began with some of the aristocrats, but they soon lost control as the movement was given direction by the Zealots.

In Roman times the high priest was ordinarily Sadducean. The later Hasmoneans as well as the families of the illegitimate high priestly aristocracy were Sadducean. The

---

[12]Ibid., 105.

[13]See Jeremias, *Jerusalem in the Time of Jesus*, 222-32. Also "Sadducees," vol. 14, *Encyclopedia Judaica* (1971), 620-22; and Emil Shurer, *The History of the Jewish People in the Age of Jesus Christ*, revised and edited by Geza Vermes, *et al*, vol. 2 (Edinburgh: T. and T. Clark, 1979), 404-14.

lay aristocracy was mostly Sadducean. The Sadducees *were* the aristocracy. They lacked the popular support of the people. They were a small group, but significant, an elite, centered in Jerusalem. After the destruction of the Temple in 70 C.E., they disappeared.

From a religious point of view, the Sadducees were a more conservative party than the Pharisees, their major rival. The major point of theological difference between the Sadducees and the Pharisees was that of the oral tradition and oral Law, accepted by the Pharisees, rejected by the Sadducees. The Law had been and still was the Torah, the books of Moses, the first five of the Hebrew Scriptures. But many writings had developed since that time and were considered Scripture as well. In addition, through the centuries, the Law had been in need of interpretation. Thus there had developed in addition to the written Law, an oral Law, later codified into the Mishnah in the latter half of the second century C.E. The Sadducees considered this oral Law as lacking in authority.

A rejection of the development of the oral tradition included a rejection of the later angelology, resurrection and afterlife, and thus a rejection of the system of future punishments and rewards. Of course, Sadducees did not need to look toward heavenly rewards; they had received theirs in this life. Their denial of the resurrection is the issue that Paul used to split the Sanhedrin when he was brought before them, gaining the support of the Pharisees by proclaiming that what he preached about Jesus was a problem only because he preached Jesus raised from the dead (Acts 23:6-10). We hear of the Sadducees after the reign of John Hyrcanus (135-104 B.C.E.) who had supported them since the Pharisees had become critical of his illegitimate high priesthood. Later Alexandra (76-67 B.C.E.) shifted her support to the Pharisees.

The *Pharisees*, in contrast to the Sadducees, were a popular party, more representative of the people.[14] They were

[14]John Bowker, *Jesus and the Pharisees* (Cambridge: University Press, 1973). Jacob Neusner, *From Politics to Piety; the Emergence of Pharisaic Judaism*

essentially but not exclusively a lay group and staunch supporters of the oral Law including the doctrines of resurrection and rewards or punishments. Although the theological differences with the Sadducees are significant, the Pharisees are probably better understood as those who upheld a strict observance of the Law.

There are many questions about Pharisaism which are difficult to answer and yet are of great interest because of its link with post 70 C.E. Rabbinic Judaism and its frequent role as foil in the New Testament where Pharisaism was concerned for the purity of Israel. Some have held that the Pharisees were descendants of the Hasidim who were perhaps also the ancestors of the Essenes before they broke with worship in Jerusalem because of the illegitimate Hasmonean priesthood. During the rule of the Hasmoneans, from John Hyrcanus (135-104 B.C.E.) to Alexander Janneus (103-76 B.C.E.), the Pharisees grew in support among the people but were prevented by the Hasmoneans from having any effective political power. They were critics of the illegitimate Hasmonean priesthood but did not reject it as completely as did the Essenes. By the time of his death, Alexander Janneus recognized the growing strength of the Pharisees and advised his wife, Salome Alexandra (76-67 B.C.E.), to reconcile herself with them. They then grew in political significance. It was probably at this time that their scribes were allowed seats on the Sanhedrin prior to which the Sanhedrin would have been exclusively Sadducean. Herod the Great recognized their power as well and tried not to push them too far.

The Pharisees became guardians of racial purity and a symbol for the true Israel. Yet the Pharisees were not as separatist as the Essenes (who completely refused to worship in Jerusalem) nor as the later Zealots (who refused to accept the Roman occupation) nor aristocrats like the Sadducees. In one sense, they were political and religious mod-

(Englewood Cliffs, N.J.: Prentice-Hall, 1973). A classic is Louis Finkelstein's *Pharisees*, 2 vols. (Philadelphia: Jewish Publication Society of America, 1962). Also see the article and bibliography, "Pharisees," vol. 13, *Encyclopedia Judaica* (1971), 363-66a; Emil Schurer, vol. 2, 388-403. Also see n. 8 in this chapter.

erates. In the beginning it seems as if they may have been closed communities of brotherhoods not unlike the Essenes.[15]

While the Pharisees can be somewhat defined over against the Sadducees, they saw themselves as the racially pure ones in Judaism over against the *am ha-aretz* and thus, socially speaking, represented a middle segment in society. Thus the first centuries, B.C.E. and C.E., saw something of a shift from the power of the old ruling aristocratic families to the more popularly based Pharisees, a shift which represented a struggle for political power where religious issues played a major role. Although it is common for Christians to associate all Pharisees with hypocrisy, there were many good Pharisees. The later Talmud speaks of seven kinds of Pharisees. Jesus was a friend of some Pharisees, and in Luke 13:31 some Pharisees warned Jesus about Herod's seeking his life. Pharisaism in itself manifested a variety of views with respect to the interpretation of the Law. The two most prominent schools of opinion in the age of Herod the Great were those of Hillel and Shammai (c. 20-10 B.C.E.).[16]

Given the extensive amount of material made available and the number of articles since the discoveries at Qumran and in the Judean desert as a whole, it is difficult to present any adequate summary of the *Essenes*.[17] They, like the Pharisees, may have had a relation to the ancient Hasidim. They may indeed have broken away from the Pharisees when the Hasmoneans usurped the high priesthood. The

[15]See Jeremias, *Jerusalem in the Time of Jesus*, 251-54; Sandmel, *Judaism and Christian Beginnings* (New York: Oxford University Press, 1978), 161; Geza Vermes, *The Dead Sea Scrolls, Qumran in Perspective* (Cleveland: World Pub. Co., 1978), 120-21.

[16]Sandmel, *Judaism and Christian Beginnings*, 237-42. Also "Sages," vol. 14, *Encyclopedia Judaica* (1971), 636-56.

[17]See Jerome Murphy-O'Connor, "The Judean Desert," in *Early Judaism and Its Modern Interpreters*, ed. Robert A. Kraft and George W. E. Nickelsburg, vol. 2 of *The Bible and Its Modern Interpreters*, forthcoming; and "Qumran and the New Testament," in *The New Testament and Its Modern Interpreters*, ed. Eldon Jay Epp and George W. Mac Rae, vol. 3 of *The Bible and Its Modern Interpreters*, forthcoming. Also Geza Vermes, *The Dead Sea Scrolls, Qumran in Perspective*. Also see "Essenes," vol. 6, *Encyclopedia Judaica* (1971), 899-902.

movement seems to have been a Palestinian phenomenon originating in conjunction with the religious persecution of the Seleucids.

The Essenes seem to have been a movement or sect located in the varied towns of Judea and in the wilderness west of the Dead Sea, especially at Qumran. Both the desert and town members followed the same leader and Qumran was the site of the leadership. At Qumran they lived a fairly communal or monastic life, without private property, with a three year period of probation, and with the practice of celibacy, although some married. Having repudiated the illegitimate worship at the Temple in Jerusalem, they were seen as having withdrawn from the larger Jewish society. Their *Community Rule* describes the way of life at Qumran.[18] Their religious life involved ritual washings and baptism, common prayer, and the study of the Hebrew Scriptures. Their interpretation of the Law was stricter than that of the Pharisees. The Essenes were both politically and religiously non-compromising.

It is almost unanimously accepted today that the people associated with the Qumran scrolls are the Essenes. The Qumran manuscripts antedate 68 C.E., when the community was dispersed during the Jewish War after which time the Essenes fade from history. The movement existed for approximately twenty years before the coming of the Teacher of Righteousness who became its leader. This leader was a particular individual and contemporary of Jonathan (161-143 B.C.E.). The manuscripts speak not only of this teacher but also of the wicked priest whom the Teacher and sectarians opposed. This wicked priest has been variously identified as Hyrcanus II, Alexander Janneus, Simon Maccabeus, but the brother Jonathan presently has the most support. There also seems to have been another wicked figure other than the priest, the Man of Lies, who seems to have been an Essene himself but one who broke away from the group that followed the Teacher of

[18]See Geza Vermes, *The Dead Sea Scrolls in English*, second edition (New York: Penguin Books, 1975), 71-94.

Righteousness. The Man of Lies gives evidence of hostile groups and a split within the Essene movement. Such a split may have followed upon the Teacher of Righteousness insisting on a complete break with the Temple or proposing to move to Qumran.

The Sadducees were a socio-economic elite in contrast to the Pharisees who were more the party of the common people. The Essenes represented a religious conservatism or radicalism with respect to the Pharisees; they were uncompromising about the illegitimacy of the cult in Jerusalem. In addition to these three major "parties," there were other ascetical as well as resistance movements. The anti-Roman political stance was taken up by resistance fighters.[19] They manifested a "Maccabean spirit," opposed the payment of taxes to the foreign oppressors, gave themselves to the cause of Jewish independence, and were frequently armed militants and nationalists. They were especially involved in the 66-70 C.E. war. Today we are very conscious of their patriotic spirit symbolized in their final stand at Masada, Herod's old fortress, where Zealots held out for three years after the fall of Jerusalem.[20]

The Am ha-aretz

It has been sufficiently recognized that from a social point of view the whole community of Judaism at the time of Jesus was dominated by the fundamental idea of the mainte-

---

[19]Marcus Borg, *Conflict, Holiness and Politics in the Teaching of Jesus*, 27-49, argues against seeing the resistance movement as already an organized party at the time of Jesus. Resistance fighters came from a cross section of society. Also see Gerd Theissen, *Sociology of Early Palestinian Christianity*, trans. John Bowden (Philadelphia: Fortress Press, 1978), 38, 48-58, 61, 80-81. Also see Martin Hengel, *Die Zeloten* (Leiden: E. J. Brill, 1961); Sean Freyne, *Galilee from Alexander the Great to Hadrian*, 208-09.

[20]Yigael Yadin, *Masada* (New York: Random House, 1966). For a recent study on the unreliability of Josephus at this point, see Shaye Cohen, "Masada: Literary Tradition, Archaeological Remains, and the Credibility of Josephus," *Journal of Jewish Studies* 33 (1982), 385-405.

nance of racial purity.[21] Social stratification existed not
only at the top of the ladder with the aristocracy, but
throughout the society, culminating with the *am ha-aretz*.[22]

The principle for social status was that of racial purity,
which led to a tri-partite division: pure ancestry, slight
blemish, grave blemish.[23] The first rung of society comprised those of pure ancestry, the priests, Levites, the laity
with pure descent. The ordinary Jew knew his immediate
ancestors and the tribe from which he descended. In the
post-exilic period there was great interest in family trees and
genealogy and not only within the aristocracy. Most families at this time came from either the tribe of Judah, in which
the line of David was of particular significance because of its
messianic implications, or the tribe of Benjamin. Mordecai
of the book of Esther, Paul, Paul's teacher Gamaliel I, were
all Benjaminites. Only a few could trace lineage to one of the
ten lost tribes. Even for the laity, genealogical tradition was
not only kept but frequently recorded. Family ancestry was
not curiosity or nostalgia; it carried with it social and legal
implications. It was a social and legal privilege for one's
daughter to be able to marry a priest. Only those of pure
descent could do so. Pure ancestry was also demanded for
members of the Sanhedrin, for public offices, for signing
marriage contracts. Also, only those of pure ancestry could
be *assured* of future salvation.

Next on the social ladder were the socially impure, but
those only slightly so. This included the illegitimate children
of priests (children born of a marriage between a priest and a
woman who was not of pure descent), the proselyte converts
(Gentiles converted to Judaism who had been both baptized
and circumcised if male, and baptized if female), and freed
Gentile slaves (Gentile men and women who had become

[21]Jeremias, *Jerusalem in the Time of Jesus*, 270. Also see Borg, 51-72.

[22]A. Oppenheimer, *The Am Ha-Aretz. A Study in the Social History of the Jewish People in the Hellenistic-Roman Period* (Leiden: E. J. Brill, 1977). Also "Am Ha-Aretz," vol. 2, *Encyclopedia Judaica* (1971), 833-36.

[23]See Jeremias, *Jerusalem in the Time of Jesus*, 275-344.

slaves in service of Jews and then accepted baptism and circumcision, and for some reason later freed). These slightly blemished people could not marry a priest or hold an important office, but in everyday life the restrictions were not burdensome.

On the bottom of the social scale were those seriously blemished, the "excrement of the community," not only those forbidden to marry priests, but also forbidden to marry Levites or any Israelite of pure ancestry or even an illegitimate descendant of a priest. These included bastards (children conceived in adultery, who could then only marry Gentile converts or freed Gentile slaves or other Jews seriously blemished), the fatherless (those whose father was unknown) and eunuchs. These indeed were outlaws, social outcasts, kept apart. The social importance of racial purity was also manifest in the attitude toward the Samaritans.

Although racial purity was the major principle determinate of social status, it was not the only one. Independent of ancestry was the question of certain professions and the role of women. There were a series of despised trades with varying lists of such occupations. The most serious of these were the gamblers, usurers, and tax collectors, all public sinners. But for varied reasons, and with varied degrees of stigma, also mentioned are launderers, barbers, weavers, peddlers, tanners, and dung collectors. The social position of a woman was also that of an inferior.[24] When she was in public, her face and head were hidden and covered and she was not to converse with anyone. Her education was restricted to the tasks of domestic life. Her father and later her husband had rights over her. In marriage the man "acquired" the woman. Polygamy was permitted and the wife had to accept concubines. Only the husband had the right to divorce.

As we look back over the socio-economic picture, we find within Judaism itself an aristocratic power elite, priestly and lay; an increasingly burdensome system of tithes and taxes

[24]Ibid., 359-76. Also see Benedict Viviano, *Study as Worship* (Leiden: E. J. Brill, 1978), 11.

carried by the many, with a growing gap between rich and poor; a carefully acknowledged system of social status based on racial purity, with many social outcasts. In addition to these phenomena within Judaism, there was the continuing presence of foreign domination, the Roman occupation with its additional burden of taxes. The situations in Galilee and Judah were not exactly the same. After 6 C.E. there was a more direct Roman presence in Judah; Galilee remained under Herod Antipas. An emerging middle class in Jerusalem accompanied urbanization in general. In Galilee, a strong gap continued between the large landowners and the peasants, whether tenants or holders of family farms. Given the inseparable social and economic problems, F. C. Grant's description is apt: "the little land of Palestine with its poverty, overpopulation, declining food supply, wasteful government, and recurrent rebellion."[25]

The majority of Palestinian Jews were not directly affiliated with any of the three major groups or parties. Population estimates for this period must be taken as just that — as estimates.[26] The population of the whole of Palestine during the first century C.E. has been estimated as having been between one and a half to two million. Of these the Jewish population in Palestine may have numbered from 500,000 to 600,000. The Jewish population would have been far less than half of the total population of Palestine (anywhere between 25 and 40 percent). The Sadducees, a significant socio-economic and political group, were a small number numerically. The number of Essenes has been estimated at approximately 4,000. There were perhaps no more than 150 to 200 of these at Qumran at any one time. The Pharisees

[25]F. C. Grant, "The Economic Background of the New Testament," *The Background of the New Testament and Its Eschatology*, ed. W. D. Davies and D. Daube in honor of C. H. Dodd (Cambridge: University Press, 1956), 114. This essay, 99-114, provides a good summary of the literature pertinent to the economic background.

[26]I emphasize that our figures are estimates. See Jeremias, *Jerusalem in the Time of Jesus*, 27, 83-84, 203-5, 252; Bruce Metzger, *The New Testament, its Background, Growth and Context* (Nashville: Abingdon Press, 1965), 39-45; Geza Vermes, *The Dead Sea Scrolls, Qumran in Perspective*, 88, 119, 125.

have been estimated at approximately 6,000. These figures provided by Josephus refer only to adult males. It is difficult to provide any estimate for the Zealots since it is difficult to determine when they came into existence and whether they were in fact a unified movement or whether the term is an umbrella term covering several movements. Their numbers varied with the times.

A good guess with respect to the three "parties" is no more than 10,000 to 25,000, while the entire Jewish population of Palestine may have been 500,000 to 600,000. Thus probably more than ninety-five percent were not directly affiliated with these "major Jewish parties."[27] It is best, however, not to think of all of the others as *am ha-aretz*. These "people of the land" failed to observe the whole of the Law. In some cases it was someone whose Judaism was mixed and with whom the more strict Jew would not intermarry, or someone uneducated and hence ignorant of details of the Law from whom exact observance could not be expected, something of a religious lower class which often included many of the poorer sections although even a rich person could be one of these religious outcasts.

Both Sean Freyne and Benedict Viviano have pointed out that the term *am ha-aretz* changed meanings. Freyne distinguishes between pre-70 C.E. and post-70 C.E. usage while Viviano indicates a lengthier history.[28] In general, however, it had the connotation of the common people, the ignorant and uneducated, the unobservant of the Law and ritually unclean. This segment would certainly have included much of the Galilean peasantry but would not have been limited to them alone. In general, the religious pluralism must simply

[27] If we consider the two larger groups, the Essenes and Pharisees 4000 and 6000, then 10,000 is a base estimate. If we take an estimate including women, we could double the figure. We could estimate the Sadducees as a much smaller group. Given previous estimates, if we take 25,000 as a high figure for membership in the three parties, and 500,000 as a low figure for the Jewish population, it seems as if at most the population of the three groups may have been only 5% of the total.

[28] The pre-70 C.E. implication is failure to observe the purity laws; the post-70 C.E. implication is failure to study the Torah. See Freyne, *Galilee from Alexander the Great to Hadrian*, 307; Viviano, *Study as Worship*, 42.

be seen to have included a large number of outcasts, marginals for diverse reasons and on diverse social and religious grounds.

Jesus seems to have had a widespread following of widely diversified people cutting across both social and religious barriers. Indeed, his following was so diversified that some have come close to identifying Jesus with the Pharisees[29] while others have maintained that he was one of the *am ha-aretz*.[30] Jesus was a man of the people, for the people, sought after for a wide variety of reasons, even by Samaritans. Not all of his following can be considered disciples who accepted his teaching and considered him the one for whom they had been waiting, who accompanied him on his journeys or even preached and healed in his name. But the wider group of his associates included the spectrum of Israel and Palestine. Gradually there emerged, in addition to the wider circle of followers and the narrower circle of explicit disciples, a growing circle of opposition as well, coming from the upper class and especially from the religious establishment. But even after the emergence of an opposition, his following was large. The sociology of those who interacted with Jesus leads to three groupings: (1) the multitudes and crowds, which include many *am ha-aretz*; (2) the disciples, various people who followed after Jesus; and (3) the opposition, which must be variously interpreted, perhaps more from the Pharisees in Galilee but more from the Jerusalem aristocracy in Judea.

Those who were attracted to Jesus, who longed to hear him, who chose to follow him as their prophet and teacher were not one homogeneous group. Yet what emerges is how popular Jesus was, how sought after by the poor or the

---

[29]Viviano, 43, suggests the possibility that Jesus may have maintined a Pharisaic level of observance of the Law.

[30]At least it is maintained that Jesus would have been classed as one of the *am ha-aretz* by the Pharisees. See G. F. Moore, in *The Beginnings of Christianity*, eds. Jackson and Lake, vol. 1 (New York: Macmillan, 1920), 445; S. S. Cohon, "The Place of Jesus in the Religious Life of His Day," *Journal of Biblical Literature* 48 (1929), 82-108.

common and ordinary people, the religiously marginal people, by the masses, simply by the people, by those without status from economic, social, or religious points of view. They loved him. He made them laugh. He respected their tears. He knew their pain. He associated with them, respected them, enjoyed their company. They listened to him, learned from him, believed in him, had hope because of him, and he lived for them. He taught them, spoke of the nearness of God to them, made them feel holy and righteous. He reached out to them, compassionately, generously, faithfully, humbly, joyfully. He healed their sick. He made them feel human again. He preached an impending social reversal. They were his people, and he was their teacher.

Albert Nolan in his portrait of Jesus before the "theologization" of Christianity has described these disparate associates of Jesus: "The people to whom Jesus turned his attention are referred to in the gospels by a variety of terms: the poor, the blind, the lame, the crippled, the lepers, the hungry, the miserable (those who weep), sinners, prostitutes, tax collectors, demoniacs (those possessed by unclean spirits), the persecuted, the downtrodden, the captives, all who labor and are overburdened, the rabble who know nothing of the law, the crowds, the little ones, the least, the last and the babes or the lost sheep of the house of Israel."[31]

We may not be able to situate Jesus within the *am ha-aretz* himself. Nor can we easily and precisely specify who the *am ha-aretz* were at differing periods in Judaism's history. But we can say that Jesus was "for them," manifested by his willingness to be "with them," and to be with them gladly. Jesus was a religious man, a man of prayer, of religious observance, of God. He was a learned man, however he acquired that learning, knowledgeable with respect to the Law, the Scriptures. It would not have been noteworthy that Jesus had associates or followers from among the Pharisees. What evidently stood out was that he was so

[31]See Albert Nolan, *Jesus Before Christianity* (Maryknoll: Orbis, 1978), 21. See esp. 21-42.

present to and spoke to the social and religious outcast, those on the margin of society and periphery of Judaism. That *he*, a *religious* man, one who spoke so authoritatively on behalf of God, that this man, this particular practicing, learned, holy, prophetic messenger of God *associated with them* was the significant reality. It evidently was unusual, unexpected and notorious that "religion" could actually be "for the people."

The Opposition

Jesus' following appears to have been large and varied. As he increasingly became good news for many people, however, he also triggered the development of a growing opposition. How gradual, pronounced, or widespread the opposition was is difficult to determine. Eventually , however, a gulf developed between Jesus and many of the "leaders" of Judaism. This opposition cannot be identified with Judaism as a whole. Jesus himself was Jewish and saw himself as a faithful and practicing Jew. It appears as if the Jewish people as a whole respected him as a prophet and teacher. Nor can the opposition to Jesus be identified with the Pharisees.[32] One of the great injustices of Christian preaching has been to identify the Pharisees with hypocrisy. Not all, not even the majority of Pharisees, were hypocritical.

Two factors have led Christians to think wrongly with respect to Pharisaism. The first is that it ordinarily appears as if the charges or condemnations were directed by Jesus against them as a whole body (Lk 11:42-44). I agree with T. W. Manson that such was probably not Jesus' intention, given his friendly association with them and also a certain commonality with them in many instances.

---

[32]For clarification with respect to Jesus' relation to the Pharisees, see in particular John Bowker, *Jesus and the Pharisees* (Cambridge: University Press, 1973); Benedict Viviano, *Study as Worship*, 40-44, 171-175; Paul Winter, on *The Trial of Jesus*, (Berlin: Walter de Gruyter, 1961), 111-35.

The woes against Pharisees are all concerned with the practice rather than with the interpretation of the law. As the Greek text stands, the sweeping denunciations are directed against the whole Pharisaic party. Whether this was the case in the original Aramaic is a question which cannot be answered. All that can be said is that "Woe unto you Pharisees! for ye tithe..." represents Aramaic which could equally well be rendered "Woe unto you Pharisees who tithe..." ... The reference could thus be not to the whole body of Pharisees, but to those among them who were Pharisees only on the surface... The Pharisaic ideal was a genuine religious ideal; and the men who gave themselves to it were mostly sincere and earnest. To maintain that all Pharisees were *ipso facto* hypocrites is as absurd as to claim that they were all saints. The truth is that some of them were men of eminent saintliness, many kept a worthy standard both in piety and morality, and some were complete frauds. It is to this last class that the woes really apply .[33]

The second factor distorting Christian perception of the Pharisees is that the writing of the Gospels took place to a great degree after 70 C.E., after the destruction of the Second Temple, and during the formative period of Judaism, a time when Judaism and Christianity were separating from each other, when Judaism was attempting to rebuild itself, and when the Gentile mission had obviously become central to Christian preaching. It is particularly after 70 C.E. that the Pharisaic party becomes more or less coterminus with Judaism. Essenes and Sadducees did not survive the war and the future of Judaism was in the hands of the rabbis and Pharisees. Thus Christian anti-Jewish polemic was at that time anti-Pharisaic polemic. One cannot simply identify the anti-Pharisaisms of the Gospels with the teaching of Jesus himself. Jesus' teaching in the first third of the

[33]T. W. Manson *The Sayings of Jesus* (Grand Rapids, Mich.William B. Eerdmans Co., [1937] 1957), 97-99.

first century had a different social context than the Christian preaching in the latter third of that same century.

The Synoptics do not attribute any negative role to the Pharisees in the trial and passion of Jesus. Thus it is probably accurate to say that they were not overly involved in it. Morton Smith writes, "Given the hostility to the Pharisees already apparent in Mark, and the demonstrated practice of adding references to them for polemic purposes to the gospel texts, it is incredible that, if any of the synoptic evangelists had heard anything of Pharisees participating in the actual proceedings against Jesus, he should not have reported it."[34] Thus it appears as if the "enemies" of Jesus ought not be quickly identified with "the Pharisees." The anti-Pharisaic attitude of the Gospels manifests the *Sitz im Leben* of the Church.

Yet Jesus' integrity and single-mindedness, his radicality and faith, his love of God and neighbor, his uncompromising attitude toward *religious* hypocrisy and its failure to practice the central command of Scripture and tradition to love neighbor, all these aspects of his teaching attracted opposition, an opposition bound to be even greater in Jerusalem than anywhere in Galilee. The outcome of this opposition will be the starting point for the next volume in this series. This present volume is concerned with the mission and earthly ministry of Jesus.

One of Us

Jesus was a human being just as we are human beings. This does not imply that he was a sinner in the way that we are sinners, but rather that he searched and struggled and suffered as we all do. One characteristic of Jesus' humanness, or consequence of his identity with us and our struggle, was his compassion. His humanity was not an abstract humanity, but the sweat and blood and fear and joy within

---

[34]Morton Smith, *Jesus the Magician* (New York: Harper and Row, 1978), 156.

which he worked out the direction and meaning of his life. No docetism here. Whatever else we may say about Jesus on the pages ahead, we cannot let go of his identity and solidarity with us. He had the limitations of a physical body. He felt the feelings we feel. He learned by experience. He relied upon faith and prayer. He was culturally and socially situated.

As a human being, Jesus was inevitably a historical being, rooted in a particular culture and ethos at a particular period of human history. He was a Jew, a Palestinian Jew, a Galilean, who lived some time between 6-4 B.C.E. and 30-33 C.E., during the Roman occupation of Palestine.

The world into which Jesus of Nazareth was born and in which he grew up was quite varied — politically, economically, religiously. There were both hasidic and hellenist groups. On the hasidic side there were the Pharisees and Essenes with their own differences. Many, but not all, were influenced by a wide variety of expectations for the future of Judaism — eschatological, messianic, and apocalyptic hopes.

Although Jesus' joys and sorrows, fears and insights, friends and family, mission and message and experience of God were peculiar to him and not exactly the same as any other human being's, he shared totally in the burdens and the privilege of what it means to be one of us. The purpose of a theology of Jesus is to understand more fully the life of this particular human being, and such a theology begins with the awareness that Jesus is human, someone like us, the compassionate one who feels our weaknesses with us (Heb 4:15). We now move into our first christological task, Jesus research and interpretation, but we are already aware of the humanness, historicality, and Jewishness of Jesus.

Part Two

Solidarity With God

4

The Origins of a Mission

Having set the stage for Jesus with his humanness and historicality, we now need to say more. Yet, whatever more we say, we never want to let go of this foundation. Jesus' humanity is the base upon which we build. Yet it is the base and not the whole building.

Jesus was not only someone like us; he was someone called and sent by God. We begin with early events in the public life of Jesus: his baptism, a period in the wilderness, the return to Galilee. Then we focus on Jesus as a man of prayer and a prophet. In all of these Jesus is found in his humanness but as a human being called by God. This call from God, however, does not make him any less one of us.

The Baptism of Jesus

The baptism of Jesus of Nazareth by John is one of the first facts in the story of Jesus.[1] It leaves us with two questions: What was the relationship between Jesus and John? What was the significance of the baptism for Jesus?

---

[1]Concerning the baptism of Jesus, see Joseph Fitzmyer, *A Christological Catechism, New Testament Answers* (New York: Paulist Press, 1981), 39-43; Joachim Jeremias, *New Testament Theology, The Proclamation of Jesus,*trans. John Bowden (New York: Charles Scribner's Sons, 1971), 49-56; Walter Kasper, *Jesus*

Many have suggested an Essene influence on John, and he may have joined an Essene community as a young man.[2] The evidence for the latter suggestion is not conclusive however. Similarities between John and the Essenes do exist. They were an ascetical and devout community, calling themselves "the penitents of Israel." They had a strong dislike for "official" Judaism and had broken away from worship in Jerusalem. Their beliefs included the expectation of an imminent coming of the Lord. Yet today many scholars are skeptical about a direct relationship between John and the Essene community at Qumran itself.[3]

Whether or not John spent time in an Essene community, whether or not he spent time as a solitary either after leaving the community or at some other time, the traditions are unanimous in associating John with the wilderness (Mt 3:1; Mk 1:4; Lk 3:2; Jn 1:23, 28), preaching and baptizing there. He had the gift of the Spirit and was seen as a prophet. Prophecy in Israel had faded out with the prophetic writings replacing living prophecy and the spoken word. Prophecy and the gift of the Spirit were considered by many to be eschatological phenomena that would accompany the end

The Christ, trans. V. Green (New York: Paulist Press, 1977), 65-71; Wolfhart Pannenberg, *Jesus—God and Man*, trans. Lewis Wilkins and Duane Priebe (Philadelphia: Westminster Press, 1968), 137-41; Edward Schillebeeckx, *Jesus, an Experiment in Christology*, trans. Hubert Hoskins (New York: Seabury Press, 1979), 136-39.

[2]Joseph Fitzmyer, *The Gospel According to Luke, I-IX*, Anchor Bible, vol. 28 (Garden City, N.Y.: Doubleday, 1981), 388-89, respects the hypothesis of a relationship between John and the Essenes while recognizing that we cannot make such a suggestion more definitive. Jean Steinmann, *Saint John the Baptist and the Desert Tradition* (New York: Harper and Brothers, 1958), 51-61, hypothesized that John had joined the Essenes during late adolescence, had been fully initiated into their life, and then became a dissenter from the community.

[3]Raymond Brown, *The Birth of the Messiah* (Garden City, N.Y.: Doubleday, 1977), 376, n. 2. Jerome Murphy-O'Connor, "Qumran and the New Testament," in *The New Testament and Its Modern Interpreters*, eds. Eldon Jay Epp and George W. MacRae (in preparation). Geza Vermes, *The Dead Sea Scrolls, Qumran in Perspective* (Cleveland: World Pub. Co., 1978).

times (Joel 2:28).[4] The appearance of John as a prophet indicated to those influenced by messianic expectations that the eschatological age was close at hand. Matthew 17:10-13 and Mark 9:11-13 identify John as Elijah, which shows that John had come to be seen among the disciples of Jesus as an eschatological prophet. In Luke, the Elijah role assigned to John is ambiguous, not explicitly denied as in the Fourth Gospel (1:20-21), nor affirmed as in Mark and Matthew.[5]

John's message proclaimed the coming of the Lord as a time of judgment. It was the time to prepare and repent as the anger of God would soon manifest itself (Mt 3:7-12; Lk 3:7-9, 16-17). John used the example of a farmer with his winnowing fork separating the wheat from the chaff (Lk

[4]Oscar Cullmann, *The Christology of the New Testament*, revised edition, trans. Shirley Guthrie and Charles Hall (Philadelphia: Westminster Press, 1959), 14; Jeremias, *New Testament Theology*. 80-82. C. H. H. Scobie, *John the Baptist* (Philadelphia: Fortress Press, 1964), writes, "Prophecy was dead; its rebirth will be a sign of the new age" (123).

[5]Cullmann concludes that John's disciples considered John to be the prophet, especially the prophet like Elijah, a direct forerunner of the Lord (God); but that Jesus and his disciples saw John as the forerunner of the Messiah or of another; and that John saw himself either as a forerunner only in the second sense or quite simply as a Prophet (Cullmann, *The Christology of the New Testament*, 26-28). Brown states that John saw himself as directly preparing the way of the Lord. Christian interpretation, however, assigned to him the role of Elijah as found in Malachi and of a forerunner to Jesus. As time passed and the disciples of John and a Baptist community continued to persist and perhaps even became hostile to the disciples of Jesus and vice-versa, the subordination of John to Jesus became even more explicit, as in the Fourth Gospel, where John is not even Elijah (1:20-21), where John gives explicit witness to Jesus (1:7, 30-31), and where John becomes an incipient Christian. With respect to Luke, Brown suggests two stages of development. An early stage (4:25-26, 9:54) identified *Jesus* with Elijah, a stage represented in Luke's portrayal of the ministry of Jesus. A later stage, dominant in the infancy narrative, composed after the Gospel as a whole, stressed Jesus as God's Son and *John* as Elijah (Brown, *The Birth*, 275-79, 2822-85).
In the sources behind the Fourth Gospel, J. Louis Martyn identifies a tradition identifying Jesus as the Elijah-prophet, and concludes that "it is the fourth evangelist who bears the responsibility for the disappearance from subsequent Christian thought of the identification of Jesus as the eschatological Elijah"(53). *The Gospel of John in Christian History* (New York: Paulist Press, 1978), 9-54. Also see Walter Wink, *John the Baptist in the Gospel Tradition* (Cambridge: University Press, 1968).

3:17-18). Through baptism John gathered together those who repented into a people who awaited the coming of God. During the century prior to Jesus there were penitential and baptist movements of varied sorts along the Jordan River. The centrality of baptisms and ritual baths in lieu of Temple sacrifices was common to many of the movements.[6] Those baptized by John immersed themselves in his presence, a symbolic action which signified conversion or repentance, a turning to the Lord to await the last days. Unlike ritual bathing among the Jews, John's baptism was performed but once. Some of those baptized followed John, while others returned to their homes to live a new life and await the coming of the end times. John's message included repentance, baptism, the imminent reign of God, a call to ethical living,[7] and may also have included the expectation of another whose way he himself was preparing.[8]

Edward Schillebeeckx situates John within the post-Maccabean, apocalyptic, penitential, baptismal, conversion movements of pre-Christian Judaism. John was "a penitential preacher prophetically announcing the imminent judgment of God."[9] It was not so much God's imminent reign but God's imminent judgment that John announced. Yet,

[6]See Wink, *John the Baptist in the Gospel Tradition*, 108. Also Frederick Houk Borsch, *The Son of Man in Myth and History*, New Testament Library (London: SCM Press, 1967), 177-218, esp. 201-18; Schillebeeckx, *Jesus*, 117-18, also 116 for the bibliography under conversion and baptismal movements.

[7]The ethical aspect of John's repentance and preaching can sometimes be neglected. E.g., Lk 3:10, concerning sharing food and clothing; 3:12-13, concerning tax collectors; 3:14, concerning soldiers.

[8]This aspect of John's preaching is not primary and is difficult to determine. See footnote 5. How much of this aspect of his message was "historically John" and how much "Christian interpolation"? It could be either. John could well have spoken of "one to come"; the idea was common in the Judaism of that time. Yet it could be the way in which Christian tradition would reconcile the popularity of John and his relationship to Jesus. That John identified the coming one with Jesus is most probably a Christian perspective. Schillebeeckx suggests that the coming one for John was "the son of humanity"; here John "borrows" an apocalyptic idea (*Jesus*, 132). Even if John did preach another one to come, this was probably a secondary aspect of his preaching.

[9]Schillebeeckx, *Jesus*, 127. For Schillebeeckx's discussion of John, see *Jesus*, 126-36, and *Christ, the Experience of Jesus as Lord*, trans. John Bowden (New York: Seabury Press, 1980), 368-72.

according to Schillebeeckx, John does not manifest Jewish apocalyptic motifs as much as earlier, classical, prophetic ones. He was not an apocalypticist, but a prophet of the old school.[10] Apocalyptic thought may have influenced John's perception of the imminence of the divine judgment, but John was more typically a prophet of the older tradition. John's innovation with respect to the old school or earlier Israelite prophecy, however, was baptism. He preached baptism (Mk 1:4; Lk 3:3; Acts 20:37; 13:24), and this baptism of repentance and its accompanying *metanoia* (change of heart) was the one thing necessary for participation in the imminent reign of God.

John was an ascetical and prophetic preacher of repentance who baptized and proclaimed the closeness of the impending judgment. Jesus evidently was less ascetical (Mk 2:18; Lk 7:31-35) and did not baptize as extensively as John (John 3:22, 26 presents Jesus as baptizing; however see John 4:1-2). Both Jesus and John, however, were prophets and preachers. Both, unlike the scribes, preached out of doors and both called people to repentance. Repentance was not the center of the preaching for Jesus as it was for John but was still part of his message. In submitting to John's baptism, Jesus recognized John's prophetic quality, and many of Jesus' early disciples had been disciples of the baptizer

[10]Schillebeeckx, *Jesus*, 129. Schillebeeckx points to the fact that three key words used in the New Testament to denote John's proclamation of judgment — the axe, the winnow, and fire — belong not to apocalypticism but to ancient prophecy. How apocalyptic or non-apocalyptic John was will remain an open question. There is little doubt that John comes across quite clearly as a prophet. Raymond Brown states that the lamb of God to which the Baptizer refers in John 1:29 can best be interpreted as the conquering lamb who will destroy evil in the world of Jewish apocalyptic *(The Gospel According to John I-XII,* [Garden City, N.Y.: Doubleday and Co., 1966] 58-60). However, this reference is probably not the historical John. Yet Josephine Massingberde Ford attempts to trace the major New Testament apocalypse, The Book of Revelation, to the Baptizer and his disciples. See Massingberde Ford, *Revelation,* The Anchor Bible, vol. 38 (Garden City, N.Y.: Doubleday, 1975), 28-37, 50-57. Massingberde Ford acknowledges John's traditional prophetic character. She writes, "John the Baptist, without doubt, was regarded as a prophet *par excellence*" (28). Yet she also sees the expression "Lamb of God" associated with John the Baptizer as the apocalyptic lamb (30-31) as does Brown, and speaks of "the Baptist's prophetic apocalyptic and 'fiery' tendencies" (56).

first (Lk 7:29-30; Jn 1:35-39, 3:26). Jesus expressed respect
for John and solidarity with his movement (Mt 11:7-11).
Both John and Jesus would have been interpreted by many
as "eschatological prophets."

In his literary and critical study of the Synoptic accounts
of the baptism of Jesus, Fritzleo Lentzen-Deis points both
to the facticity of the baptism and also to the interpretative
elements within the text, such as the dove and the voice. He
judges the literary form to be that of the "Deute-Vision," an
interpretative vision for which there are parallels in the
targums in which a synagogue translator abandoned the
exact text and interpreted it for the hearers.[11] In targumic
versions of Genesis 22:10 and 19:12, for example, the event
is interpreted by means of a vision in which one hears a
voice. This interpretative vision (a distinct literary form, in
contrast to a theophany narrative or a call narrative), presents Jesus as the beloved son rather than as a disciple of
John. Yet Jesus is still aligned with the eschatological movement of John.

The baptism was a significant religious event in the life of
Jesus. Undoubtedly he had already become aware of the
significance of John's preaching and baptism (Mk 11:30; Mt
11:9, 11;21:32; Lk 7:28,29). As Joachim Jeremias points out,
"The sayings that betray such a high estimate of the Baptist
are certainly authentic."[12] His baptism signified his conviction that the reign of God was close at hand, as well as his
desire to number himself among "those who wait." The
baptism must have been more than he had anticipated,
however. Jesus received the gift of the Spirit on this occasion and thus was anointed as a prophet to Israel as John
had been, even if the full effect of this would take time for

[11]Fritzleo Lentzen-Deis, *Die Taufe Jesu nach den Synoptikern. Literarkritische
und gattungsgeschichtliche Untersuchungen* (Frankfurt: Verlag Josef Knecht,
1970). Feuillet speaks of Jesus' baptism as a theophany. See "Prophetic Call and
Jesus' Baptism," *Theology Digest* 28 (1980), 29-33; A. Feuillet, "Vocation et
mission des prophetes, Bapteme et mission de Jesus: Etude de christologie biblique," *Nova et Vetera* 54 (1979), 22-40.

[12]Jeremias, *New Testament Theology*, 47.

him to fully understand. [13] John's baptism was not necessarily accompanied by the gift of the Spirit; Jesus' baptism was unique in that regard. Jesus himself was driven by the Spirit into the wilderness from whence John himself had come. [14]

Historiographically we can maintain that Jesus was baptized by John, but we can say nothing of his motivation —

[13]The imparting of the Spirit signifies prophetic inspiration and vocation. Jeremias, *New Testament Theology*, writes, "Jesus experienced his call when he underwent John's baptism in order to take his place among the eschatological people of God that the Baptist was assembling" (49). Also, "At his baptism, Jesus experienced his call" (55). I agree with Jeremias here. Yet it is going too far when he writes, "From the time of the baptism he was conscious of being God's servant promised by Isaiah" (55). Jesus genuinely experienced the gift of the Spirit at his baptism, yet it also took time for him to sort out the complete significance of this — hence the wilderness motif.

In my point of view there is no basis for pushing the reception of the gift of the Spirit and hence the prophetic vocation back prior to the baptism by John (as Schillebeeckx implies); at the same time one should not read too much into the baptismal event, as Jeremias is wont to do. We probably cannot locate on critical grounds alone the reception of the Spirit by Jesus. This remains unknowable to scientific investigation. But we can say that Jesus was aware of the gift of the Spirit and that his Spirit-consciousness very possibly originates with his experience of the baptism. This initial Spirit-consciousness, however, is not yet so articulate that he sees clearly a specific role.

For Schillebeeckx, *Jesus*, the baptism was Jesus' first public act as a prophet, a symbolic-prophetic action like those of old, in which he "intimates that Israel as a whole does indeed require a change of heart" (138). For Schillebeeckx, Jesus would have been aware of his call to be a prophet prior to his baptism. But, although possible, there is no basis in the texts for this view. Schillebeeckx does not diminish the role of the baptism for Jesus, however. He writes, "For him this baptism must have been a disclosure experience, that is, a source experience that was revelatory" (137). And he recognizes that, "In the absence of sources the historian can neither affirm nor gainsay anything about the life of Jesus pror to his baptism" (137). Yet he maintains, "His undergoing that baptism was not of course his first religious experience" (137). Granting this, and its vagueness, he attempts to sustain both, "We know nothing of what he understood about himself up to that moment" (137), and "Nothing would allow us to see in this step taken by Jesus the first breakthrough of his prophetic self-awareness" (138). All his examples of these symbolic actions, however, are of those who have been prophets prior to such actions. It is this previous, pre-baptismal awareness for which there is no basis. Jesus was baptized and received the gift of the Spirit. This does not mean that the baptism account is a call narrative either. It is, however, the occasion in which Jesus receives the gift of the Spirit, the sign of a prophetic vocation, and is led by the Spirit into the wilderness.

[14]That Jesus was baptized by John does not mean he necessarily became a disciple of John or that he baptized as a disciple alongside John. This is impossible to determine. See Schillebeeckx, *Jesus*, 136-37. Jeremias (*New Testament Theol-*

whether he left Nazareth with the intention of returning there after being baptized, since not all of the baptized remained with John; or whether he had decided to become a disciple of John, and perhaps temporarily was one; whether he came simply to hear the preaching of John and was then moved to receive the baptism; or whether he already had seen himself as a prophet and the baptism was a symbolic act reinforcing John as also God's messenger. At any rate, after his time in the wilderness, Jesus eventually preaches on his own authority, and returns to Galilee, perhaps only after the imprisonment and death of John (Mk 1:14 suggests that John's arrest was the occasion for Jesus' return to Galilee). Both John and Jesus preached God, and both risked death out of fidelity to their messages.

The Wilderness Experience

A major portion of the Pentateuch, part of Exodus and all of Leviticus and Numbers, interprets the origins and experience of the Hebrew people in the wilderness. The Lord's name, the Law, and the covenant all have their roots there. A fairly elaborate form of Israel's creed, Joshua 24:2-13, includes the sojourn in the wilderness.[15] Amos 2:10, Hosea 9:10 and 12:9, Jeremiah 31:2, and Deuteronomy 32:10 show the importance of the desert tradition in Israelite history. Ulrich Mauser writes, "The wilderness is the womb of a fundamental datum of the religion of the Old Testament without which its development would be unintelligible."[16]

The desert was not only the scene of God's revelation but also of Israel's sin. Deuteronomy recalls not only the help of

ogy, 45-47) points out the contrast between the Synoptic and Johannine images of Jesus and John. In the Synoptics, the contrast is limited to the moment of baptism. In John's Gospel, Jesus is a follower of John and baptizes alongside John (3:22-4:3). On this point the Fourth Gospel may well be more historical.

[15]See Ulrich Mauser, *Christ in the Wilderness* (London: SCM Press, 1963), 15-18. Also Gerhard von Rad, *Old Testament Theology*, trans. D. M. G. Stalker, 2 vols. (New York: Harper and Row, 1962-65), 1: 121-28, 226-31.

[16]Mauser, *Christ in the Wilderness*, 29.

the Lord (7:18, 8:2, 18), but also the rebellion of the people (9:7). Psalm 78 portrays Israel's history, and the wilderness theme of the sin of the ancestors is emphasized. Psalm 106 links Israel's exile to the sin in the desert.

The prophets introduced another element — the expectation of another time that Israel would have to spend in the desert (Hos 2:3, 14). Israel, for Hosea, would have to return to the wilderness because she had refused to be faithful to the Lord (2:14, 11:5). Ezekiel spoke of this second exodus and saw it as fulfilled in his own days with the exile (20:34-36). Deutero-Isaiah also used the motif of a second exodus (40:3, 48:20-21). In both Ezekiel and Deutero-Isaiah the wilderness became a symbol — a time of judgment, purification, and a new outpouring of the Spirit of the Lord.

Later, in early Judaism, the Messiah was expected to come forth from the wilderness. The Judean desert was often the site of messianic movements. Matthew 24:26 reflects this belief. The Qumran community saw itself as a wilderness people and the *Community Rule* stated: "And when these become members of the Community in Israel according to all these rules, they shall separate from the habitation of ungodly men and shall go into the wilderness to prepare the way of Him; as it is written, 'Prepare in the wilderness the way of . . . make straight in the desert a path for our God' (Is 40:3)."[17]

We can say on historiographical grounds that Jesus spent time "in the wilderness," although we cannot with confidence put together the details. Questions remain. Exactly when did this sojourn in the wilderness take place (immediately after the baptism or not)? How long a time was it (forty days is symbolic)? Where was this wilderness (the geographic description is not precise)? What happened (the temptation accounts are more theologically significant than historically factual)?

To understand the significance of Jesus' sojourn in the

---

[17] I QS 8:12-16. Translation that of Geza Vermes, *The Dead Sea Scrolls in English*, Second edition (New York: Penguin Books, 1975), 85-86. I QS refers to the Rule of the Community or the Manual of Discipline.

wilderness, we begin with the prologue to Mark's Gospel (1:1-13).[18] The setting is the area around the Dead Sea and the Jordan valley. Verse two of the prologue is a quotation from the Hebrew Scriptures. It is an amalgamation of three sayings, two from the prophets (Is 40:3 and Mal 3:10), and one from Exodus (23:20). Exodus 23:20 and Isaiah 40:3 have as their context the wilderness tradition of the Hebrew Scriptures. For Mark, the messenger of the Lord of which Isaiah 40:3 speaks is John, "a man of the desert." The detail in verse 6 about the leather girdle around John's waist helps Mark to establish an identity between John and Elijah (In 2 Kings 1:8 this is a feature of Elijah's dress). John's message of repentance was rooted in the wilderness tradition.

> The Baptist's call to repentance and his call to come to him in the wilderness to be baptized are but two aspects of one and the same thing. Going out into the wilderness and repentance are not two different ideas which could only be related to one another as form and content or as condition and result. Rather they are essentially one and the same — the march out into the wilderness is the repentance to which John calls.[19]

The Marcan account sets the scene for Jesus. How will the wilderness relate to the call and ministry of Jesus? Is the wilderness for him a transition to a ministry elsewhere whereas for John the ministry remained in the wilderness? Will Jesus remain associated with the wilderness?

Jesus too went to the wilderness as a sign of repentance. He fully realized what it meant to go there; to be determined to live under the judgment of God. Going into the wilderness itself was symbolic. Jesus was aware of what he was doing by going into the wilderness to be baptized. He was already prompted by God-consciousness when going there. Did he receive the call once there but prior to being baptized? Did it come during the experience of the baptism?

---

[18]Ulrich Mauser, *Christ in the Wilderness*, 77-80, identifies Mark 1:1-13 as a unit and as a prologue to the Gospel.

[19]Ibid., 87-88.

During the days in the wilderness after the baptism? How much time had he spent in the wilderness prior to the baptism? After the baptism? To these questions there is no answer from the data available. Baptism and wilderness, although historical, have two sides to them, the factual and the symbolic.

To penetrate more deeply into the wilderness episode in Jesus' life we must thus let go of historiography and enter theology. According to the account in Mark, the Spirit drives Jesus into the wilderness after his baptism. This suggests going more deeply into the wilderness, but this need not be primarily geographical. It is symbolic of what lies ahead — Jesus' wrestling with the powers of evil and with his own call by God.

"Forty days" is symbolic. Moses spent forty days on Mount Sinai; Elijah wandered forty days through Mount Horeb (Ex 24:18; 34:28; 1 Kgs 19:8, 15). Nor for any of these was the forty days something passed through once and for all, but rather a symbol of more to come, a focused look at who they are as God's servants. Temptation or testing was at the core of the wilderness experience. In the Hebrew Scriptures, God tested and purified the people there. In the New Testament, Satan was often the tempter. For Mark, Jesus continued to be tempted; his whole life embraced the struggle that the wilderness theme symbolized. He was not victorious until the end.

The content of the ordeal Jesus underwent in the wilderness, the character of the struggle, the so-called temptations are not recorded in Mark. Mark simply writes:

> The Spirit immediately drove him out into the wilderness. And he was in the wilderness forty days, tempted by Satan; and he was with the wild beasts, and the angels ministered to him. (1:12-13)

Matthew and Luke flesh out this period in the wilderness with three struggles in particular, although for them not all three are located in the wilderness itself; one was at the Temple in Jerusalem. Although the particular character of Jesus' struggle in the wilderness is not something which can be arrived at historiographically, it is well not to dismiss the content of Matthew's and Luke's narratives too quickly. They are certainly symbolic of the struggling Jesus who was still in the midst of that same struggle as he went to Gethsemane before his death, the struggle to know and persevere in following the will of God. "Not my will, but Thine be done," was a prayer Jesus learned in the school of struggle (Heb 4:15-5:10). Although the particular character or content of Jesus' wilderness experience cannot be determined historiographically, nevertheless the fact that struggle was central to the life of Jesus is historical. David Hill writes, "Although the narrative [Matthew's] is thus theological (strictly, Christological) rather than biographical, it certainly implies the reality and historicity of Jesus' temptation and spiritual struggle, else it could hardly have been composed."[20]

One of the more thorough and historically sensitive discussions of the temptation narratives is Birger Gerhardsson's discussion of the Matthean text. He maintains that the shorter narrative in Mark and the longer narratives in Matthew and Luke are two versions of one tradition and that the Marcan version is an abbreviated form of a longer narrative. He holds for the priority of the Matthean version.[21] No agreement on the relationship between Mark and Matthew exists, however. Gerhardsson suggests that Matthew is earlier. Mauser, however, says that Mark is earlier and that Matthew and Luke rely upon Mark.[22] Murphy-O'Connor considers them as independent traditions.[23]

[20]David Hill, *The Gospel of Matthew*, New Century Bible (Greenwood, S.C.: The Attic Press, 1972), 99.

[21]Birger Gerhardsson, *The Testing of God's Son: An Analysis of an Early Christian Midrash* (Lund, Sweden: CWK Gleerup, 1966), 10-11. Fitzmyer holds that the order of the temptations in Matthew's version is more original than Luke's, *The Gospel According to Luke, I-IX*, 507. For the opposite point of view, see T. W. Manson, *The Sayings of Jesus* (Grand Rapids, Mich.: William B. Eerdmans Pub. Co., 1979), 42-43.

[22]Mauser, *Christ in the Wilderness*, 144-49.

[23]Jerome Murphy-O'Connor, class notes. Also see this opinion in Jacques Dupont, "L'Origine du récit des tentations de Jésus au desert," *Revue biblique*, 73 (1966), 30-76, esp. 45-47. Dupont gives a detailed study of the temptations in *Les Tentations de Jésus au désert* (Bruges: Desclée de Brouwer, 1968)

> And he fasted forty days and forty nights, and afterward
> he was hungry. And the tempter came and said to him, "If
> you are the Son of God, command these stones to become
> loaves of bread." But he answered, "It is written, 'People
> shall not live by bread alone, but by every word that
> proceeds from the mouth of God'." (Mt 4:2-4)

The first of the temptations took place in the wilderness.
Its background was in Deuteronomy 8 in which the Lord led
Israel into the wilderness for forty years to test them. Jesus'
forty days corresponded to Israel's forty years. The Matthean narrative was a Christian midrash on Deuteronomy
6-8. For Gerhardsson, the key term in the Matthean narrative is "son of God." Jesus' sonship was being put to the test.
Jesus remembered what his people had learned during the
desert wandering, and his response to the tempter was a
quotation from that precise passage in Deuteronomy
(8:3).[24]

But what had Israel learned? What was the sin with which
Jesus was being tempted? The sin of Israel was that of
having a divided heart, a discontent with what the Lord had
provided, hence a lack of trust in and fidelity to the Lord (Ps
78:18-22). In Deuteronomy 8 and in this first temptation,
the wilderness was a setting for a trial designed to reveal
what lay in one's heart. Israel did not pass the test; Jesus did.
Jesus' trust was in the Lord. He did not grumble, but
remained faithful.

It was not only a question of Jesus' fidelity, however, but
also of Jesus' struggle. Jesus was quite aware that "people
do not live by bread alone." His response almost sounds
easy. And it would have been easy for Jesus, had he not been
portrayed as having been fasting for forty days. The account
is almost humorous when it informs us that Jesus was
hungry. Jesus saw the suggestion coming from the devil
rather than from God. All three temptations involved that
same aspect — the choice between following the suggestion

[24]Gerhardsson, *The Testing of God's Son*, 42.

of the devil and doing the will of God. But what was the will
of God for Jesus? That question lies at the core of his
struggle. That was what Jesus had come into the wilderness
to discern. The wilderness represents Jesus' struggle with his
call and the origins of his mission.

Was Jesus perhaps tempted to live an ascetical, penitential life from which the tempter tried to dissuade him? Given
the ascetical, penitential movements of Jesus' day, this must
have been a possibility for him. John himself was something
of an ascetic; the Essenes even more so. Was this the direction that Jesus himself should follow as he prepared for the
coming of the Lord? Later Jesus comes out of the desert,
preaching and healing and driving out demons and criticized for not being as ascetic as John.[25] Did his own consciousness of his mission begin here to part company with
that of John's? Later Jesus fed the hungry and taught others
to do likewise. Neither in asceticism (perhaps a real temptation for Jesus) nor in comfort is life to be found, but only in
fidelity to God.

The context for understanding both the Matthean and
Lucan versions of the story is the wilderness experience of
Israel itself as developed in Hebrew tradition. Matthew 4:4
is a quotation from Deuteronomy 8:3 in the Septuagint
form of the Scriptures. Likewise the second and third temptations parallel Deuteronomy 6:16 and 6:13. Jesus was not
unlike Moses (Dt 9:9-18). The fasting of Jesus recalls that of
Moses (Ex 34:28). In the tradition behind both Matthew
and Luke, however, Jesus was seen more in contrast to
Israel as a whole. Israel was tested in the desert and found
wanting. Jesus was tested and found faithful. Jesus' will was
to do the will of the Lord. But we cannot presume at this
point that Jesus knew what that will was. He was still in the
process of discovering that.

> Then the devil took him to the holy city, and set him on
> the pinnacle of the temple, and said to him, "If you are the

[25]Mt 11:18-19; Lk 7:33-34. See Jeremias, *New Testament Theology*, 48-49. Also
Schillebeeckx, *Jesus*, 201-18.

Son of God, throw yourself down; for it is written, 'He will give his angels charge of you,' and 'On their hands they will bear you up, lest you strike your foot against a stone'." Jesus said to him, "Again it is written, 'You shall not tempt the Lord your God'." (Mt 4:5-7)

There is a difference in the order of the temptations within Matthew and Luke. For Matthew, the order is desert, Jerusalem Temple, a high mountain. For Luke it is desert, view of kingdoms of the world, Jerusalem Temple. The first temptation in Matthew's narrative would have led to the sin of infidelity because it would have tempted God, would have put God to the test. So likewise the second was another temptation to put God to the test. Rather than tempting God to satisfy one's hunger, however, it was tempting God to provide protection. The setting here was the Temple because the Temple was the presence of God to God's people. The background is again Deuteronomy 6-8 and also Psalm 91. The reply of Jesus is specifically Deuteronomy 6:16.

John typified the ascetical movements in Judea. Not all of John's disciples remained itinerant with him, however; some returned home to await there the dawning of the end times. Could this have been what God was asking of Jesus? Certainly this would have been an attractive possibility for Jesus, to return to Nazareth and continue to live his "hidden life." Just as Jesus could have been drawn toward a more ascetical life, so he could have been pulled toward a peaceful and quiet life. Yet it was a public ministry the Lord had in store for Jesus. He was not to return to Nazareth and would never have that kind of life again. In resisting the temptation of the devil to test God, it was becoming clearer to him what God might be asking of him. Jesus resisted the diabolical temptation to be the occasion for the working of a great miracle. Just as there were ascetics enough, so there were wonder workers enough in those days. Jesus resisted two extremes: he would not be leaving the wilderness in order "to stay at home" or "to perform miracles." He was being called to a ministry for the sake of others. Throwing himself down from the pinnacle of the Temple would have been a marvel indeed. But in resisting it, he was beginning to get some sense of his own mission and he remained faithful to God.

> Again the devil took him to a very high mountain, and showed him all the kingdoms of the world and the glory of them; and he said to him, "All these I will give you, if you will fall down and worship me." Then Jesus said to him, "Begone, Satan! For it is written, 'You shall worship the Lord your God and him only shall you serve'." (Mt 4:8-10)

The setting this time is a mountain. Deuteronomy depicted Moses on a high mountain beholding the glories of Canaan. And Jesus' response came from Deuteronomy. "You shall fear the Lord your God; you shall serve him, and swear by his name" (Dt 6:13).

Certainly the kingdom of the world that the devil offered Jesus must have been something to pass through his mind. His world not only had its ascetics, and its wonder workers, but also its messiahs or messianic expectations. Jesus must have wondered about and feared that he might be that Messiah. He may not have been tempted by earthly kingdoms so naively offered by the devil, but to be the Messiah of Israel, the liberator of God's people and to set up God's reign on earth may indeed have been what the Lord was asking. The Lord was calling him not to an ascetical life in the wilderness, not to a quiet life at home, perhaps then to this earthly mission for which he felt so ill prepared. Moses after all felt the same way.

Yet by this time in his search Jesus may have become willing to accept a ministry rather than the ascetical life, and willing to accept a public ministry for his people rather than a quiet ministry back in Nazareth, but at least a public ministry that might be non-offensive, non-political, and non-violent: a public ministry that would not create conflict. Certainly God would spare him the personally offensive, politically dangerous, and potentially violent character that his mission eventually involved. But no. His was to become a most delicate balance to maintain — neither a strictly messianic mission nor religious compromise. His heavenly Father was calling him into the thick of this religiously varied and controversial world, this politically tense and potentially explosive world. No, he was not to be the Messiah in the sense that most of Israel expected one. In fact, God was calling him to run the risk of being a heretic as Jeremiah had been. The devil offered comfort and fame and power; Jesus may have preferred solitude and quiet and staying out of trouble. Yet these are not to be his either. God would lead him out into the world where the battle was to take place. The struggle remained with Jesus throughout his life. The ordeal never went away.

One's approach to the Matthean and Lucan narratives is legitimately imaginative, midrashic as the narratives themselves are. The narratives are symbolic of Jesus' historical but inaccessible struggle — inaccessible in its innermost depths. It is not a question of psychologizing, nor of assuming as historiographical what has been interpretatively developed. It is, however, a question of an encounter with the Jesus who struggles, in this case with his call and his mission. For it is from within this wilderness experience, whatever it consisted in, that Jesus' sense of call gets further clarified and his sense of mission originates — even if that mission and its particularities only get further clarified during the course of the life and ministry which still lay ahead. The wilderness experience was a time of search, of questioning, of struggle — with himself, with the devil, and with his God. The unfolding of the mission will continue beyond the wilderness events themselves. We will later see the search continue and the mission further clarified when Jesus is with his disciples in the region of Caesarea Philippi.

Deuteronomy 6-8 provides the background for the Matthean temptation narrative. Deuteronomy 6:4-5 is the famous *Shema* of the Jews.

> Hear, O Israel: The Lord our God is one Lord; and you
> shall love the Lord your God with all your heart, and with
> all your soul, and with all your might.

Jesus realized at his baptism or in the wilderness that he was
being called to be a prophet, like unto Moses but at a much
different period of history. *Jesus was being asked to live by
faith alone.* He had to trust and not resist the Lord. He had
been given the gift of the Spirit. Jesus had come through his
time in the wilderness, strengthened, afraid, ready, with a
heightened experiential knowledge of the Father's love:
God *only* shall you serve. Yes, he would be a servant of the
Lord — even until death if that was where it would take him,
although he was still not yet fully aware where in fact it was
all going to take him. That part of the story had to be lived.

All three narratives, Mark, Matthew, Luke, are more
theology than they are history or geography — although
this does not mean that the historical and geographical
reality is to be dismissed. Mark, Matthew and Luke each
has a theological purpose and all use earlier traditions for
that purpose. Gerhardsson reminds us of an important
aspect of biblical exposition, namely, the "inexhaustible
wealth of meaning" within the sacred writings, meaning
"additional to and beyond that which was traditionally
ascribed" to a text. He writes, "We must remember that no
rabbi assumed that the text could only have one meaning.
The same expositor could on different occasions, or even on
the same occasion, demonstrate that a single passage had
many different things to say. This is particularly true of the
haggadic exegesis."[26] In other words, the historical basis of
the text and the theological intentions behind them still do
not exhaust the possible approaches to the text.

What we find is that both critical biblical study and a
theological imagination move us in the same direction. Both
approaches suggest that in the wilderness after the baptism,
and throughout his ministry, Jesus' faith and fidelity were

---

[26]Gerhardsson, *The Testing of God's Son*, 72-73.

put to the test: was he willing to put the will of his Father first? Was he willing to be God's son, which did not mean doing what the Essenes did, or what John was doing, or what others expected, but doing what the Father asked of him? In the wilderness Jesus learned to pray, "Thy will be done." Jesus left the wilderness a new man, a servant of the Lord, God's son, the obedient one who had been put to the test and remained faithful. Here was a human being willing to entrust his life to the Father, who trusted the Father no matter where this would lead, who lived by faith.

These temptations not only had a basis in the life of the Christian community, but also in the life of Jesus himself. It is highly unlikely that a Christian community with its post-resurrection exalted understanding of Jesus would have developed this tradition from nowhere. Elsewhere the Scriptures give witness to the struggle of Jesus to be God's son, as in the prayer in Gethsemane and in *Hebrews*. In the wilderness Jesus was put to the test and this was an ordeal he would not forget. Jesus himself may well have spoken of it.

Joachim Jeremias helps us to appreciate the genuinely trying character of this experience for Jesus.

> "Temptation" is a misleading designation. The word *peirasmos* occurs twenty-one times in the New Testament. In no less than twenty of them, however, it has the meaning of "trial, testing, ordeal"; only in one passage does it clearly denote "temptation to sin" (1 Tim 6:9). It is to be rendered "testing, ordeal" even in Luke 4:13. For the meaning of the so-called "temptation story" is not that Jesus was put in the way of sin and resisted it; rather, the story is about Jesus' acceptance of his mission. It is better, therefore, to avoid the term "temptation story," the moralizing tone of which can easily be misunderstood. The Jesus who confronts us is not the one who has been tempted, but the *one who has emerged from his ordeal.*[27]

[27]Jeremias, *New Testament Theology*, 74. See 68-75 for Jeremias' discussion of the temptation narratives. For Jeremias "all three variants of the story are con-

There is both a historical and also a symbolic or theological side to Jesus' being driven into the wilderness. The historical side consists in the fact of his being tested, perhaps shortly after his baptism, while still in the wilderness.[28] The actual character of this ordeal, however, is not historiographically ascertainable.[29] Jesus left Nazareth and Galilee for the wilderness area wherein John was baptizing. While there he received the baptism of John as well as the gift of the Spirit. Called by God as a prophet to Israel, the Spirit drives him further into the wilderness during which time his faith and fidelity and sonship are put to the test. In that ordeal Jesus may have experienced God more personally as his Father. His prayer may have been to do his Father's will. He is willing to trust whatever the Father will ask. He, unlike Israel, is the obedient one, the Son in whom the Father is well pleased. Mauser's interpretation of Mark is that Jesus clashed with Satan who attempted to direct him from an unswerving obedience to the Father's will. Gerhardsson's interpretation of Matthew is that Jesus was tried in every way that Israel was, but remained faithful. Fitzmyer's interpretation of Luke is that Jesus was obedient to his Father's will by refusing to be seduced into using his power of authority as Son for any reason other than that for which he has been sent. I suggest in addition that Jesus had to learn from experience God's will and to live by faith.

In attempting to understand Jesus, we cannot leave this desert/wilderness motif behind once Jesus moves into his Galilean ministry. There were in Israelite and Judean history two particularly formative traditions: the Moses-

cerned with one and the same temptation: *the emergence of Jesus as a political messiah*" (71). Also see Fitzmyer, *The Gospel According to Luke, I-IX*, 514, concerning the word for temptation, test. Jeremias, *The Parables of Jesus*, revised edition, trans. S. H. Hooke (New York: Charles Scribner's Sons, 1963), 122-23, suggests that the three temptations or episodes originally existed in separate forms. "It is preferable, therefore, to speak of three versions of the account of the temptations, rather than of three temptations. The subject of all three ... is the overcoming of the temptation to entertain a false messianic expectation" (123).

[28]T. W. Manson, *The Sayings of Jesus*, 46, suggests that the stories do report a genuine experience of Jesus.

[29]See Fitzmyer, *The Gospel According to Luke, I-IX*, 509-10.

exodus-wilderness tradition especially significant in the north, and the David-Jerusalem-Zion tradition of greater value in the south or Judea.[30] Of these two, the former will remain more important for interpreting and understanding Jesus than the latter, the Mosaic prophet-servant more important than the Davidic king-messiah. As we proceed, we will see that Jesus is better understood in the context of prophecy than in that of messianism. The ordeal in the wilderness may have already involved Jesus in struggle with a messianic call — one which he so far effectively resists and interprets as diabolical. Both Jesus' baptism and the wilderness experience are stories that point to the origins of a mission which is still to unfold, and to be further elaborated even for Jesus himself. The wilderness and the symbolic value which it held in the history of Jesus' people, the ancient tradition of prophecy and the prophets of old, particularly the historical and symbolic roles of Moses: all of these will continue to be influential as Jesus enters upon his mission and ministry.

A Man of the Shema

According to the Gospel of Mark, Jesus was baptized (1:9-11), then went further into the wilderness where he was put to the test (1:12-13), then left the wilderness and returned to Galilee after the arrest of John (1:14). After the wilderness experience Jesus was found in Galilee proclaiming the good news of the closeness of God's reign (1:15). In the first chapters of Mark Jesus is portrayed as preaching, healing, and casting out devils. He also attracted four significant disciples — Simon, Andrew, James and John. Much of this ministry took place in Capernaum. Verses 35-39 of the first chapter of Mark provide us with the two sides of Jesus which are closely interwoven throughout his public life — prayer and ministry.

[30]Gerhard von Rad, *Old Testament Theology* I, 46-48, 69-77, 334-47.

> [35]And in the morning, a great while before day, he rose
> and went out to a lonely place, and there he prayed. [36]And
> Simon and those who were with him pursued him, [37]and
> they found him and said to him, "Every one is searching
> for you." [38] And he said to them, "Let us go on to the next
> towns, that I may preach there also; for that is why I came
> out." [39]And he went throughout all Galilee, preaching in
> their synagogues and casting out demons. (Mk 1:35-39)

Verse 35 presents Jesus alone at prayer. Before the day's
work began, Jesus went off to a place where he could be
alone with God, where he perhaps recaptured the nearness
of God that had been his experience in the wilderness.

Jesus participated in the annual festive religious celebra-
tions of the Jewish people, the traditional festival of Pesach
or Passover, the greatest and oldest of the Jewish festivals;
and the Feast of Sukkoth or Tabernacles (Tents, Booths, or
Ingathering), the autumn agricultural festival. Both of these
were pilgrim festivals that brought thousands to Jerusalem.
We can assume that Jesus as a practicing and devout Jew
often went to Jerusalem for these festivals during his life,
perhaps annually.[31] Jesus also observed the sabbath.

> And he came to Nazareth, where he had been brought up;
> and he went to the synagogue, as his custom was, on the
> sabbath day. (Lk 4:16)

In addition to the sabbath, Jewish men prayed three times
daily. This seems already to have been a custom by the time
of Jesus — prayer at sunrise, in the afternoon around 3 p.m.,

---

[31]On the Jewish festivals, see Roland de Vaux, *Ancient Israel*, vol. 2 (New York:
McGraw-Hill, 1965), 484-517; Theodor Gaster, *Festivals of the Jewish Year* (New
York: William Sloane Associates, 1953); Hans-Joachim Kraus, *Worship in Israel,
A Cultic History of the Old Testament*, trans. Geoffrey Buswell (Oxford: Basil
Blackwell, 1966); George Foot Moore, *Judaism in the First Centuries of the
Christian Era*, vol. 2 (New York: Schocken Books, 1971), 40-54; Henry Renckens,
The Religions of Israel, trans. N. B. Smith (New York: Sheed and Ward, 1966);
Hayyim Schauss, *Guide to Jewish Holy Days, History and Observance*, trans.
Samuel Jaffe (New York: Schocken Books, [1938] 1962).

and at sunset. The daily prayer involved the recitation of the *Shema* (*sh^{e}ma'*) twice a day, at the morning and evening hours, and the *Tephillah* (*t^{e}phillāh*) three times a day at all three hours.

The *Tephillah*, or "Prayer," is a litany of benedictions known at the end of the first century C.E. as the *Shemoneh Esreh* (sh^{e}moneh 'esrēh), "Eighteen Benedictions," to which one could add personal petitions. It was to be prayed by all including women and children.[32] The *Shema* we have met as the background and context for the testing of Jesus in the wilderness.

> Hear, O Israel: The Lord our God is one Lord; and you shall love the Lord your God with all your heart, and with all your soul, and with all your might. And these words which I command you this day shall be upon your heart; and you shall teach them diligently to your children, and shall talk of them when you sit in your house, and when you walk by the way, and when you lie down, and when you rise. And you shall bind them as a sign upon your hand, and they shall be as frontlets before your eyes. And you shall write them on the doorposts of your house and on your gates. (Dt 6:4-9; also Dt 11:13-21, Nm 15:41)

This was to be recited twice daily by men and boys over twelve. Jesus would have been taught, would have recited, and would have meditated upon these words for at least twenty years prior to his baptism. No wonder he would have felt them in his heart and found them ready at hand during the test in the wilderness. These words above any others were the ones upon which Jesus based his life. His own restatement or the summary of Jesus' teaching on the Law involves the *Shema* as the first of the commandments. In

[32]Joachim Jeremias, *The Prayers of Jesus* (Naperville, Ill.: Alec R. Allenson, 1967), 70-72; *New Testament Theology, The Proclamation of Jesus,* trans. John Bowden (New York: Charles Scribner's Sons, 1971), 185-88. For a translation of the benedictions, see Ernst Lohmeyer, *Our Father* (New York: Harper and Row, 1965), 302-4. Also see Evelyn Garfiel, *Service of the Heart, A Guide to the Jewish Prayer Book* (North Hollywood, Calif.: Wilshire Book Co., 1978), 94-106.

some ways, in response to the question "Who is Jesus of Nazareth?" one might best reply by saying: Jesus is someone who loved the Lord his God with all his heart, all his soul, and all his might — a man who lived the *Shema*. There are many references to Jesus also praying in solitude, often for extended periods. We have noted Mark 1:35 and could include Mark 6:46 (// Mt 14:23). Luke frequently adds the motif of prayer to Mark's text (Lk 3:21; 5:16; 6:12; 9:18, 28).

With respect to Jesus' prayer, all five strata of the Gospels present him as addressing God as Father: Mark 13:36 (// Mt 26:39, Lk 22:42); Q, Matthew 6:9 (// Lk 11:2), Matthew 11:25, 26 (// Lk 10:21); special Luke, 22:34, 46; special Matthew, 26:42 (repetitions of 26:39); John 11:41, 12:27f, 17:1, 5, 11, 21, 24, 25. The *only* exception to this form of address on the part of Jesus is Mark 15:34 (// Mt 27:46), the cry from the cross, "My God, my God, why have you forsaken me," in which Jesus alludes to Psalm twenty-two. In addressing God in his personal prayer, Jesus used Aramaic rather than Hebrew, and thus addressed God as *Abba*. This is explicit in Mark 14:36 and is also reflected in the life of the early Church (Gal 4:6; Rom 8:15).

Jeremias maintained that Jesus' use of *Abba* in addressing God was the most important linguistic innovation on the part of Jesus.[33] James D. G. Dunn indicates that Jeremias has overstated his case, yet agrees that *Abba* was a characteristic feature of Jesus' prayers and that it distinguished him to some degree from his contemporaries.[34] Ferdinand Hahn states, "the Aramaic form of address *Abba* can be regarded with certainty as a mark of Jesus' manner of

---

[33] *New Testment Theology*, 36. There is an important distinction here when referring to Old Testament and post-biblical sources. For example, although there is little evidence for someone *addressing* God as *Abba* prior to Jesus, there are instances in which God is spoken of as a father. The difference is between the one spoken to (in prayer) and the one spoken of (in the sacred traditions). James D. G. Dunn modifies Jeremias' overstatement. See *Christology in the Making*, (Philadelphia: Westminster Press, 1980), 26-29; and *Jesus and the Spirit* (London: SCM Press, 1975), 20-40.

[34] Dunn, *Christology in the Making*, 26-29.

speech."[35] The significance of Jesus' use of *Abba* rises from
the fact that the word is very familial and familiar. Jesus
prayed to God as an adult child would talk to or colloquially
address dad or mom.[36]

Another characteristic of the prayer of Jesus was its
obediential quality reflecting a submission to the will of God
(*Abba*). This quality is reflected in Luke's portrayal of Jesus'
mother's life: "Behold, I am the handmaid of the Lord; let it
be done to me according to your word" (Lk 1:38). It was the
core of Jesus' prayer at Gethsemane: "Abba, Father, all
things are possible to thee; remove this cup from me; yet not
what I will, but what thou wilt" (Mk 14:36; // Lk 22:42; Mt
26:42). In the Synoptic Gospels we really have only two of
the personal prayers of Jesus, Mark 14:36 quoted above,
and the prayer of thanks in Matthew 11:25-30. Both mention the will of the Father (Mt 11:26), as does the prayer
which he taught his disciples. Thus understandably and
faithfully his disciples recalled this aspect in the life and
prayer of the Teacher when they have him say: "I seek not
my own will but the will of him who sent me," (Jn 5:30) and
"I have come to do thy will" (Heb 10:9).[37]

As we reflect upon the prayer Jesus taught, we can consider it both as a prayer and as a summary of his teaching.
The prayer is not a prayer which Jesus taught publicly for
everyone, but rather a prayer for his disciples in response to
their request (Lk 11:1). Matthew places the prayer within his
compilation of Jesus' teaching (the "sermon on the mount").
But Luke sees Jesus teaching the prayer in response to the
request of his disciples. Although it is nowhere explicitly
stated, one can assume that the prayer Jesus taught reflects

[35]Ferdinand Hahn, *The Titles of Jesus in Christology, Their History in Early Christianity*, trans. Harold Knight and George Ogg (London: Lutterworth Press, 1969), 307.

[36]The use of *Abba* in the time of Jesus was not necessarily limited to babies or small children. See Jeremias, *New Testament Theology*, 67; *The Prayers of Jesus*, 58-63. Also Schillebeeckx, *Jesus, An Experiment in Christology*, trans. Hubert Hoskins (New York: Seabury Press, 1979), 159; 693, n. 210. Also T. W. Manson, *The Sayings of Jesus* (Grand Rapids, Mich.: William B. Eerdmans, 1957), 168.

[37]See also John 4:34; 6:38. Schillebeeckx, *Jesus*, 263; Jeremias, *The Prayers of Jesus*, 18, 62; Dunn, *Jesus and the Spirit*, 15-21.

Jesus' own personal way of praying himself. Jesus' prayer (the one he taught) reflects Jesus' prayer (his own way of praying).

Jeremias has helped to provide us with a possibly original form of the prayer.[38] We have two versions of the prayer which vary slightly. It is generally considered that Luke's version (11:2-4) is the more original. His is the shorter and it is more probable that the prayer would have been expanded rather than that the disciples would have omitted something. Also, Matthew's version reflects a more liturgical setting. While Luke's version may be more original with respect to length, Jeremias maintains that Matthew's version (6:9-13) is more original with respect to wording, given its more difficult reading and its Aramaic flavor. Accepting these two principles, Luke's length and Matthew's wording, Jeremias has reconstructed a possible Aramaic original by translating the prayer as based on Luke's length and Matthew's words back into Aramaic. This may be the prayer as actually taught by Jesus. Translated into English, it would be something like:

> Dear Father,
> Hallowed be thy name;
> Thy kingdom come;
> Our bread for tomorrow, give us today;
> And forgive us our debts, as we also here and now
>   forgive our debtors;
> And let us not fall into temptation.[39]

This reconstruction, however, is only probable.[40] We can take hypotheses with respect to Jesus' prayer too defini-

---

[38]Jeremias, *The Prayers of Jesus*, 85-94. Michael Goulder, *Midrash and Lection in Matthew* (London: SPCK, 1974), 296-301, suggests that the Lord's Prayer is composed by Matthew from Jesus' prayers in Gethsemane and teaching on prayer (Mk 11:25).

[39]John Reumann, *Jesus in the Church's Gospels* (Philadelphia: Fortress Press, 1968), 95. Also see T. W. Manson, *The Sayings of Jesus*, 266.

[40]Even Jeremias speaks of probability, *The Prayers of Jesus*, 89, 91. Yet he does not always emphasize the probable aspect, *New Testament Theology*, 195-96. For

tively. For example, we suggested that the prayer was one taught to the disciples, as suggested by Luke. The evidence for this is the assimilation of the prayer into a sermon setting in Matthew, the restricted post-baptismal use of the prayer in the early Church,[41] and the probability that Jesus only taught the prayer once. All of this makes it probable that Jesus did teach the prayer to his disciples and the Church treasured this prayer and reserved it for the baptized. On the other hand, we cannot simply dismiss the real possibility that Jesus did teach the prayer twice — once earlier in his ministry to his disciples in response to their request and again later to a larger audience.

We note that Jesus tells his disciples, when they are praying, to address the God of Israel and Lord of the Universe with the familial *Abba*. The Lord is the Father of Jesus, and our Father as well. The prayer can be divided into the God-conscious reverence in the first part and the self-conscious needs or fears in the second. This division is similar to that within the New Testament's twofold summary of the Law, the first part of which concerns our love for God and the second part which concerns our love for neighbor and self. Although we could reserve an analysis of Jesus' prayer until we discuss the teaching of Jesus, it is also

excellent points which make one more skeptical of the effort to determine the original version, see Lohmeyer, *Our Father*, 131-33, 275, 291-95.

[41]In the *Didache*, which probably dates from the first century, there is the instruction to pray Jesus' prayer three times a day (8:3). The early Christians took over the Jewish custom of praying three times daily, but they used the prayer Jesus taught rather than the Jewish *Tephillah*. See *The Didache*, trans. James A. Kleist, *Ancient Christian Writers*, vol. 6 (New York: Neuman Press, 1948), 3-25. Also, *The Apostolic Fathers*, in *The Fathers of the Church*, vol. 1 (New York: Christian Heritage, Inc., 1947), 167-84. The fact that the prayer itself may have been reserved for those who had already been baptized is reflected in the catechesis of Cyril of Jerusalem (fourth century), the earliest witness to the fact that the prayer was used in the celebration of the Eucharist and in that portion of the liturgy reserved for the baptized, in contrast to catechumens. See Cyril's 24th catechetical lecture. Lectures 1-19 were prebaptismal instructions. Lectures 20-24 were given during Easter Week and were post-baptismal. See Johannes Quasten, *Patrology*, vol. 3 (Utrecht: Spectrum Publishers, 1966), 362-77. Also, and for a translation, *St. Cyril of Jerusalem's Lectures on the Christian Sacraments*, ed. F. L. Cross, trans. R. W. Church (Crestwood, New York: St. Vladimir's Seminary Press, 1977).

appropriate here as we reflect upon Jesus as a man of prayer and the *Shema*.

1. "Hallowed be thy name" (Lk 11:2; Mt 6:9). Reverence is shown — may your name, Father, be hallowed, praised, respected, revered, rightly feared, made holy, sanctified, glorified. The prayer begins by acknowledging respect for the name of God. Raymond Brown suggests that the prayer concerns an action on the part of God: may God "make manifest the sanctity of His own name," akin to Jesus' cry in John's Gospel, "Father, glorify your name" (12:28).[42] This petition is not original with Jesus. It is the first petition of the *Kaddish*, one of the prayers of Judaism: "Exalted and hallowed be his great name in the world which he created according to his will."[43] The Kaddish was a prayer which immediately followed the sermon which was given in Aramaic in the synagogue. Jesus would have been familiar with the Kaddish and would have prayed it from his childhood on.

2. "Thy Kingdom come" (Lk 11:2; Mt 6:10a). "Thy will be done on earth as it is in heaven" (Mt 6:10b). In this second petition, Matthew's text includes two petitions for Luke's one. The two in Matthew, however, are practically synonymous and reinforce each other. They express two aspects of the God-consciousness of Jesus in relationship with *Abba* — God's reign and will. They express the same heartfelt desire. We see here the reverent, obediential, hopeful posture of Jesus. Although only the first may reflect the prayer as originally taught by Jesus, both reflect accurately aspects from the life of Jesus. "May your reign begin and your kingdom come" reflects something he is asking of God. Come quickly, Father — a *maranatha* (Rv 22:20) addressed to the Father.

[42]Raymond Brown, "The Pater Noster as an Eschatological Prayer, " *New Testament Essays* (New York: Paulist Press, 1965), 229. Also see Lohmeyer, *Our Father*, 63-87.

[43]Jeremias, *New Testament Theology*, 198. Lohmeyer, *Our Father*, 66-67. *The Lord's Prayer and Jewish Liturgy,* ed. Jakob J. Petuchowski and Michael Brocke (New York: Seabury Press, 1978), esp. 59-72.

Just as in Jesus' own personal prayer he learned "but not as I will" (Mt 26:42), so here he teaches "thy will be done." The God-consciousness in the first half of the prayer reflects both our hope — may thy kingdom come — and also our response — may thy will be done. This expression, "Thy will be done on earth," is also an act of resignation. As "May your kingdom come" reflects something that we are asking of God, so "May your will be done" is something we are asking of ourselves. Whether our Father's will is or is not done on earth will depend on us.

The first half of the prayer is an expression of hope, and an eschatological awareness. Both "May your reign begin" and "May your will be done" express hope, and one can say that these expressions of hope are the core of prayer. The "God-consciousness" is an "eschatological consciousness" as well. The resigned and committed aspects of this petition are rooted in the hope: may your kingdom come; may your will be done.

3.   The second half of the prayer involves three petitions. The first is, "Give us each day our daily bread" (Lk 11:3); or "Give us this day our daily bread" (Mt 6:11). One notices a variation between the Matthean and Lucan versions.

The petition is eminently practical: Feed us. Grant us today the bread we need to live. Help us to get through today. We pray this prayer daily, and our prayer today is for bread today (at least in Matthew). There is also a tone of hope and expectation here. There is no hint that our Father will not see that sufficient bread for today is provided. This is an expression of trust. The simplicity and practicality of the petition point to it as an expression on behalf of those whose daily food was not secure. It was a petition that reflected the socio-economic reality of the petitioners, as well as dependency upon God. It was not a prayer taught the rich; it would too readily smack of irony or arrogance. Nothing would suggest that Jesus himself did not pray in this way. He often could not be sure where his next meal would come from; he was certainly conscious that this was true of many who gathered to hear him preach; it must have been the condition of his disciples who had left much behind to follow him. They all had this in common — their only hope was in the Lord.

The "us" here ought not be defined individualistically or narrowly. Given the multitudes who came to Jesus, it is likely that the "us" included all those in need, himself, his disciples, the poor of whom he was so conscious. "Give us, all of us, enough to eat. Give especially those most in need sufficient bread for this day."

If we, his disciples today, reflect upon the number of times we pray this prayer in one week or one month, it cannot help but have an air of insincerity or triviality about it unless we have that consciousness in us which was in Jesus, namely a more social religious awareness. Given the reality of the overwhelming number of poor and starving in our world, and given the reality that so many of us who call ourselves disciples of Jesus in fact need not worry about where our next meal may come from, if we pray as Jesus taught and in a heartfelt way, it must involve a global consciousness: Give us the food we need for this day. Give especially those most in need sufficient bread for this day. We too pray the "us" not only for ourselves but for all who have been entrusted to our care, for ourselves and our families, for all disciples of Jesus and our brothers and sisters in the faith, for the hungry and needy, our neighbors wherever they may be.

One will notice in my interpretation a very present and existential character. A tendency in recent years, however, has been to interpret this petition in an eschatological sense. We have already seen hopefulness and eschatology in the first half of the prayer. The eschatology in the second half of the prayer, while present, is balanced with other concerns. Let us look at the texts more closely to see the basis for an eschatological interpretation. Matthew writes, "Give us *this* day," and Luke writes, "Give us *each* day." In Luke the petition appears broadened or generalized. Matthew's version, according to Jeremias, reflects the original petition. Also, in Mathew, an aorist imperative is used, in Luke a present imperative. Elsewhere in the prayer the aorist is used, hence Matthew appears to be more consistent. The aorist implies a single action: today, this day, once. Luke's expansion to every day, each day, would require the present imperative for repeated actions. Hence it appears that Luke made an adaptation. Matthew's version, with the one time request, is open to an eschatological interpretation.

But the crucial factor with respect to an eschatological interpretation is the meaning of the word *epiousion*. The Greek word is rare. It is also a later tradition. The Aramaic original can only be hypothetical. Thus one cannot be sure of the exact meaning of *epiousios*.[44] Etymologically , does the word derive from *epi* and *einai* or *ousia* (to be) or from *epi* and *ienai* (to go, come)? The first two imply bread for existence of some sort; the latter bread to come, or for the coming day, or for tomorrow. The first interpretation appears more existential; the latter more eschatological.

Jeremias takes his clue for the latter interpretation from a gloss in Jerome which speaks of the word *mahar* in a lost Aramaic Gospel of the Nazarenes, which word means tomorrow. Jeremias therefore translates *artos epiousios* as "bread for tomorrow."[45] I grant the validity of this translation, but there is a further step taken when one goes from "bread for tomorrow" to "bread for *the* tomorrow, the end times." What is the basis for the eschatological leap?

Jeremias points out that *mahar* literally denotes the next day. Certainly it could mean bread for the future. But to move from "tomorrow's future bread" to "the bread of the end times" is a major leap. Granted an early eschatological interpretation of this bread as bread of the age of salvation, or heavenly manna, these post-resurrection and liturgical settings cannot necessarily be read back into Jesus. Raymond Brown sees a biblical background in Exo-

---

[44]Brown, "The Pater Noster as an Eschatological Prayer," 239-43; Jeremias, *New Testament Theology*, 199. A good discussion of the *epiousios* problem is that of Lohmeyer, *Our Father*, 141-46. Also see W. F. Arndt and F. W. Gingrich, *A Greek-English Lexicon of the New Testament and Other Early Christian Literature* (Chicago: U. of Chicago Press, 1957), 296-97.

[45]Jeremias, *The Prayers of Jesus*, 100; *New Testament Theology*, 200. Also see Lohmeyer, *Our Father*, 155.

dus 16:4 ("I will rain bread from heaven for you; and the people shall go out and gather a day's portion every day").[46] The manna would come on the morrow. Granted such background, this does not necessitate or even favor an eschatological or a Eucharistic interpretation. The manna in the desert was a very existential, life-giving, needed, daily bread. Brown gives an eschatological importance to the aorist tense in all the petitions, but this one-time request can reflect existential as well as eschatological urgency. The interest of the petition in each case is *now*, even if prayed daily.

There is no need to deny the eschatological sense to this petition completely. Lohmeyer maintains a balance between both meanings, physical hunger and eschatological hunger, physical bread and eschatological bread. He writes, "The bread, then, is earthly bread, the bread of the poor and needy, and at the same time, because of the eschatological hour in which it is prayed for and eaten, it is the future bread in this today, the bread of the elect and the blessed."[47]

I myself see more evidence for the existential character of the petition: "Give us today tomorrow's bread," or "Give us today bread for the future." "As you fed our ancestors in the desert, and thus prevented them from starving, give us this heavenly, physical bread that will prevent us from starving." John Reumann accepts the sense of "for tomorrow," and yet writes, "The most likely answer is that it means 'bread for tomorrow, give us today' — i.e., give us enough to see us through the next step on the way."[48]

---

[46]Raymond Brown, "The Pater Noster as an Eschatological Prayer," 242.

[47]Lohmeyer, *Our Father*, 157; also see 150-59.

[48]Reumann, *Jesus in the Church's Gospels* 104; cf., 351. Perrin prefers the eschatological interpretation of the petition; see *The Kingdom of God in the Teaching of Jesus* (London: SCM, 1963), 191-98, and *Jesus and the Language of the Kingdom* (Philadelphia: Fortress Press, 1976), 47-48. T. W. Manson, *The Sayings of Jesus*, 167-71, 265-66, interprets it as referring to the necessities of life, which I prefer, not to the exclusion of the other. Also see *The Lord's Prayer and Jewish Liturgy*, 98-104, where Vogtle suggests that the eschatological interpretation is an over interpretation.

4. "Forgive us our sins, for we ourselves forgive every one who is indebted to us" (Lk 11:5); "Forgive us our debts, as we also have forgiven our debtors" (Mt 6:12).

From the perspective of a balance which takes into consideration both the physical and spiritual or social and religious needs of a human being, one could not formulate two requests more to the point: Give us today and tomorrow sufficient bread. Forgive us our sins. Just as Jewish men or women would have been aware of their material needs, so they would have been aware of their condition before God. They were a religious people, and religious reality was as real as economic reality. There was no reason to separate the two or isolate one over against the other or exalt one above the other. Both were very real and felt needs.

This petition links our own need to be forgiven with our need to forgive, our relation with God and with our brothers and sisters. Matthew 6:14-15, which immediately follows the prayer, makes this point as well. Jesus again and again declared that you cannot ask God for forgiveness if you are not prepared to forgive. It is not a question of bargaining with God. It is a question of restoring proper relationships with our heavenly Father, and with our brothers and sisters — another very existential and felt religious request.

5. "Lead us not into temptation" (Lk 11:4); "Lead us not into temptation, but deliver us from evil" (Mt 6:13). Again, as in the second petition, Matthew's version is expanded. This is another very existential request: Do not let us be put to the test.

Although the two previous petitions can be universalized, this third is best seen as a petition on the part of the committed disciples. The background involves Jesus' own struggle, test, and ordeal through which he was put in the wilderness. Please, *Abba*, never let us be put to the test like that. Never try our faith and fidelity to see how sincere and deep it really is. We have already acknowledged our sinfulness. Up against the command of the *Shema* we are found wanting.

Jesus was quite aware that the struggle which began with him in the wilderness was not finished once and for all. It

remained with him in his life and up to his death. This is one
of his own reasons for prayer — his continued need to rely
on his heavenly Father and surrender over and over again.
The same surrender was still needed in Gethsemane, and it
seemed no easier: *Abba*, if only this cup could pass me by.
Jesus learned experientially what it meant to live by faith
alone. The disciples were called to this same life, that of faith
and trust in God. But this life of faith is often accompanied
by fear. This last request arises out of reverence and out of
fear. Spare me, O Lord.

We are not talking about flimsy temptations here. We are
talking about the temptation from Satan, the father of lies,
the temptation to do our own selfish will. Jesus taught his
disciples to pray to be spared. Jesus prayed the same prayer.
There is no question but that the prayer is a prayer of the
heart of all disciples. No one welcomes a prophetic call
without fear. Do not put us to the test. It is not a question
here of God's tempting us, but of God's allowing us to be put
to the test by the Evil One. The word, *peirasmos*, does not
mean minor temptation or struggle, but the test or ordeal
through which Jesus was put in the wilderness, the testing of
the depth of faith. The Matthean expansion recognizes this
need to be delivered from the power of the evil one.[49] This
peirasmos (test, ordeal) is found in Mark 14:38 — Jesus tells
his disciples, "Pray that you may not enter into trial, be put
to the test."

The concluding doxology with which we are familiar
reflects the prayer as it is already found in the *Didache* (8:2).
The *Didache* has generally followed the more liturgical and
expanded Matthean text. The doxology, "For thine is the
kingdom and the power and the glory, for ever and ever," is
lacking, however, both in Luke and in the oldest manuscripts of Matthew.

Let us return to the one to whom the whole prayer is
addressed: "Father" (Lk 11:20), "Our Father who art in

---

[49]Brown, "The Pater Noster as an Eschatological Prayer," 251-53; Reumann, 96.
For a discussion of why to translate evil as the evil one, see Lohmeyer, *Our Father*,
213-17.

heaven" (Mt 6:9). Again we see a longer Matthean form which may reflect Jewish prayer customs or formulae. The Aramaic which Jesus used could simply have been *Abba*. Jeremias writes, "It is possible to conclude that the giving of the Lord's Prayer to the disciples authorized them to say '*Abba*,' just as Jesus did."[50] The privilege of being able to pray in this fashion and the boldness it implies is reflected in the liturgy. The Liturgy of St. John Chrysostom introduces the Lord's Prayer with, "Grant that we may dare to call on thee as Father and say . . . . " The present Roman Liturgy begins, "We are bold to say. . . . "

Addressing God as Father, although not common within Palestinian Judaism, did have Near Eastern precedents in Sumerian prayers long before the time of Moses. The deity was seen as both powerful and merciful. Jeremias writes, "For Orientals, the word 'father,' as applied to God, thus encompasses, from earliest time, something of what the word 'mother' signifies among us."[51] The richness and uniqueness of the word *abba* makes it difficult to translate. Following Jeremias' suggestion about its setting in an Oriental world, *imma* (mother) as readily captures the felt sense: *abba, imma*, our heavenly father and mother, our darling God.

We often think of the way Jesus prayed, or the prayer he taught. Yet it is also helpful to ask why Jesus prayed. What prompted it? There is no question here of psychoanalysis, nor of historiographical data either, but of allowing the biblical portrait to present itself. The prayer of Jesus involved thanks and praise (Jn 11:41; Mt 11:25) as well as petition (Mk 14:36). Thomas Clarke mentions five reasons or occasions for prayer within the life of Jesus.[52] The first was that of his search for self-understanding or self-identification (e.g., the wilderness experience). Prayer was a heightening of Jesus' consciousness of who he was. Jesus'

[50]Jeremias, *The Prayers of Jesus*, 63.

[51]Ibid., 95.

[52]Notes from an unpublished series of lectures by Thomas Clarke, Monroe, New York, June, 1974. I build upon the five reasons he suggested.

self-understanding cannot be separated from the prayer of Jesus. In prayer he wrestled with all aspects of his identity and especially his religious identity, his relationship to God. Prayer was thus a means by which he achieved personal identity.

Second, prayer helped him to sustain his relationship to the Father, that filial and obediential posture that he had become aware of. It enabled him not only to be conscious of his sonship but to persevere as son, and thus discover and do the Father's will.

Third, prayer also helped him to maintain a fraternal posture toward fellow men and women. He achieved a greater understanding of the people who were part of his life and the people whom his Father loved. In prayer he came to love and to sustain love for his brothers and sisters, and to transcend the anger and hurt and pain he would feel because of them. He was able to forgive them. He prayed for them (Jn 17:15, 20; Lk 22:31f, 23, 34).

Fourth, Jesus prayed in order to make decisions, especially the difficult and significant decisions in his life. He prayed before choosing disciples (Lk 6:12); he brought this choice to the Father. He prayed over his own mission in the wilderness as he struggled with the temptation to be the Messiah.

Fifth, there is an element of passing over into life with the Father and returning to share what he received (Lk 9:29). In his union with the Father in prayer, he became aware of the Father and gained knowledge of the Father. This is akin to what we may have called infused knowledge, but not a special knowledge granted to Jesus; rather a knowledge granted to him in the midst of deep prayer, a revelatory effect of prayer. A man or woman in prayer is the one to whom God discloses God's own self. Thus, in his life of prayer, Jesus more and more became aware of his relationship to God, strove towards union with the Father, and became a more effective messenger and minister of the Father. He became more and more God's son and servant, more and more one with God.

In our discussion concerning the prayer of Jesus, one prominent note is that of Jesus' addressing God in prayer as *Abba* and of Jesus' teaching his disciples to pray by addressing God as *Abba* as well. Thus already we have some sense of Jesus as son. The notion of sonship ought first be seen in a Semitic, Hebrew, Jewish context. In the Scriptures the Hebrew *ben* (Aramaic *bar*) is primarily an expression of subordination, in contrast to the Greek *huios* which denotes physical descent. The biblical concept of sonship could also express "belonging to God."[53] God's people, Israel, were seen as children of God. The Davidic king as well as expected Davidic Messiah were sons of God. In the wisdom tradition, the wise ones were sons of God, as well as the righteous ones (Sirach 4:10; Wisdom of Solomon 2:18). The son of God is a servant of God. In Jesus' prayer, as in the baptism and wilderness experience, Jesus manifests himself as God's son, a man of faith and the *Shema*.

---

[53]Martin Hengel, *The Son of God*, trans. John Bowden (Philadelphia: Fortress Press, 1976), 21-23, 41-45.

5

A Prophet from Nazareth

In writing history, historiography and interpretation go together.[1] We cannot do one without doing the other. As we attempt to understand the Jesus of history, we rely on certain concepts which help us to understand and situate Jesus, concepts that are both interpretative and also rooted in historical data. An interpretation is reliable because it purports to be the best interpretation of the facts. The relationship is such that the facts point to this interpretation and this interpretation points to these facts. Such is the concept of prophet. It is both hermeneutical and historiographical. To speak of Jesus of Nazareth as a Galilean prophet involves both interpretation for the sake of our understanding him and also data which point toward such an interpretation.[2]

In chapter two we saw the need to root Jesus within Palestinian Judaism. But, within early Judaism, Jesus was

[1]In volume two I will consider the relationships among faith, history, and historiography at greater length. I ordinarily prefer the word historiography rather than history when referring to the research and methodology of historians. Historiography is what historians do.

[2]Important to any discussion of Jesus as prophet is the classic essay by C.H. Dodd, "Jesus as Teacher and Prophet," in *Mysterium Christi*, ed. Bell and Deissmann (London: Longmans, Green and Co., 1930), 53-66. Also see James D.G. Dunn, *Jesus and the Spirit* (London: SCM Press, 1975), 82-84, Reginald Fuller, *The Foundations of New Testament Christology* (New York: Charles Scribner's

not Sadducee or Pharisee or Essene or Zealot. Jesus had "Zealots" among his disciples and he was quite aware of the delicate political and religious situation within which he lived.[3] He, however, was not one of the "brigands" himself. Jesus was undoubtedly aware of the Essenes and may have even been tempted to join them. The wilderness played a role in his spirituality, yet he evidently was not an ascetic like John (Mk 2:18; Lk 7:31-35). In many ways Jesus was like the Pharisees.

He practiced his religion, studied Torah, and respected Temple worship.[4] Yet his program for the renewal of Judaism differed significantly from theirs.[5]

The earlier traditions of Israel had spoken of kings, priests, prophets, and sages. These were the ones who played the role of God's agents in history. The monarchy no longer existed in the time of Jesus, although there was the hope for its restoration. But Jesus was not a king, and the royal ideology and its terminology do not help us to "situate" him. Nor did Jesus function as a priest. In "the religion of old," of pre-exilic days, these two, kings and priests, were the institutionally established religious agents. The domain of the former was the kingdom itself; the domain of the latter was the Temple and cult. In post-exilic Judaism, since the

Sons, 1965), 125-31. Whatever one may say about other aspects of their interpretations, the prophetic character of Jesus' life and ministry is solidly established by A.E. Harvey, *Jesus and the Constraints of History* (Philadelphia: Westminster Press, 1982); and Edward Schillebeeckx, *Jesus, an Experiment in Christology*, trans. Hubert Hoskins (New York: Seabury Press, 1979), esp. 105-319, 439-515. For remarks pertinent to Jesus as an eschatological preacher, see W.D. Davies, *The Sermon on the Mount* (Cambridge: Cambridge University Press, 1966), 131-34.

[3]Oscar Cullmann, *Jesus and the Revolutionaries*, trans. Gareth Putnam (New York: Harper and Row, 1970); also *The State in the New Testament* (New York: Charles Scribner's Sons, 1956), 8-23.

[4]John Bowker, *Jesus and the Pharisees* (Cambridge: University Press, 1973). Benedict Viviano, *Study as Worship, Aboth and the New Testament* (Leiden: E.J. Brill, 1978), 171-95.

[5]Marcus Borg, *Conflict, Holiness and Politics in the Teachings of Jesus* (New York: Edwin Mellen Press, 1984). Gerd Theissen, *Sociology of Early Palestinian Christianity*, trans. John Bowden (Philadelphia: Fortress Press, 1978).

monarchy no longer existed, the priesthood grew in importance. As such, there was no institutionalized religious role into which Jesus moved.

There were two other traditional religious roles arising out of the prophetic and sapiential traditions. Both of these traditions, however, were less institutionalized (though not completely uninstitutionalized); the prophets were charismatic, and the sages were critical and in dialogue with international thought. As we will see, Jesus had roots in both wisdom and prophecy, in the more "charismatic" Israelite and Judean traditions.[6]

Prophecy had died out in Israel during the fifth century B.C.E., after the post-exilic prophecy of Haggai, Zechariah, and Malachi. The gift of the Spirit of prophecy had come to be associated with eschatological times. John seemed to be perceived as a prophet and to have manifested the gift of the Spirit. Jesus seems to have received the gift of the Spirit at his own baptism. Many Palestinian Jews perceived Jesus as a prophet. Who did people say that he was? Some said John the Baptizer; others said Elijah, or Jeremiah; others said one of the prophets (Mk 8:28; Mt 16:14; Lk 9:19).

A prophet was a messenger of God, one who spoke the word of God, who gave God's very own word to the people, and who was an interpreter of that word for these people or this king at this time in history and in these circumstances. The prophets in Israel, par excellence, were Moses and Elijah.[7] The classical prophets of old were Amos, Hosea, Isaiah and Micah, of the eighth century B.C.E. The prophets associated with the exile were Jeremiah, Ezekiel and Deutero-Isaiah. Zechariah, Haggai, and Malachi were all post-exilic prophets. Malachi seems to have been the last of these prophets. Like the priests and kings, the prophets were a sacred part of Israel's history and traditions.

---

[6]See Gerhard von Rad, *Old Testament Theology*, trans. D.M.G. Stalker, 2 vols. (New York: Harper and Row, 1962-65), 1:93-102. Martin Hengel, *The Charismatic Leader and His Followers*, trans. James Grieg (New York: Crossroad, 1981).

[7]See R.B.Y. Scott, *The Relevance of the Prophets* (New York: Macmillan Co., 1971), 68-69, for his discussion of the five stages of prophetic succession.

Abraham Heschel describes the prophet as one "who feels fiercely," one "intent on intensifying responsibility," often "an iconoclast," both "a messenger of God" and one "who stands in the presence of God." "We will have to look for prophetic coherence, not *in what* the prophet says but *of whom* he speaks ... The ultimate object and theme of his consciousness is God."[8]

> The prophet is not a mouthpiece, but a person; not an instrument, but a partner, an associate of God. Emotional detachment would be understandable only if there were a command which required the suppression of emotion, forbidding one to serve God "with all your heart, with all your soul, with all your might." God, we are told, asks not only for "works," for action, but above all for love, awe, and fear. We are called to "wash" our hearts (Jer 4:14), to remove "the foreskin" of the heart (Jer 4:4), to return with the whole heart (Jer 3:10). "You will seek Me and find Me, when you seek Me with all your heart" (Jer 29:13). The new covenant which the Lord will make with the house of Israel will be written upon their hearts (Jer 31:31-34).
>
> The prophet is no hireling who performs his duty in the employ of the Lord. The usual descriptions or definitions of prophecy fade to insignificance when applied, for example, to Jeremiah. "A religious experience," "communion with God," "a perception of His voice" — such terms hardly convey what happened to his soul: the overwhelming impact of the divine pathos upon his mind and heart, completely involving and gripping his personality in its depths, and the unrelieved distress which sprang from his intimate involvement. The task of the prophet is to convey the word of God. Yet the word is aglow with the pathos. One cannot understand the word without sensing

[8]Abraham Heschel, *The Prophets* (New York: Harper and Row, 1962), 23. For the quoted references in the text, see chapter one, "What Manner of Man Is the Prophet," 3-26.

the pathos. And one could not impassion others and remain unstirred. The prophet should not be regarded as an ambassador who must be dispassionate in order to be effective.

An analysis of prophetic utterances shows that the fundamental experience of the prophet is a fellowship with the feelings of God, a *sympathy with the divine pathos*, a communion with the divine consciousness which comes about through the prophet's reflection of, or participation in, the divine pathos. The typical prophetic state of mind is one of being taken up into the heart of the divine pathos. Sympathy is the prophet's answer to inspiration, the correlative to revelation.

Prophetic sympathy is a response to transcendent sensibility. It is not, like love, an attraction to the divine Being, but the assimilation of the prophet's emotional life to the divine, an assimilation of function, not of being. The emotional experience of the prophet becomes the focal point for the prophet's understanding of God. He lives not only his personal life, but also the life of God. The prophet hears God's voice and feels His heart. He tries to impart the pathos of the message together with its logos. As an imparter his soul overflows, speaking as he does out of the fullness of his sympathy.[9]

The Greek word *prophētēs* means one who speaks on behalf of someone else. That someone else is the Lord: it is the Lord who speaks. The prophet is not primarily a predictor of future events, although sometimes God's word is addressed to a future close at hand. R. B. Y. Scott writes, "The prophets were primarily *preachers* in the highest sense of that term" (italics in original).[10]

Some of the prophets gathered disciples about them (Is 8:16). They took issue with the policies of the state, yet they

[9]Heschel, *The Prophets*, 25-26.
[10]R.B.Y. Scott, *The Relevance of the Prophets*, 14.

did not engage in revolutionary activity. They "carried out their criticism of society with a moral insight and a radical consistency never known before."[11] They came to their work with a sense of divine vocation, with some definite experience of call. The prophet was a human being who stood in tension between two poles or two worlds; they stood both in the presence of God and also in the world of history. They spoke *God's word* to *this world*.

There can be little question but that Jesus was seen by his contemporaries as being a prophet. We have already referred to Mark 8:28 (// Mt 16:14; Lk 9:19). After raising the son of the widow of Naim from the dead, the crowd proclaimed, "A great prophet has arisen among us" (Lk 7:16). The Pharisee, Simon, on the occasion of his dinner during which a prostitute poured ointment on the feet of Jesus, thought to himself, "If this man were a prophet, he would have known who and what sort of woman this is who is touching him, for she is a sinner" (Lk 7:39). At the time of his entry into Jerusalem, the crowds said, "This is the prophet Jesus from Nazareth of Galilee" (Mt 21:11). Members of the Sanhedrin wanted to get rid of Jesus, but "they feared the multitudes, because they held him to be a prophet" (Mt 21:46).

A Prophetic and Social Consciousness

Not only did Jesus' contemporaries consider Jesus to be a prophet. It would appear as if this is a fundamental way in which Jesus perceived himself as well. Jesus presented himself as a prophet. He spoke with the authority of the prophet. His mission, as he himself understood it, was primarily that of preaching (Mk 1:38-39). He interpreted the failure and lack of acceptance in his home territory in prophetic terms: "A prophet is not without honor, except in

[11]John Bright, *Jeremiah*, The Anchor Bible, vol. 21 (Garden City, N.Y.: Doubleday, 1965), XXIII.

his own country, and among his own kind, and in his own house" (Mk 6:4; // Mt 13:57; Lk 4:24). After the reference to a prophet's lack of acceptance in Luke's version, Jesus continues and contrasts himself with Elijah and Elisha (Lk 4:24-27).

Jesus' conscious intent not to avoid Jerusalem manifested a prophetic consciousness as well.

> At that very hour some Pharisees came, and said to him, "Get away from here, for Herod wants to kill you." And he said to them, "Go and tell that fox, 'Behold, I cast out demons and perform cures today and tomorrow, and the third day I finish my course. Nevertheless I must go on my way today and tomorrow and the day following; for it cannot be that a prophet should perish away from Jerusalem.' O Jersualem, Jerusalem, killing the prophets and stoning those who are sent to you! How often I would have gathered your children together as a hen gathers her brood under her wings, and you would not! Behold, your house is forsaken. And I tell you, you will not see me until you say, 'Blessed is he who comes in the name of the Lord.'" (Lk 13:31-35)

In the world of early Judaism, Jesus was a prophet.

An important aspect of any prophet's consciousness was their social consciousness. One evident fact about Jesus is that he related to and was concerned for the social outcasts of his world. C. H. Dodd, in choosing nine Gospel passages, diverse with respect to form and motive for inclusion in the tradition, concludes, "All of them in their different ways exhibit Jesus as an historical personality distinguished from other religious personalities of his time by his friendly attitude to the outcasts of society."[12] Jesus was a prophet particularly concerned for society.

[12]C.H. Dodd, *History and the Gospel* (London: Nisbet and Co., 1983), 94, also 92-103. The passages he is referring to are Mk 2:14; 2:15-17; Lk 19:2-10; 7:36-48; Jn 7:53-8:11; Lk 15:4-7 (// Mt 18:12-13); Lk 18:10-14; Mt 11:16-19 (// Lk 7:31-35); Mt 21:32.

Social consciousness is, of course, one of the distinctive characteristics of a prophet. The classical eighth century prophets — Amos, Hosea, Isaiah, and Micah — were supreme exemplifications of that. Amos is often referred to as the prophet of social justice; Micah has been described as the Amos of the south. Amos 2:6-8; 3:10; 4:1; 5:7-12; 5:21-24; 8:4-7; Hosea 6:5-6; Isaiah 1:11-17; 1:23; 2:4; 3:12-15; 5:1-7; 10:1-2; 29:13-14; 32:6-7; Micah 6:8; Jeremiah 6:13-15; 6:20; 7:5-7; 8:8-9; 22:13-17 are only a few of the texts which show how deeply based the thirst for justice was within the prophetic consciousness.

> What to me is the multitude of your sacrifices? says the LORD: I have had enough of burnt offerings of rams and the fat of fed beasts; I do not delight in the blood of bulls, or of lambs, or of he-goats.
>
> When you come to appear before me, who requires of you this trampling of my courts?
>
> Bring no more vain offerings; incense is an abomination to me. New moon and sabbath and the calling of assemblies — I cannot endure iniquity and solemn assembly.
>
> Your new moons and your appointed feasts my soul hates; they have become a burden to me, I am weary of bearing them.
>
> When you spread forth your hands, I will hide my eyes from you; even though you make many prayers, I will not listen; your hands are full of blood.
>
> Wash yourselves; make yourselves clean; remove the evil of your doings from before my eyes; cease to do evil; learn to do good; seek justice, correct oppression; defend the fatherless, plead for the widow. (Is 1:11-17)

Within this tradition the prophetic and social anger of Jesus comes as no surprise. Abraham Heschel writes, "That justice is a good thing and a supreme ideal is commonly accepted. What is lacking is a sense of the monstrosity of injustice. The distinction of the prophets was in their remorseless unveiling of injustice and oppression."[13] This is a description of Jesus as well. Jesus was not identified with any of the major socio-political, religious parties within Palestinian Judaism. Yet he was willing to be identified with the *am ha-aretz* (the people, literally, the people of the land). Benedict Viviano writes, "With respect to the *am ha-aretz* or religious lower class of Palestinian Jewry, our hypothesis would run: Jesus was sensitive to their needs, he judged that the Pharisees could never meet them, and he directed his mission to them in a special way (Mt 15:25; 11:25 par; Mk 2:17 par; 6:34 par). Little wonder then that many of them received him as a messenger of God sent directly to them (Mk 1:45; 1:22; 12:37)."[14] Jesus of Nazareth was a socially conscious prophet in an eschatologically conscious period of history.

Any understanding of Jesus as prophet must be within the context of the "quenching of the spirit" or absence of prophecy in late post-exilic Judaism. First Maccabees refers to this tragedy: "A terrible oppression began in Israel; there had been nothing like it since the disappearance of prophecy among them" (9:27, also 4:46, 14:41). Oscar Cullmann wrote, "Prophecy as a profession no longer existed in New Testament times. In fact, there were rarely prophets at all any longer in the specifically Israelitic sense of spiritually inspired men who had received a special calling from God. Prophecy had died out more and more until by this time it really existed only in the written form of the prophetic books."[15] Joachim Jeremias also wrote, "This view took the following form: In the time of the patriarchs, all pious and upright men had the spirit of God. When Israel committed sin with the golden calf, God limited the Spirit to chosen men, prophets, high priests and kings. With the death of the

[13] Heschel, *The Prophets*, 204.

[14] Viviano, *Study as Worship*, 173.

[15] Cullmann, *The Christology of the New Testament*, trans. Shirley C. Guthrie and Charles A.M. Hall, revised edition (Philadelphia: Westminster Press, 1963), 13.

last writing prophets, Haggai, Zechariah and Malachi, *the spirit was quenched* because of the sin of Israel."[16]

The spirit of prophecy had been replaced by that of the Law, and the Law gradually became normative from the times of Ezra and Nehemiah on.[17] Even the prophetic canon existed pretty much as it does today by 200 B.C.E. In the post-exilic period, prophecy was judged in terms of whether it was in accord with the Law, not vice-versa. The author of Zechariah 13 envisioned the death penalty for a false prophet. John and Jesus appeared as prophets in an era of the Law.

At the same time that there was *a felt absence* of the Spirit there was a *longing hope* for its return which, given the eschatological character of early Judaism, became an eschatological hope. "Everywhere in Judaism at this period the hope of the end was united with the expectation of the renewal of prophecy."[18] This eschatological hope for a return of the Spirit can be traced to prophetic utterances like those of Joel: "I will pour out my spirit on all flesh. Your sons and daughters shall prophesy, your old men shall dream dreams, and your young men shall see visions. Even upon the menservants and maidservants in those days, I will pour out my spirit" (2:28-29).

This expectation of the return of the Spirit, of the return of prophecy, became the expectation of *the* prophet of the eschatological times, an eschatological prophet distinct from the royal and priestly messiahs. This expectation of an eschatological prophet eventually moulded itself into two forms, that of Moses on the basis of Deuteronomy 18:15-18, and that of Elijah on the basis of Malachi 3:1; 4:5-6.

The starting point for the expectation of Elijah was 2 Kings 2:1-12, his miraculous removal to heaven. Then the prophecy in Malachi 3:1 was interpreted early to be Elijah in Malachi 4:5 and in Ecclesiasticus 48:10.

---

[16]Jeremias, *New Testament Theology, The Proclamation of Jesus*, trans. John Bowden (New York: Charles Scribner's Sons, 1971), 80-81.

[17]R.H. Charles, *Eschatology* (New York: Schocken Books, 1963), 196-205, 235.

[18]Cullmann, *The Christology of the New Testament*, 22.

> Behold, I send my messenger to prepare the way before
> me, and the Lord whom you seek will suddenly come to
> his temple; the mesenger of the covenant in whom you
> delight, behold, he is coming, says the Lord of hosts. (Mal
> 3:1)
> Behold, I will send you Elijah the prophet before the great
> and terrible day of the Lord comes. (Mal 4:5)

The prophet like Elijah was not equated with the Davidic
Messiah. Sometimes he was seen as the forerunner of the
Messiah, sometimes as the forerunner of the Lord. He was
to appear as the preacher of repentance and to establish the
spiritual conditions necessary for the end. Later, in Ecclesiasticus, he also acquired the function of restoring the tribes
of Israel. His essential function, however, was preaching
repentance.

Besides the Elijah expectation, there was the expectation
of a prophet like Moses, based on Deuteronomy 18:15-19.

> The Lord your God will raise up for you a prophet like me
> from among you, from your brethren — him you shall
> heed — just as you desired of the Lord your God at Horeb
> on the day of the assembly, when you said, 'Let me not
> hear again the voice of the Lord my God, or see this great
> fire any more, lest I die.' And the Lord said to me, 'They
> have rightly said all that they have spoken. I will raise up
> for them a prophet like you from among their brethren;
> and I will put my words in his mouth, and he shall speak
> to them all that I command him. And whoever will not
> give heed to my words which he shall speak in my name, I
> myself will require it of him.' (Dt 18:15-19)

This text originally did not refer to an eschatological
prophet but to historical prophets who would come after
Moses. Evidence of the expectation of an eschatological
prophet like Moses is not found in the Hebrew Scriptures
themselves; it comes later. There is evidence for the expectation in the New Testament (Mk 8:27-28), and Qumran

discoveries indicate an expectation based on Moses or one like him, along with messianic expectations.

Jesus clearly saw himself in prophetic terms (Mk 6:4; Lk 13:34-35). The question remains open as to whether he saw himself in eschatological terms, as an eschatological prophet. It would be going too far to say that he thought of himself as a definite, particular prophet, like Moses or Elijah. In the initial stages of his ministry, he may have seen himself more as a prophet like John, and his ministry as a continuation of John's: preaching, repentance, proclaiming the reign of God. The wilderness context at the origins of Jesus' own mission had Elijah and Mosaic overtones, and as we suggested there, Jesus seems to have spiritually identified more with the wilderness, Moses-prophet, exodus tradition than the Jerusalem, David-Messiah, Zion tradition.

Jesus and Messianism

We have situated Jesus within Israel's charismatic and prophetic tradition. In the course of our discussion we have found ourselves describing Jesus' very own consciousness as prophetic and social. Jesus' self-understanding is a question of great interest, but there are two misunderstandings which any discussion needs to avoid lest the question be falsely posed: (a) a misunderstanding of consciousness and (b) a misunderderstanding of Jesus.

First, there is the question of the nature of consciousness itself. Whatever particular philosophical or psychological perspective one may take, there is a quality of consciousness that is difficult to deny: its fluidity. Consciousness, as we know it in ourselves, is movement. Although this is particularly a Bergsonian way of speaking, whether we are "existentialist" or "essentialist," "realist" or "idealist," consciousness does not stand still. We need not develop or agree on a particular phenomenology of consciousness in order to make the point. Consciousness is a reality that cannot be pinned down. It is too alive and active to be fixed.

Bergson's analysis of *durée* makes us aware that pinning consciousness down to being "this" or "that" is to attempt to stabilize that which is by nature movement, to spatialize that which is by nature temporal, to solidify that which by nature flows. One cannot describe a river by stopping it or a liquid by solidifying it or life by killing it or consciousness by atomizing it. Thus one cannot describe the "self-consciousness" of someone in too fixed, mechanical, or stagnant a way and still be describing consciousness. To segmentalize duration, for Bergson, is no longer to have duration. To compartmentalize consciousness can mean losing what we seek to grasp. Still life is no longer life, and a photograph cannot capture movement. This is not to advocate a particular philosophical perspective. It is simply to caution us against pinning "self" or "consciousness" down too tightly. Jesus' self-awareness was on the move. He was alive. One day flows into but is not the same as the next. That which is so prone to change cannot be best understood in terms of tightly fixed categories. Thus an approach to the self-understanding of Jesus through neatly delineated and fixed categories or titles is doomed to failure. One is attempting to fix that which in life is not fixed. Clarification of different concepts, expressions, or titles is of intellectual importance. One cannot eliminate conceptual clarity, but neither can one make rigid that which in life and history move. We can also go too far in the direction of saying that nothing can be said at all. We may well be able to describe the flow or direction of consciousness, but we must be careful not to picture it as fixed once and for all.

Secondly, a quest for the self-understanding of Jesus can too readily be based on a concern that was not there at that period of history — personal identity is a modern concern — and especially not there in Jesus of Nazareth, biblically pictured as an un-self-preoccupied person. Jesus was what he was without being self-preoccupied. He was not ego-dominated. Much modern discussion about "the self" does not help us to understand the historical Jesus because his primary concerns did not include himself. He was not self-

focused, but focused on others, the poor, his heavenly
Father. His self-consciousness was much more God-
consciousness. His concern was to do the will of his Father
in heaven. The dominant emphasis for him was trusting in
God. This does not imply that he had no identity, but that
self-identity was not a primary focus of his consciousness.
His Father, his Father's will, were his concern, as were those
to whom the Father sent him. We learn more about the
consciousness of Jesus from his prayer and ministry than we
do from attempts to pin or not pin certain titles on him.
Certainly Jesus may well have thought of himself as a
prophet or servant of God, but this only says that he thought
first of God. Not "who am I?" but "Thy will be done," better
reflects the concerns of Jesus. This does not mean that a
description of Jesus as prophetic and socially conscious is
inaccurate. It simply cautions us to be careful about what
and how we say something about the fluid psychic contents
of so un-self-preoccupied a human being.

We encourage caution in talking about the consciousness
of Jesus. Yet we can describe him as a prophetic figure. Let
us go one step further and see what can be said about Jesus
as a messianic figure.[19] Although the expression Christ
(Messiah) became the common way of describing Jesus in
the early Christian traditions, to the extent that it eventually
became a part of his name, Jesus himself as far as we can tell
rarely used the expression. Only three times in the Synoptic
Gospels do we find some response on the part of Jesus to
this title as applied to himself, twice during his "trial" when
the high priest and Pilate asked him, "Are you the Christ?"
and earlier in the confession of Peter at Caesarea Philippi.
The implication in these instances is that some people had
begun to think of Jesus as more than a prophet. They saw
him as the Messiah.

[19]See Oscar Cullmann, *The Christology of the New Testament*, 111-36; Reginald
Fuller, *The Foundations of New Testament Christology*, 23-31, 109-11; Ferdinand
Hahn, *The Titles of Jesus in Christology, Their History in Early Christianity*,
trans. Harold Knight and George Ogg (London: Lutterworth Press, 1969), 131-
222; A.E. Harvey, *Jesus and the Constraints of History*, 134-51; and Geza Vermes,
Jesus the Jew (Philadelphia: Fortress Press, 1973), 129-59.

Jesus certainly never claimed in any unambiguous fashion to be the Messiah himself. He seldom referred to the awaited Messiah in his own teaching. In Mark 12:35-37 (Mt 22:41-46; Lk 20:41-44) we have a polemical exchange between Jesus and the Pharisees concerning the relationship between the Messiah and the house of David but no definite teaching of Jesus himself. Matthew 24:5, 23-24 and Mark 13:6, 21-22 are concerned with false messiahs, but teach nothing about Jesus' own beliefs and they are most probably not authentic Jesus material. Luke 24:26, 46 are sayings of the risen Jesus. Mark 9:41 is the only other reference of Jesus himself to the Messiah and it is generally considered Christian interpolation. Geza Vermes' conclusion seems reliable: "It is clearly not an exaggeration, therefore, to suggest that Messianism is not particularly prominent in the surviving teaching of Jesus."[20]

Jesus seems not to have taught a particular messianic doctrine. In reference to the attitudes of others toward Jesus, perhaps some of his disciples thought of him as the Messiah, as reflected in the response of Peter to Jesus' question at Caesarea Philippi (Mk 8:29). Otherwise there does not appear any such accusation or suggestion prior to Jesus' arrest and trial when he was handed over to Pilate as a messianic pretender. The three main texts which concern us in which Jesus has to face the opinion of others that he is the Messiah are: Mark 8:27-33 (Mt 16:13-23, Lk 9:18-22); Mark 14:60-62 (Mt 26:62-64, Lk 22:67-70); and Mark 15:2-5 (Mt 27:11-14; Lk 23:2-5).

There is no need to treat the two references from the arrest and trial at length since they leave us with the same conclusions as the study of the profession of Peter at Caesarea Philippi. Mark 14:60-62 and Mark 15:2-5 both pertain to the arrest and trial of Jesus, the former Jesus' response to the high priest and the latter Jesus' response to Pilate. A characteristic of Jesus' response during the arrest and trial is his silence, Mark 14:61; 15:5 (also the parallels, Mt 26:63; Mt 27:12; Lk 23:9). Or the response is ambiguous, such as,

[20]Vermes, *Jesus the Jew*, 143.

"You have said so" (Mt 26:64; 27:11; Mk 15:2; Lk 22:70; 23:3). There is also the response, "If I tell you, you will not believe" (Lk 22:67). The only text to record an unambiguous response ("I am") is Mark 14:62.[21]

We will thus confine ourselves to a more detailed reflection on the confession of Peter. The earliest version of this event is Mark's.

> [27]And Jesus went on with his disciples, to the villages of Caesarea Philippi; and on the way he asked his disciples, "Who do the people say that I am?" [28]And they told him, "John the Baptist; and others say, Elijah; and others one of the prophets." [29]And he asked them, "But who do you say that I am?" Peter answered him "You are the Christ." [30]And he charged them to tell no one about him. [31]And he began to teach them that the son of humanity must suffer many things, and be rejected by the elders and the chief priests and the scribes, and be killed, and after three days rise again.[32]And he said this plainly. And Peter took him, and began to rebuke him. [33]But turning and seeing his disciples, he rebuked Peter, and said, "Get behind me, Satan! For you are not on the side of God, but of humanity." (Mk 8:27-33)

The above incident seems to have occurred while Jesus was alone with his disciples (Lk 9:18) in the territory of Philip near Caesarea Philippi (Mk 8:27; Mt 16:13). Jesus was concerned about how he was being perceived by others. The responses reflect varied prophetic images. When he addressed the disciples directly about their own perception, Peter spoke up and said: "You are the Christ." Jesus' response (v. 30) is quite significant and the major object of discussion. There are three things to note in verse 31 — Jesus did not directly speak of himself as the Messiah, as Peter had proclaimed, but rather referred to the son of

---

[21]Morna Hooker, *Jesus and the Servant, the Influence of the Servant Concept of Deutero-Isaiah in the New Testament* (London: SPCK, 1959), 88-89, interprets the Synoptic trial material as being less ambiguous than I do.

humanity; Jesus taught that he would suffer much, be rejected and be put to death; he taught that he would rise again. Mark insists that he taught these things quite clearly.

This teaching must have been so straightforward that Peter was taken aback. After his recent messianic proclamation, he must have thought: How can this be? The Messiah suffer and die?[22] So Peter reprimanded Jesus for the comments about his suffering and death. Peter's rebuke leads Jesus in turn to reprimand Peter, and to do so quite strongly: "Get behind me, Satan." Peter's insinuations angered Jesus for they were diabolical, perhaps temptations akin to the testing in the wilderness. The Evil One had put these things in Peter's mind.

Contemporary interpretation of this text must concern itelf with the messianic secret.[23] Jesus knew that he was the Messiah but did not want others to realize or proclaim this lest they misinterpret or misunderstand what this meant. Jesus was not the Messiah in the royal sense in which the Jews expected the Messiah and Jesus rebuked Peter because Peter himself did not seem to understand. Was this secretiveness an expression of Jesus' own desire and self-undertanding? Or was it a Marcan convention to hold together the fact of Jesus' disowning the messianic title and Mark's own intention in the Gospel to proclaim Jesus to be the Messiah?

The more common current interpretation of the text interprets verse 30 on secretiveness as Marcan and then interprets the text as a whole as an explicit rejection on Jesus' part of the messiahship.[24] In other words, the text

[22]See Mowinckel, *He That Cometh*, trans. G.W. Anderson (Nashville: Abingdon Press, 1954), 325-33, about a suffering messiah. For the notion of the slain messiah, see Vermes, *Jesus the Jew*, 139-40.

[23]The notion of the messianic secret goes back to W. Wrede who maintained that Mark was the one who introduced into the tradition Jesus' command not to be proclaimed as Messiah. See William Wrede, *The Messianic Secret*, trans. J.C.C. Greig (Greenwood; S.C.: Attic Press, [1901] 1971). Also see *The Messianic Secret*, ed. Christopher Tuckett (Philadelphia: Fortress Press, 1983).

[24]Bruce Metzger, *The New Testament — Its Background, Growth, and Content* (Nashville: Abingdon Press, 1965), 151, presents the traditional point of view. Jesus was reluctant to use the title of Messiah, but not because he did not believe

does not teach that Jesus is the Messiah but does not want people to know. Instead it makes clear Jesus' rejection of any messianic claim and consciousness.

Verses 27-33 are to be read as a unit. Read the text and skip verse thirty for a moment. Peter proclaimed Jesus to be the Messiah. Jesus then continued to teach. There is a significant shift, however. Jesus did not teach that *the messiah* would have to suffer and die, but rather that *the son of humanity* would do so. Jesus spoke of himself as the "son of humanity." In fact, "son of humanity" occurs on the lips of Jesus over sixty times in the Synoptic Gospels. Thus, if anything, Jesus saw himself as the "son of humanity." When Peter objected, Jesus' rebuke was extremely strong. The whole messianic interpretation of Peter was diabolical, and Jesus recognized it for what it was — a work of Satan. Jesus' exhortation to secrecy (v. 30) is a Marcan way of holding together Jesus' explicit rejection of a messianic designation in his lifetime and the early Church's explicit affirmation of Jesus as being the Messiah.

himself to be the Messiah. Jesus' reluctance arose from the political and national expectations associated with the concept of Messiah which he did not want to be associated with his own teaching.

Oscar Cullmann, *The Christology of the New Testament*, 122-25, concludes that Jesus showed extreme restraint toward, and possibly even rejection of, the *title* Messiah. Yet Jesus, and not the Church, is the source of the messianic secret. Cullmann maintains that Jesus neither affirms nor denies Peter's messianic confession. In rooting Jesus' command to secrecy in Jesus himself, Cullmann is taking the traditional opinion. By interpreting Mark 8 as being noncommittal on the part of Jesus, he opens the door, however, to a new direction for interpreting the text, which interpretation he moves further by suggesting that Jesus may have even *rejected* the *title* Messiah.

This newer and quite common interpretation of Mark 8 as Jesus' explicitly rejecting messiahship can be found in Fuller, Hahn, Vawter and Vermes. Reginald Fuller, *The Foundations of New Testament Christology*, 109. Ferdinand Hahn, *The Titles of Jesus in Christology*, 157-61, 223-28. Bruce Vawter, *This Man Jesus*, (Garden City, N.Y.: Doubleday, 1973), 89. Geza Vermes more or less takes the same stand, *Jesus the Jew*, 145-53. On the one hand he writes in reference to Mark 8, "It would admittedly not be correct to deduce that Jesus thereby denied that he was the Messiah" (146). Also in reference to the arrest and trial texts, "Jesus is not claimed positively to have asserted that he was the Messiah" (149). Yet, "If the Gospels have any coherent meaning at all, his comment on Peter's confession and the answers to the high priest and Pilate are only to be understood as a denial of messiahship" (154).

But let us return to the text itself: Jesus was in the region of Caesarea Philippi and asked the disciples what the people were saying about him (v. 27). The disciples replied that people were talking about him as being a prophet (28). Jesus then addressed the question to the disciples and Peter responded that Jesus was the Messiah (29). Jesus asked that they not repeat this (30). In and of itself, this is a quite explicable response. The only reason it would not fit would be if Jesus did not in any way at all think of himself as messiah. But we cannot yet assume that. Nor is it appropriate to excise this verse, and then show how the remaining text could so prove a rejection of any messianic association, and then return and justify the excision of the text on the basis of its incompatibility with a non-messianic consciousness. This is obviously a circular argument. If we come to a non-messianic interpretation of Jesus' consciousness we must do so on some other basis. Within this text, a messianic secrecy as originating with Jesus himself does make sense.[25]

After instructing his disciples not to speak of him as messiah, Jesus continued to instruct them about the suffering, death, and resurrection (31). The text seems to indicate that Jesus was simply continuing to instruct them about

[25]Although secrecy is an obvious and prominent aspect of Mark's Gospel and thus suggests his redactional work, it cannot be ruled out that it also was present in the teaching of Jesus himself. Since Wrede (1901) it is often assumed that the secrecy motif has been imposed on the tradition by Mark rather than flowing from the life of Jesus himself (William Wrede, *The Messianic Secret*). H.C. Kee points out, however, that there are expressions which indicate that "Jesus took his followers aside or away from the crowds to give them special instructions or interpretation" (*Community of the New Age*, [Philadelphia: Westminster Press, 1977] 52, also 3-7, 50-54, 93-96, 165-75). Not all of the secrecy in Mark can be summed up under the phrase of "messianic secret." For instance, instructions following healings and exorcisms (5:43; 7:36; 8:26) do not serve the same purpose as the silencing of demons (1:23-25; 1:34; 1:43-45; 3:11f.), and neither of these are the same as the messianic secret strictly speaking, the effort to restrict the messianic consciousness to the circle of disciples (8:30; 9:9). Another valuable study is that of T.A. Burkill, "The Hidden Son of Man in St. Mark's Gospel," *New Light on the Earliest Gospel—Seven Markan Studies* (London: Cornell University Press, 1972), 1-38. Burkill attempts to trace the secrecy motif prior to Mark and concludes that it is not a Marcan invention but rather a situation of Marcan adaptation of a pre-Marcan tradition which may have some basis in the life of Jesus himself.

what lay ahead for him. Peter, however with an understanding of Messiah that excluded the way Jesus was speaking (there was no notion of a suffering Messiah in early Judaism), objected to what Jesus was saying (32). Jesus' forceful rebuke of Peter then simply referred to the teaching that Jesus would suffer and die (33). Jesus' words in verse 33 were a response to Peter's behavior in verse 32, and not to Peter's statement in verse 29. To see Jesus' response as a rejection of what Peter said in verse 29 does violence to the text by excluding verse 30, by denying the order in the fact that verse 33 follows verse 32 and not verse 29, and by denying that verse 30 does make sense in response to 29 and verse 33 does make sense in response to 32. To assume a great discontinuity between the (un-messianic) mind of Jesus and the (messianic) mind of the early Church is gratuitous at this point. The more obvious sense is that Peter reacted to Jesus' teaching about his future suffering and Jesus' rebuked Peter for not accepting or hearing what lay ahead.

The meaning of the text does not depend upon whether Jesus' consciousness ought to be described as messianic or unmessianic. In fact the text as such cannot answer that question either way. Neither can the ambiguous response of Jesus during his trial before Pilate. Other than the three ambiguous references, during the incident at Caesarea Philippi and during his arrest and trial, Jesus nowhere spoke of himself as being the Messiah. Thus it hardly constituted a part of his teaching. Whether interiorly, however, he knew himself to be the Messiah is another question, but one to which there is no historiographical access, especially given our cautions above.

We need to avoid extremes: (1) Jesus thought of himself explicitly as a suffering Messiah whose true identity was to remain hidden until after the resurrection although revealed earlier to his disciples; and (2) The secrecy associated with Jesus' life and teaching is thoroughly Marcan, therefore Marcan innovation. The truth probably lies between these two. As presented in Mark, it is undoubtedly Marcan. Yet a pre-Marcan tradition may well have maintained a *memoria Jesu* about Jesus' teaching which was reserved for the circle of his disciples in which he spoke more freely and more explicitly about suffering to come.

An *argument against a messianic consciousness in Jesus* would go as follows. The concept of the messianic figure varied from a royal to a priestly to a prophetic figure. The more prevalent concept, however, was that which patterned itself after the expectation of a future king, with its Davidic, nationalistic, political, and royal implications. There was great inconsistency between the conception of the awaited Messiah and what Jesus taught and how he presented himself. He was concerned with a coming kingdom, but one not like the kingdoms of this world. As in the traditions of Israel and Judah, and even at the time of the decision whether Samuel ought to anoint a king in the first place (1 Samuel 8: 4-7, 10-22), the Lord God is King. For Jesus the coming kingdom was God's and the kingdom of God was not like the kingdoms of this world. Jesus in fact seems explicitly to have stayed away from such a notion. It hardly seems possible that secretly Jesus thought of himself as the royal Messiah. And thus it would be accurate to say that Jesus did not think of himself as the Messiah in any way in which that was understood within the Judaism of his day.[26]

[26]See Reginald Fuller, *The Mission and Achievement of Jesus* (London: SCM, 1967), 116: "'The life of Jesus was un-Messianic' — such was Bultmann's conclusion about the Jesus of History. At best this statement conserves an important half-truth. The life of Jesus was un-Messianic in any sense of that term previously recognized in Jewish eschatological hope. The life of Jesus was un-Messianic in the sense that Jesus never proclaimed himself to be the Messiah. The life of Jesus was un-Messianic in the sense that Jesus did not possess what modern critics have called 'Messianic consciousness' or make a 'Messianic claim'(except perhaps right at the end, at the supreme, paradoxical moment of his humiliation). The life of Jesus was un-Messianic in the sense that he did not impose a Christology upon his disciples. But what was the life of Jesus? It was a life wrought out in conscious obedience to the eschatological will of God, a life in which proclamation of the impending advent of the Reign of God and the performance of the signs which heralded its approach culminated in the suffering of the cross as the decisive event by which the eschatological process should be inaugurated. Was that life un-Messianic? It would be truer to say it was 'pre-Messianic,' for it was the outcome of the lowly history of Jesus that he was, in the belief of the Church, exalted to be the Messiah."

I would agree with Fuller that the life of Jesus was unmessianic in the sense in which that was commonly understood within Judaism and in the sense that Jesus never explicitly proclaimed himself to be Messiah. Whether Jesus possessed a messianic consciousness is another question, however. The expression "pre-messianic" shows an attempt on Fuller's part toward a balanced and reasoned statement.

But, it has never been argued that Jesus was the Messiah precisely in the way or in any of the ways in which such a figure was expected within Judaism. The early Jewish hope and the early Christian proclamation were not coextensive, even though the Christians proclaimed a fulfillment in Christ Jesus. But, as with all of God's promises, there was no simple correspondence between the promise and its fulfillment. God is a God of surprises, and the ways in which God fulfills God's promises do not always correspond to our expectations. Thus it can be well granted that there is a "missing link" between Jewish messianism and Christian proclamation, even though the latter claims to have been the fulfillment of the former. That missing link was Jesus. The Christians did not claim that Jesus was the Messiah *in the way that* the Messiah was understood or awaited within the Judaism of his day. He was the Messiah but in a different, unexpected way. Jesus was the one who realized God's future plans for Israel and who realized that he was the awaited one who would inaugurate its accomplishment. And he also realized that it would not be accomplished in the ways expected. Thus Jesus was the Messiah, thought of himself as the Messiah, but not the Davidic Messiah as such. Rather he was one who would have to suffer and die. Within the teaching (or theology or messianology or christology) of Jesus, the very concept of messiah was being changed.

On the other hand, we must concern ourselves with the Judaism of Jesus' day and not post-resurrection Christian theology. We have already situated Jesus within Judaism and it is within that context that we must understand him. We all know that the meaning of words changes and language evolves and develops. Take the word *oaf*.[27] An old superstition speaks of a changeling child — a misshapen child whom the fairies have left in place of a child they have stolen. In Old Norse, such a child was an elf. The word became oaf and the meaning changed; it referred to any mentally or physically abnormal child. Then the meaning

---

[27]See William and Mary Morris, *Dictionary of Word and Phrase Origins*, vol. 2 (New York: Harper and Row, 1967), 195.

changed again; it now refers to a clumsy or lazy person. We must pin the language down to the way in which it was used and available to Jesus within early Judaism. He did not think of himself as the Davidic royal Messiah.

But there is *a further objection*. Grant the messianic conceptions of Judaism and the "discontinuity" between these and the early Christian conception. But the question is whether Jesus provided the "continuity." The "sources" for the Christian conception cannot be limited to those within Judaism as it existed before or during the times of Jesus, but must be thought of as Judaism plus Jesus, a particular Jew who was keenly perceptive, present to God, and from any historiographical point of view a transition to something new. Therefore Jesus must be understood within but cannot necessarily be reduced to pre-Christian Judaism. Thus the issue is not the Jewish conception, nor the Christian conception, but what was Jesus' conception of the awaited one, and did he see himself as in fact fulfilling that role?

We must come after such discussion to some conclusions. Although both of the above sides of the argument can be defended, both involve their own assumptions. Therefore, my opinion is that it is better to describe Jesus' consciousness neither as messianic nor as unmessianic, for the following reasons:

1.   Even within Judaism the concept of Messiah was varied and fluid at the time of Jesus. To "fix" it too tightly is untenable even on historiographical grounds. It allowed, within limits, room for maneuver and would have allowed rethinking and flexibility. If we introduce apocalyptic thought, as well as Essene, Zealot, and Samaritan thought, there was much room for creativity within Jewish eschatology.

2.   Even apart from the variety within Judaism, we must given attention to the outstanding stature and prophetic character of the man Jesus. However one might evaluate him, he was associated with the origins of a new movement within Judaism which later separated from it. We cannot assume that the Jewish wineskins could contain the new wine of the man Jesus (Mk 2:18-22).

3.   We must give some attention to our cautions above. Even if the concept of Messiah could be more fixed, the consciousness of Jesus could not be. He was human, changing himself, trying to understand, listening to God, and a fixed or precise concept or adjective or self-description or self-understanding simply become less workable or apt. It easily becomes too narrow to apply if we make it precise, or too broad to be meaningful if we leave it more fluid. One can rightly describe Jesus' consciousness as prophetic and social. These terms are applicable. But what does messianic mean when applied to Jesus? We see the difficulty. It is not that Jesus' consciousness was not messianic but that the expression messianic is not sufficiently clarified a concept when applied to Jesus to be helpful. It must always be qualified. We must keep in mind that we are talking about consciousness or awareness, a very fluid reality, and in this case that of a very creative and prophetic individual.

4.   We can conclude by saying that Jesus' self-identity was not messianic in the sense that this was most commonly understood within his Judaism. He certainly did not see himself in a royal or priestly role. The messianic notion, however, was open to prophetic and new understndings as well. Jesus may have seen himself as messianic in the sense that he was offering in a definitive way God's salvation to Israel — and their responses to him and his message would be crucial to their salvation. One cannot describe Jesus' consciousness as messianic in the same way that we can describe it as prophetic or social. But this is not the same as saying it was not messianic. We must be open to the possibility that it was messianic *in a new way*. But we cannot know whether this new way would have been considered by Jesus himself as particularly messianic. Jesus' own eschatology is something to which we will come in a later chapter.

The question for Jesus was not what he thought of himself, but how did he envision what the God of Abraham and Isaac and Jacob was doing at this point in history. He saw himself as preaching a social and religious message which people interpreted in prophetic terms. We can see how difficult it would be for Mark 8 or the trial texts to be interpreted either as support for or refuting of a messianic self-understanding on the part of Jesus. Jesus means *both* Judaism *and* newness.[28]

Preacher and Healer

Jesus was called by God, but called for the sake of others. Prayer and mission, being "of God" and "for the people," were two sides of the same person. Jesus was one of us, called by God, for our sake. Which is more important for a proper understanding of Jesus? His being "from" or "of" God; or his being "with" or "for" the people? Which is more important: inhaling or exhaling? One can distinguish but cannot separate in Jesus of Nazareth his relation to and love for his heavenly Father, and his relation to and love for the people.

Mark's Gospel weaves together these two sides of Jesus — prayer and ministry.

> And in the morning, a great while before day, he rose and went out to a lonely place, and there he prayed. And Simon and those who were with him pursued him, and they found him and said to him, "Everyone is searching for you." And he said to them, "Let us go on to the next town, that I may preach there also; for that is why I came out." (Mk 1:35-39).

Who was Jesus? He was of God. This identity is clear within the first chapters of the Gospel of Mark (1:1, 11, 14; 2:7; 3:11). Disciples did not always recognize that he was from God and were astonished at his authority (1:22, 27; 2:10, 12). Yet his own claim was that his authority and power came from God (2:3-12). Also, Jesus lived for others, a life of ministry which consisted in preaching (1:38), healing (1:31),

---

[28]We may not be able to improve much upon C.H. Dodd's statement, *The Founder of Christianity* (New York: Macmillan, 1970), 102-3.

and exorcising demons (1:23). His ministry was especially devoted to outcasts and sinners (2:16-17). He also called disciples to himself (1:16; 2:13; 3:14) and was an itinerant teacher. Toward chapter four of Mark, the shift is toward Jesus as teacher (4:1, 38; 5:35), and his teaching pertains to the reign of God (4:26, 30).

This picture of Jesus also comes through in the Gospel of Matthew.

> And he went about all Galilee, teaching in their synagogues and preaching the gospel of the kingdom and healing every disease and every infirmity among the people. (Mt 4:23-24; also Mt 9:35; 10:5-8)

Luke also perceives Jesus as being "of God" and "for others." In chapter four, which opens with the wilderness experience, we find Jesus at prayer (4:42, also 5:16; 6:12), preaching (4:18, 43, 44), teaching (4:15, 31-32), healing (4:38-39, 40) and casting out demons (4:35, 41). His ministry is seen especially as a mission to the poor (4:18-19). Evidence indicates two very closely related activities in Jesus' life: 1) preaching and teaching, 2) healings and exorcisms.

Jesus' life was so much for the people that his death came to be understood in those terms as well. Paul writes, "And he died for all, that those who live might live no longer for themselves but for him who for their sake died and was raised" (2 Cor 5:15).

It is clear that the earthly Jesus cured people of varied illnesses.[29] The Synoptic Gospels speak of Jesus healing multitudes in Capernaum (Mk 1:32-4) and throughout Galilee (Mk 3:7-12 and 6:53-6). They also speak of twelve very specific healings: three cases of blindness (Mk 8:22-26; 10:46-52; Mt 9:27-31), two cases of leprosy (Mk 1:40-44; Lk 17:11-19), one case each of fever (Mk 1:29-31), hemorrhage

[29]Cf., Norman Perrin, *Rediscovering the Teaching of Jesus* (New York: Harper and Row, 1978), 8-20. Donald Senior, *Jesus* (Dayton, Ohio: Pflaum Press, 1975), 113-31. Geza Vermes, *Jesus the Jew, A Historian's Reading of the Gospels* (Philadelphia: Fortress Press, 1973), 22-25, 59-69.

(Mk 5:25-34), a withered hand (Mk 3:1-5), deafness (Mk 7:31-7), paralysis (Mt 8:5-13), another case of paralysis which also involves the forgiveness of sin (Mk 2:3-11), lameness (Lk 13:10-13), and dropsy (Lk 24:1-6).

As prominent as was Jesus' power over disease, so was his authority over the demonic world. He was both healer and exorcist. The synoptics record six specific cases of exorcism (Mk 1:23-28; 5:1-20; 7:24-30; 9:14-29; Mt 9:32-4; 12:22-24). In addition, the first three Gospels speak of numerous exorcisms accompanying the healings (Mk 1:32-4, 39).

One ought not draw a sharp distinction between the healings and exorcisms. Matthew lists the demoniacs along with the epileptics and paralytics as examples of "those afflicted with various diseases" (Mt 4:24). How many of the diseases stemmed from "psychic" or "spiritual" causes? To what extent were some diseases understood to be cases of possession? Some descriptions of demoniacs seem to describe epileptics (Mk 1:23-28; 9:14-29). Muteness is involved in three of the cases of demonic possession (Mk 9:14-29; Mt 9:32-4; 12:22-24), but in another instance a deaf and at least partially mute person is not presented as a case for exorcism (Mk 7:31-37).[30]

The prophetic character of Jesus' life together with the astonishing wonders he performed as healer and exorcist, wonders which are part of the tradition about prophetic activities (consider Moses, Elijah, Elisha), again indicate that Jesus of Nazareth can be situated in the context of "charismatic Judaism."[31]

[30]Was this Marcan deaf-mute a case of exorcism? See John M. Hull, *Hellenistic Magic and the Synoptic Tradition* (Naperville, Ill.: Alec R. Allenson, 1974), 78-82. For further discussion of the relation between healing and holiness, and between sickness, sin and demonic possession, see Geza Vermes, *Jesus the Jew*, 59-68.

[31]Cf., James D.G. Dunn, *Jesus and the Spirit, a Study of the Religious and Charismatic Experience of Jesus and the First Christians as Reflected in the New Testament* (London: SCM, 1975), 9-92; *Unity and Diversity in the New Testament, an Inquiry into the Character of Earliest Christianity* (Philadelphia: Westminster Press, 1977), 184-89; Martin Hengel, *The Charismatic Leader and His Followers* (New York: Crossroad Pub. Co., 1981); Geza Vermes, *Jesus the Jew*, 58-82. Bruce Molina, however, has called into question whether the expression "charismatic" is an appropriate description of Jesus' authority, "Was Jesus a Charismatic Leader?" *Biblical Theology Bulletin* 14 (1984), 55-62.

The history of Israel and Judah included many conflicting and complementary traditions, among others the royal,
priestly, prophetic and sapiential traditions. One can hardly
overestimate the role of the king, priest, prophet, and sage in
Israel's history. We would call the kingship and priesthood
"establishment." After the exile, the role and influence of
the priesthood had grown. The prophetic tradition, which
had died out, manifested a more charismatic, less institutionally controllable factor in Israel's history. The sages
gave rise to a critical wisdom as well as a folk wisdom. In
addition, in post-Maccabean Judaism, there were many
varied "enthusiasts" — martyrs, messiahs, ascetics, zealots,
wonderworkers. As an itinerant preacher and healer, Jesus
had much in common with these enthusiasts, even if he
never claimed to be *the* Messiah, even if he was less ascetical
than John, even if he never joined the resistance
movement.[32]

The astonishing deeds performed by Jesus (the *erga* of the
Synoptics) were not a phenomenon unique to Jesus. Among
others, Hanina ben Dosa, a first century C. E. Galilean like
Jesus, was known for his power of concentration during
prayer, his ability to cure illnesses as well as effect healing
from a distance, his power over demons, and his ability to
influence nature. He lived in poverty, seemed uninterested
in legal and ritual issues, and was resented by the leaders of
the Pharisees.[33]

In our attempt to understand Jesus, we must not only
acknowledge his reputation as a healer but also his hesita-
tion to present himself in this way.[34] Jesus was reticent

[32]It is almost commonplace today to describe the Judaism of Jesus' day in terms
of four "parties": Sadducees, Pharisees, Essenes, and Zealots. It is very questionable, however, whether there existed in the first half of the first century anything like
a Zealot party as an identifiable, ideologically distinct group. This does not deny
an anti-Roman resistance movement. See Marcus Borg, *Conflict, Holiness and
Politics in the Teachings of Jesus* (New York: Edwin Mellen Press, 1984), 27-49,
64-68.

[33]Geza Vermes, *Jesus the Jew*, 72-78, also 69-72 for a consideration of Honi the
Rain Maker.

[34]A continuing area of significant research is the relationship between Jesus and
the "magical tradition" attested in Palestine and the Hellenistic world. Morton

about asking God for miracles and in performing signs (Mk 2:5; 5:34; 10:52; Lk 7:50; 17:19).

> The Pharisees came and began to argue with him, seeking from him a sign from heaven, to test him. And he sighed deeply in his spirit, and said, "Why does this generation seek a sign? Truly I say to you, no sign shall be given to this generation." (Mk 8: 11-12)

Jesus hoped to evoke faith from people without signs. "It is an evil and unfaithful generation that asks for a sign!" And, "The only sign it will be given is the sign of the prophet

Smith's *Jesus the Magician* (New York: Harper and Row, 1978), however, has major flaws in its thesis which interprets Jesus primarily and almost exclusively within that context. Smith recognizes but gives too little attention in his conclusion to the difficulty of providing a precise definition for magic, and thus his argument manifests equivocation. E.g., Jesus is a magician (in a wide sense of wonder worker); therefore, Jesus is a magician (in a narrower sense, in the sense of one who practices "magical," or diabolical, or supernatural rites). Smith recognizes the diversity and wide range of meaning behind the word *magic* (68-80), yet he "jumps" from a word with a wide meaning in his discussion to a word with a quite specific and focused meaning in his conclusion.

He goes from an identification of Jesus with a *part*, an aspect, of the magical tradition to Jesus' identity with the *whole*, or wider range of meanings. Because the sky is blue, and my shirt is blue, my shirt must be in the sky. Smith verifies well: One of the main characteristics of a magician was that of performing miracles. He also verifies: Jesus worked miracles. But likewise, one of the main characteristics of the sky is its blueness. Also, the ocean is blue. Therefore . . . the ocean is in the sky. Smith recognizes the difficulty but ignores it in drawing his conclusion. Smith: "A miracle worker is not necessarily a magician" (143). There is no question of the historical stratum which recognizes Jesus as a miracle worker, but given Smith's statement, how do we jump from the fact of Jesus' working miracles to his being a magician? The "primary characteristic of a magician was to do miracles" (109). But the fact that A and B have something in common doesn't mean A is B. Smith actually makes this "jump" through an interpretation of other evidence. But, at this point, his argument runs thin (109-139). E.g., that Jesus was driven by the Spirit into the wilderness after his baptism (Mk 1:12) indicates the compulsive behavior characteristic of demoniacs (143), and the "clearest evidence of Jesus' knowledge and use of magic is the eucharist, a magical rite of a familiar sort" (152).

A more balanced study of the relationship between the magical tradition and the Christian tradition is John M. Hull's *Hellenistic Magic and the Synoptic Tradition.* The belief that Jesus *was* a magician is an ancient belief going back as far as the middle of the first century. Jewish tradition attributed Jesus' miracles to magical power. Even Christian literature records the accusation that Jesus was a magician, and a magical interpretation of the miracles was easily possible.

It is not easy to distinguish clearly between magic and miracle. Is there such a

Jonah" (cf. Mt 12:38-42; 16:1-4). [35] At the same time that we place Jesus in a tradition of healings and exorcisms, we must be careful not to overemphasize it since evidence suggests that Jesus himself did not see this as his primary mission even if it was prominent.

Jesus' healings and exorcisms, however, do give testimony to a power at work within him. Words used to describe Jesus are *dynamis* and *exousia*. Luke's use of *dynamis* refers to a power which makes the power of the spiritual world present in our world. [36] According to Luke, after Jesus' conquest of Satan, he has the "power of the Spirit" (4:14). The power was effective against demons and Jesus at times felt it going out of him (Mk 5:30; Lk 8:46). One of the difficulties Jesus faced was that his power was sometimes used against him, under the charge that it was diabolical: "He is possessed by Beelzebul, and by the prince of demons, he casts out demons" (Mk 3:22; Mt 12:24; Lk 11:15).

thing as a non-magical *religious* miracle? One cannot simply resort to saying, "God works miracles, demons work magic" (Hull, 61). The distinction then becomes one of faith and interpretation alone. Miracles and exorcisms in the ancient world were often regarded as being associated with magical rituals and powers (45-72).

Hull concludes that "the results of our investigation must not be exaggerated" (142). Yet, "we do find, however, certain aspects of the gospels which are at home in the magical world view of the first century of our era, and a number of details relevant to the central concern of magic . . . We find that the miracles of Jesus and particularly his exorcisms and healings were interpreted as being magical at an early date, that in the light of contemporary presuppositions it was inevitable that they should have been so interpreted, and that the gospels themselves witness to early stages of the interpretations" (142). "As well as using faith, prayer, knowledge of the Torah and holiness of life, the means by which God was believed to work miracles through the rabbis, Jesus was thought to have used folk remedies" (143). However, "Jesus did not think of himself as a magician," and "the most abiding impression left by the New Testament treatment of Jesus as the master-Magician is the restraint of that treatment . . . The potential of the magus-myth for Christology was not very great" (144-45).

Another valuable reference is Howard Clark Kee, *Miracle in the Early Christian World, a Study in Sociohistorical Method* (New Haven: Yale University Press, 1983).

[35]See Richard A. Edwards, *The Sign of Jonah, in the Theology of the Evangelists and Q*, Studies in Biblical Theology, Second Series (Naperville, Ill.: Alec R. Allenson, 1971). Robert Jewett, *Jesus Against the Rapture, Seven Unexpected Prophecies* (Philadelphia: Westminster Press, 1979).

[36]For a discussion of this particularly Lucan understanding of Jesus' power, see Hull, *Hellenistic Magic*, 105-15.

There is no question of the historicity of Jesus' charismatic healings and exorcisms, which is not to affirm the historicity of all the miracles or even all the details of the healing miracles. It is simply to say that Jesus did cure the sick and expel demons. His works were in continuity with the mighty and prophetic acts of God which were always on behalf of God's people. Jesus' works manifested someone opposed to, in struggle with, and overcoming the powers of evil (the exorcisms) and someone who released power for good (the healings). The struggle began in the wilderness, continued in his ministry, and was still there at Gethsemane. His opponents accused him of being possessed by Beelzebul, but Jesus' defense was in terms of his being locked in a struggle against Satan, the king of devils (Lk 11:14-22). And it was not by the power of the Evil One, whom he had early met in the wilderness and against whom he continued to pray (Mt 6:13, save us from the Evil one), that he had power over demons, but by the very power of God (Lk 11:20).

Although Jesus was not simply a repeat at a later period in history of one of the earlier prophets, not simply another Moses, Elijah, Isaiah, or John, he is nevertheless connected to that prophetic tradition and has his roots within it. In his prayer and in his mission, as a preacher and as a healer, Jesus is the prophet from Nazareth.

6

Jesus and Apocalypticism

In the previous chapter we described Jesus' self-understanding as prophetic but chose not to describe it as either messianic or non-messianic. If messianism does not aptly describe the eschatology and consciousness of Jesus, perhaps apocalypticism does. In some ways, of course, apocalypticism did make itself felt in the life and thought of Jesus. Yet Edward Schillebeeckx's Jesus study explicitly rejected situating Jesus within Jewish apocalypticism.[1]

We first encounter Jesus' public life and ministry in connection with John's ministry and baptism. Schillebeeckx notes that the motifs associated with John in the New Testament are early prophetic ones and not later apocalyptic ones. The three key words used to describe John's proclamation, the axe and winnow and fire, belong to prophecy and not apocalyptic literature.[2] Of the three images within prophecy for God's impending judgment — the burning of chaff after the harvest, a fire in which the withered and barren trees will be consumed, a metal furnace — John used the first two.[3] Nor do we find the apocalyptic doctrine of the

[1]Edward Schillebeeckx, *Jesus, An Experiment in Christology*, trans. Hubert Hoskins (New York: Seabury Press, 1979), 119-54.

[2]Ibid., 128. See Am 8:2; Is 30:24; 40:3-5; 41:15-16; Jer 15:7; 51:33; Mi 4:12-14; Joel 3:13.

[3]Ibid, 129, and notes 34-37, p. 682. The image of burning chaff — Is 5:24; 10:17; 47:14; Nahum 1:10; Ob 18; Mal 3:19. The conflagration of withered and barren

two ages in John. Rather he preaches repentance and baptism. Schillebeeckx writes, "John the Baptist then is a non-
messianic figure, no Zealot either, and a-political in his
immediate message; he stands outside Zealotism, outside
messianism, and outside apocalypticism."[4]

Jesus heard John preach, perhaps even followed John for
a while. He identified himself with John, accepted John's
baptism, may have even seen himself in the beginning as a
prophet like John. It is more accurate to describe Jesus as
akin to the prophets of old rather than to the latter-day
visionaries. It is more the Book of Isaiah than that of Enoch
which helps us to understand Jesus of Nazareth. Jesus is
portrayed as inaugurating his preaching mission by reading
from the scroll of the prophet Isaiah (Lk 4:16-21). The Book
of Isaiah is quoted more often in the New Testament than
any other book from the Hebrew Scriptures with the exception of the Psalms.[5] Jesus indeed was more akin to the
prophets of old, preaching faith and justice, and in this was
essentially and radically conservative, as prophets were:
going back to their roots in the Yahwistic faith and choosing
to live according to the covenant.

The apocalyptic visionaries legitimated their messages by
appeal through pseudonyms to ancient figures. Jesus legitimated his message by appealing to his own authority which
came directly from the Father. The apocalyptic perspective
was dualist in its teaching on the two ages and pessimistic in
its assessment of the present and earthly age. Jesus was a
prophet of hope with a concern for the here and now.
Apocalyptic attempts to interpret the coming of a new age

trees — Is 10:18-19; Jer 21:14; 22:7; Ex 21:2-23; Zec 11:1-2. The refining fire in the
furnace — Is 1:24-25. For references to John see Mk 1:4; Mt 3:2, 8; Acts 13:24;
19:4.

[4]Ibid., 135.

[5]Whether one considers the New Testament as a whole, or simply the four
Gospels, or only the Synoptics, the most frequently quoted source is Psalms, then
Isaiah, then Deuteronomy. See *Old Testament Quotations in the New Testament*,
ed. Robert G. Bratcher, revised edition (New York: United Bible Societies, 1961).

were based on a deterministic view of history. Jesus preached that no one, including himself, knew the day or the hour. God's coming reign, which is not the apocalyptic aeon, will come when least expected. Jesus did not communicate his dreams as visions; he spoke God's word.

A major aspect of Jesus life and message simply involved this present era and this earth. Although he looked toward the coming reign of God, which was already dawning, he was not other-worldly, supra-terrestrial. His radical social consciousness, a part of every prophet's consciousness, was existential living in the present. Jesus was not a dualist grounded in an either/or antagonism between this era and the age to come. He believed in *both* heaven *and* earth. He lived in both worlds, as prophets of old had done, the world of God and the world of humankind. He may have envisioned a new age but a new age did not necessarily mean the end of the earth as we know it.

We cannot help at this point but be open to the suggestion of Bruce Chilton.

> The term "apocalyptic," as applied to Jesus' preaching, is practically evacuated of content. On purely logical grounds, the propriety of its continued usage in this connexion is seriously to be questioned.[6]

Jesus starkly repudiated the faithless (diabolical?) seeking after signs, and in doing so repudiated an association between his message and that of the apocalypticists.[7]

---

[6]Bruce Chilton, "Regnum Dei Deus Est," *Scottish Journal of Theology* 31 (1978), 261.

[7]See Robert Jewett, *Jesus Against the Rapture, Seven Unexpected Prophecies* (Philadelphia: Westminster Press, 1979). Also Marcus Borg, *Conflict, Holiness, and Politics in the Teachings of Jesus* (New York: Edwin Mellen Press, 1984), 201-27.

The Human One
The Son of Humanity

In assessing the influence of apocalypticism on Jesus, the most challenging task is to determine what Jesus meant when he referred to "the human one" or "the son of humanity" (the "son of man").[8] In contrast to the very few references in which Jesus concerns himself with the question of the Messiah, there are over sixty texts in the Synoptics alone in which Jesus speaks of "the son of humanity."[9] In these Synoptic texts, the expression is almost always found in the sayings of Jesus, not spoken by others in reference to Jesus. Jesus' use of the expression did not alarm or arouse the curiosity of his listeners. They were far less bewildered by it than we are, for whom it has become one of the most difficult issues in New Testament interpretation.

The Greek expression used in the gospels (*ho huios tou anthrōpou*) is a translation of an Aramaic original (*bar*

[8]How best to translate *ho huios tou anthrōpou*, given its varied shades of meaning and the fact that it is itself a translation of an Aramaic original, is a difficult question. "Son of man" will no longer do. Literally it is best rendered as "the son of a human being," but this is awkward in English. Its basic meaning is a human being, or *the* human being. Hence, in reference to Dan 7, C.F.D. Moule speaks of "the Human One" (*The Phenomenon of the New Testament* [Naperville, Ill.: Alec R. Allenson, 1967], 89). F.W. Danker suggests "Son of Humanity" as a translation, which also seems acceptable (*Interpretation* 37 [1983], 298).

[9]The expression, "son of humanity," occurs in 66 references within the Synoptics. The incidence of the expression is higher if one counts the fact that in some of the references the expression occurs twice (e.g., Mk 14:21; Mt 24:30; 26:24). The expression is almost always found being used by Jesus himself. Lk 24:7 is an exception to this. On Mk 2:10, see Christian P. Ceroke, "Is Mk 2:10 a Saying of Jesus?" *Catholic Biblical Quarterly* 22 (1960), 369-90. See Reginald Fuller, *The Mission and Achievement of Jesus* (London: SCM Press, 1954), 96-97; Jacques Guillet, *The Consciousness of Jesus*, trans. Edmond Bonin (New York: Newman Press, 1972), 125; Geza Vermes, *Jesus the Jew* (Philadelphia: Fortress Press, 1973), 179. The sixty-six references are as follows. Mark 2:10; 2:28; 8:31; 8:38; 9:9; 9:12; 9:31; 10:33; 10:45; 13:26; 14:21; 14:41; 14:62. Matthew 8:20; 9:6; 10:23; 11:19; 12:8; 12:32; 12:40; .13:37; 13:41; 16:13; 16:27; 16:28; 17:9; 17:12; 17:22; 19:28; 20:18; 20:28; 24:27; 24:30; 24:37; 24:39; 24:44; 25:31; 26:2; 26:24; 26:45; 26:64. Luke 5:24; 6:5; 6:22; 7:34; 9:22; 9:26; 9:44; 9:58; 11:30; 12:8; 12:10; 12:40; 17:22; 17:24; 17:26; 17:30; 18:8; 18:31; 19:10; 21:27; 21:36; 22:22; 22:48; 22:69; 24:7.

'enāshā'). [10]What did Jesus mean when he referred to "the human one" or "the son of humanity?" Did Jesus' usage reflect on apocalyptic influence or did it simply reflect a common, idiomatic, Aramaic way of speaking? Opinions with respect to the interpretation of this expression must remain open to revision for some time to come. Yet there are conclusions which we can legitimately suggest as well.

Judaism Before Christianity

According to a widely held opinion, there existed in pre-Christian Judaism at the time of Jesus a fairly defined eschatological expectation associated with a supra-terrestrial figure, an apocalyptic "Son of Humanity," and that "Son of Humanity" functioned as a quasi-messianic title for a figure other than the political Davidic Messiah. Although this is a respected opinion, it is a highly questionable one. We cannot assume that such a concept or title existed at the time of Jesus.

Three texts have had major significance in affirming the existence of this concept in pre-Christian Judaism: Daniel 7, 4 Ezra 13, and the Similitudes of Enoch. Of these three, 4 Ezra provides no basis for the existence of this concept in pre-Christian Judaism simply due to its late date, the second century C.E. [11] If other sources provide a basis for the exis-

---

[10] It is generally considered that the Greek is a translation of *bar 'enōsh*, but as used in the emphatic state, which is used in Aramaic instead of the definite article with a noun, hence *bar 'enāshā'*. These forms are characteristic of Middle Aramaic. Later, during the first centuries C.E., the initial aleph disappeared, and thus from 200 C.E. onwards the expression was *bar nāsh* instead of *bar 'enāsh*, or *bar nāshā'* instead of *bar 'enāshā'*. Cf. Maurice Casey, *Son of Man, the Interpretation and Influence of Daniel 7* (London: SPCK, 1979), 224-28; Barnabas Lindars, *Jesus Son of Man, A Fresh Examination of the Son of Man Sayings in the Gospels* (Grand Rapids, Mich.: William B. Eerdmans Co., 1983), 17-28, and 194, n. 2; and Alger F. Johns *A Short Grammar of Biblical Aramaic* (Berrien Springs, Mich.: Andrews University Press, 1972), 9-10.

[11] With respect to post-biblical and intertestamental literature, the standard reference is R.H. Charles , *The Apocrypha and Pseudepigrapha in English, with*

tence of such a conception,4 Ezra may be of help in filling the concept out, but one cannot argue from it to the existence of the concept in pre-Christian Judaism.

Some have maintained that the apocalyptic concept or title has its basis in Daniel 7:13, which is pre-Christian (second century B.C.E.). The figure in Daniel 7:13, however, is either a symbolic reference to the saints of the Most High, the loyal Jews, and not an actually existent individual,[12] or perhaps a reference to an angel, an angelic leader and heavenly counterpart of the loyal Jews.[13] According to the interpretation that the heavenly but human figure in

Introductions and Critical and Explanatory Notes to the Several Books, 2 vols. (Oxford: Clarendon Press, 1913). A new edition of this literature is now available, James H. Charlesworth, ed., 2 vols. *The Old Testament Pseudepigrapha* (Garden City, N.Y.: Doubleday, 1983). Helpful aids in approaching this literature include John J. Collins, *The Apocalyptic Imagination, an Introduction to the Jewish Matrix of Christianity* (New York: Crossroad, 1984); Martin McNamara, *Intertestamental Literature*, Old Testament Message, vol. 23 (Wilmington, Del.: Michael Glazier, 1983); George W.E. Nickelsburg, *Jewish Literature Between the Bible and the Mishnah* (Philadelphia: Fortress Press, 1981); Bruce Metzger, *An Introduction to the Apocrypha* (New York: Oxford University Press, 1957).

One of the canonical books of the Old Testament is that of Ezra (1 Ezra). There is an apocryphal book called the Book of Esdras (or sometimes 1 Esdras and even at times 3 Ezra). Esdras is a Greek form of Ezra. The biblical book of Ezra is considered 1 Ezra; the biblical book of Nehemiah is 2 Ezra; and the apocryphal Esdras is 3 Ezra. The book of our present concern is either labeled as 4 Ezra or 2 Esdras. The original chapters of the book, 3-14, the Jewish apocalypse, are dated c. 100 C.E. by Nickelsburg, 187-88. For the fact that 2 Esdras/4 Ezra cannot be used as a basis for a pre-Christian Jewish "Son of Humanity" concept, see both Maurice Casey, *Son of Man*, 122-29; and A.J.B. Higgins, *The Son of Man in the Teaching of Jesus* (Cambridge University Press, 1980), 12.

[12]See the translation of Hartmann and Di Lella, *The Book of Daniel*, The Anchor Bible, vol. 23 (Garden City, N.Y.: Doubleday, 1978), 202-4.

See Maurice Casey, *Son of Man*, 7-50, for his interpretation of Daniel 7; pp. 24-40 for his interpretation of the human figure as a symbol for Israel. Also, Hartmann and Di Lella, 85-102, 202-20; and p. 97, n. 234, for other commentators who agree with this interpretation. Also J.D.G. Dunn, *Christology in the Making, A New Testament Inquiry into the Origins of the Doctrine of the Incarnation* (Philadelphia: Westminster Press, 1980), 68-75.

[13]John J. Collins, *The Apocalyptic Imagination*, 81-85, develops the main alternative to the corporate, symbolic interpretation, namely, that the Danielic figure is the angelic leader of the heavenly host, most probably Michael. The angelic interpretation does not exclude the fact that the text also implies reference to the persecuted Jews. Nor does the angelic interpretation imply that "son of humanity" was a title in pre-Christian Judaism.

Daniel 7 is a corporate symbol, the "one in human likeness" (7:13) is symbolic of "the holy ones of the Most High" (7:18). The four beasts (7:3-7) are not actually existing animals but symbolic of the Babylonians, Medes, Persians and Greeks, all conquerors of Palestine.[14] Likewise the human figure is symbolic for the holy ones of God, the faithful ones who resisted Antiochus IV Epiphanes. The "one in human likeness" of Daniel 7 cannot be interpreted as a quasi-messianic title for an individual and ought not be translated as an apocalyptic "Son of Humanity."

The four pagan kingdoms are represented by four monsters or beasts; the kingdom of the holy ones is represented by a member of the *human* race. In the vision, the "one in human likeness" is given kingship (7:14); in the interpretation it is the holy ones of the Most High who are given dominion (7:18). The one in human likeness comes with the clouds of heaven as a contrast to the beasts who came up out of the ocean. He did not descend from God as an angel might, but rather ascended to God and was brought into his presence. Thus the "son of humanity" in Daniel 7:13 is not to be interpreted as a messianic title.

The real question is whether Daniel 7:13 came to be understood or interpreted differently as times changed and apocalypses and apocalypticism developed. Maurice Casey surveyed the history of the interpretation of Daniel 7 and suggests two traditions of interpretation.[15] One tradition retained the original corporate interpretation of Daniel 7 as the faithful Jews. A second tradition of interpretation was characterized by its re-interpretation of the text, adapting it to current historical situations. In this exegesis the fourth kingdom was no longer Seleucid but became the Roman Empire, and the four kingdoms became Babylon, Medo-Persia, Greece, and Rome rather than the original interpre-

[14]Cf. Maurice Casey, *Son of Man*, 18-22, Hartmann and Di Lella, 211-17; H.H. Rowley, *Darius the Mede and the Four World Empires in the Book of Daniel* (Cardiff: University of Wales Press, [1935] 1964).

[15]For "the Syrian tradition," see chapter three of Casey, *Son of Man*, 51-70, esp. 69-70. For "the Western tradition," see chapter four of Casey, 71-98.

tation of Babylon, Media, Persia, and Greece. Christian interpreters in this tradition of interpretation understood the little horn to be the Antichrist rather than Antiochus Epiphanes and the little horn or Antichrist would be destroyed at the last judgment with the second coming of Christ.

The important question is whether the human figure, which was symbolic in Daniel 7 (or perhaps angelic), became re-interpreted (in accord with the second tradition of interpretation) as a real messianic individual, namely, the so-called apocalyptic "Son of Humanity." If there existed such a concept, it is not found within the original understanding of the author of Daniel nor the tradition which preserved that original understanding. It could have developed in the pre-Christian period in accord with the type of exegesis that led to re-interpretation. This, however, brings us to the Book of Enoch.

To maintain the existence of the "Son of Humanity" as an apocalyptic, quasi-messianic title on the basis of Enoch has serious difficulties. Chapters 37-71, the Similitudes of Enoch, have two problems. The first is whether there is in the Similitudes anything like the "Son of Humanity" used in a messianic, titular sense.[16] The second is that of dating. The absence of this section of 1 Enoch from the Qumran materials has led to a well argued post-Christian date for the

[16]There are both a First Enoch and a Second Enoch. 1 Enoch is sometimes known as the Ethiopic Book of Enoch since we only have the entire collection of material in the Ethiopic translation. Chapters 37-71 of 1 Enoch appear to have been originally a separate work and are called "The Parables of Enoch." See Nickelsburg, *Jewish Literature*, 46-55, 90-94, 145-51, 214-23.

See Maurice Casey, *Son of Man*, pp. 35, 90, 92, 112, 125-26, 128-29, 135-39, for his repeated conviction that there was no "son of humanity" concept or title in Judaism. Casey argues that "son of humanity" in Enoch is not a title, but simply the ordinary expression for a human being, 99-112. Also see Vermes, *Jesus the Jew*, 173-76. Nickelsburg, *Jewish Literature*, 215, writes in reference to the Similitudes: "'Son of Man' is not a title. It is a Semitic way of saying 'man,' and it is almost always qualified ."

Casey argues that the expression in 1 Enoch referes to Enoch. However, John J. Collins, *The Apocalyptic Imagination*, 147-54, in keeping with his interpretation of Daniel 7, argues that the "son of man" in the Similitudes is not Enoch but a heavenly, angelic representative.

Similitudes (which is not the same as maintaining that they are of Christian origin). Evidence suggests the possibility of a post-Christian Jewish document.[17] With such questions raised about the Similitudes of Enoch, the basis for a pre-Christian apocalyptic messiah is seriously weakened.

Maurice Casey accepts that the "son of humanity" in the Similitudes is no longer symbolic for a corporate group but rather refers to an individual; yet the expression is still not an apocalyptic, messianic title. The person referred to is Enoch, who was pre-existent, was born and lived on earth,

[17]The dating of the Similitudes has been much disputed since J.T. Milik, ed., *The Books of Enoch, Aramaic Fragments of Qumran Cave 4* (Oxford: The Clarendon Press, 1976), who dated the Similitudes c. 270 C.E. (p. 96). This is in sharp contrast to the date given by R.H. Charles who dated them in the first century B.C.E., *The Book of Enoch* (London: SPCK, [1912] 1947), xiv.

Nickelsburg, *Jewish Literature*, 221-23, argues that the Similitudes are a Jewish writing produced around the turn of the era or the beginning of the Common Era; also *Catholic Biblical Quarterly* 40 (1978), 411-19.

Among those inclined toward a pre-Christian date is J.A. Fitzmyer, "Implications of the New Enoch Literature from Qumran," *Theological Studies* 38 (1977), 332-45.

Among those against a pre-Christian date for the Similitudes are J. Barr, "Messiah," *Hastings Dictionary of the Bible*, 651; J.C. Hindley, "Towards a Date for the Similitudes of Enoch, An Historical Approach," *New Testament Studies* 14 (1967-68), 551-65; M.A. Knibb, "The Date of the Parables of Enoch: A Critical Review," *New Testament Studies* 25 (1978-79), 345-59; G. Vermes, *Jesus the Jew*, 175-76. J.D.G. Dunn, *Christology in the Making* (Philadelphia: Westminster Press, 1980), 75-78, suggests a post-70 C.E. date.

John J. Collins, *The Apocalyptic Imagination*, 143 and 241, suggests the early or mid-first century C.E.

Many recognize that the lack of certainty over the date presents a problem. Fuller recognizes that there is legitimate uncertainty about a pre-Christian date, and yet maintains that the Similitudes can still be used as evidence for a pre-Christian Jewish tradition, *Foundations of New Testament Christology*, 37f. On the other hand, C.F.D. Moule and M. Black would maintain that the uncertain date weakens the theory of a pre-Christian Jewish "son of humanity" concept. C.F.D. Moule, *The Phenomenon of the New Testament* (Naperville, Ill.: A.R. Allenson, 1967), 34, n. 21. M. Black, "The Son of the Man Problem in Recent Research and Debate," *Bulletin of the John Rylands Library* 45 (1962-73), 305-318, esp. 312.

Casey, *Son of Man*, 99, is open with respect to the date but argues against a titular use within the Similitudes. Thus the date is not crucial for him (p. 137).

A summary of some recent discussion can be found in "The SNTS Pseudepigrapha Seminars at Tubingen and Paris on the Books of Enoch," *New Testament Studies* 25 (1978-79), 315-23.

did not die but was taken up to heaven, would reappear at the end as eschatological judge, and would vindicate his followers and condemn their oppressors. Genesis 5:21-24 provided the basis for speculation concerning Enoch which later gave rise to the Enoch literature. "Son of humanity"in the Similitudes is a word for an individual but refers to Enoch, not an apocalyptic, messianic expectation.

There was an influence of Daniel 7:13 on the Similitudes, but there is no messianic or titular concept in Enoch because of that influence. The author of the Similitudes followed the tradition of interpretation open to re-interpretation and applied the Danielic prophecy of the human figure to his own hero Enoch. He chose the particular expression for his hero because he was influenced by Daniel 7, but there is no evidence in the Similitudes of the expression being a title for an apocalyptic messianic figure.

James D.G. Dunn comes to conclusions fairly similar to those of Maurice Casey.[18] For Dunn, the Danielic use of "one like a son of man" is a symbolic representation of Israel. Nor is there evidence in later pre-Christian Judaism of such a concept as that of an apocalyptic, messianic figure. Dunn attaches more importance to the date of Enoch than does Casey, however.

The view that there existed in pre-Christian Judaism such an eschatological, apocalyptic figure has been the opinion of Fuller,[19] Hahn,[20] Todt,[21] and others.[22] With different

[18]James D.G. Dunn, *Christology in the Making*, 65-97, esp. 95-97.

[19]Fuller, *Foundations of New Testament Christology*, 34-43.

[20]Ferdinand Hahn, *The Titles of Jesus in Christology, Their History in Early Christianity*, trans. Harold Knight and George Ogg (London: Lutterworth Press, 1969), 15-53. According to Hahn, in pre-Christian Judaism a titular use had established itself. This use was adopted by Jesus and by the primitive Christian community (20). Nevertheless, many of the "son of humanity" sayings are still secondary, and the question remains which sayings are the oldest and thus to be included in the preaching of Jesus (21). There are three groups of sayings: those which refer to the future eschatological function of judge; those which refer to the suffering, dying, and rising; and those which refer to an earthly, present activity or function. The prophecies of suffering and death, at least in their present form, arose within the Christian community, are not traceable to the preaching of Jesus himself, and are probably the latest development of the three groups (21). The question then is whether the more original sayings, those in fact traceable to Jesus,

nuances, such has been the opinion of Borsch[23] and Higgins.[24] In opposition to this perspective, maintaining that no such concept existed, we have Borg,[25] Casey,[26] Dunn,[27] Lindars,[28] and Vermes,[29] as well as Collins,[30] Dodd,[31] Leivestad,[32] and Perrin,[33] again with varied nuances. We

are the present ones or the future ones (21). Hahn accepts the priority of the eschatological, future sayings (24). These go back to Jesus himself. The "son of humanity" in these sayings, however, is not to be identified with Jesus. The "I" of the speaker in these sayings is clearly distinguished from the "son of humanity" (22). E.g., in Luke 12:8f., which is genuinely a saying of Jesus, a differentiation between Jesus and the coming "son of humanity" is made (33-34). The sayings about the earthly deeds in their present form cannot be original words of Jesus (37). Thus the process of development was: Jesus referred to the future coming of an eschatological "son of humanity" in its titular, apocalyptic sense, but someone other than himself. The early Christian community identified this coming one with Jesus. Next, the Jesus who worked on earth in power and authority was also described as the "son of humanity." Lastly, this description was extended to cover statements about his suffering and rising (28).

[21]H.E. Tödt, *The Son of Man in the Synoptic Tradition*, trans. Dorothea Barton (Philadelphia: Westminster Press, 1965). Tödt's research into the "son of humanity" sayings has been especially respected. I summarize some of his presuppositions and conclusions and include my own observations within parentheses.

"Before the concept of the Son of Man appeared within the synoptic tradition, it had already existed in Jewish apocalyptic thinking. Literary evidence for this can be found in Dan 7:13f.; 4 Ezra 13; and 1 Enoch. There can be no doubt that there was a relationship between the apocalyptic concept of the Son of Man and the synoptic sayings" (222). (This is a starting point for Tödt, not something he really attempts to prove. And yet it is a point of great controversy. It is a prominent opinion, especially in German scholarship, but must be considered unproven.)

"The Son of Man concept has commonly been treated as a constant entity possessing the same meaning throughout the synoptic tradition . . . . It will not suffice to pay attention to the way in which Jesus modified the Son of man concept in his teaching . . . one shall have to examine whether the post-Easter tradition continued to develop the Son of Man concept productively" (33). (This is one of the most constructive aspects of Tödt's research. Although I do not accept his starting point, and thus his conclusions with respect to Jesus' use, we must recognize that the sayings as we have them are not only a question of Jesus' use and that of the post-resurrection Christian community, or a question of three classes of sayings which entered the tradition at different points, but rather that the sayings serve different functions in Matthew, Mark, and Luke, as redaction criticism would lead us to suppose.) See pp. 92-94 for Tödt's summary of Matthew's usage and 108-12 for his summary of Luke's usage.

"In Jesus' sayings concerning the Son of Man the apocalyptic elaborations are radically cut down . . . At the inlet through which the Son of Man concept was primarily channeled into the synoptic tradition, i.e., in Jesus' teaching, this concept shed the features of apocalyptic elaboration and theology. There is not even an allusion to a pre-existence of the Son of Man. In Jesus' teaching all importance is

should also place Schweizer here.[34] Given the highly disputed character of this issue, we cannot assume that the existence of such an apocalyptic figure or title has been proven. I am more inclined to follow the direction set by Vermes, Casey, Dunn, and Lindars.

attached to the fact that God's reign stands at the door, that the Son of Man will come" (66). "Jesus' Son of Man sayings differ from the Jewish apocalyptic concept by reason of their soteriological nature" (227). (Although there supposedly is this definite Son of Man conception or title in pre-Christian Judaism, even Todt remarks that Jesus' teaching about the figure is stripped of its many typical, apocalyptic features.)

[22]E.g., D.E. Nineham, *The Gospel of St. Mark*, Pelican Commentaries (Philadelphia: Westminster Press, 1977), esp. 46-47.

[23]Frederick Houk Borsch, *The Son of Man in Myth and History* (London: SCM Press, 1967). Borsch holds to the existence of an apocalyptic "Son of Humanity" concept in Judaism, but comes to this conclusion by a different route. He is also open to authentic sayings of Jesus in all three of the common categories.

Borsch writes, "The mainstream of Judaism . . . had no real place for a suffering messianic figure" (175). However, "we must still search for a setting, some set of circumstances perhaps more esoteric, or, if you will, more on the fringe of what may be called *normative* Judaism, where the teaching might have taken shape" (176). Borsch comprehensively surveys the "human figure" in many non-Jewish as well as Jewish sources and concludes, "We hold that there are now many good reasons for believing that there were extant during the first century AD and probably for some time earlier a number of Jewish-oriented sects which practiced forms of baptism as an ordination/coronation rite and which were likely open to at least a measure of *foreign* (or simply indigenous but non-Jewish) influences" (218). "We believe it quite likely that Jesus could have been influenced by the beliefs of one or more groups like these" (219).

Borsch writes, "We may well have shown that this sectarian *milieu* was much concerned with the Man in one way or another, but we have not found that the specific expression *the Son of Man* was used for such a figure in the same particular milieu" (225-26). But this point is a crucial one. He continues, "In one sense we have no answer to this criticism. From the information available to us, we can hardly insist that there did exist a pre-Christian baptizing sect (or sects) which described or styled its Man hero specifically as the Son of Man and saw him as something more than a distant heavenly champion . . . Yet is it all that unlikely that such could have been the case?" (226). This is admitting an insufficient basis for his conclusion. He is saying that, based on his comprehensive research, he cannot document the existence of the hypothetical baptizing sect which he postulates. In other words the evidence does not necessitate the acceptance of such a pre-Christian "son of humanity" figure.

Of course, if there were such a sect, should we not look for it in the circle surrounding John the baptizer, simply because of all the baptizing sects this one would more probably have had the greater influence on Jesus? But Borsch writes, "It certainly does not prove that John the Baptist was a leader of the manner of sect which we are proposing, one that combined belief in the royal Man with baptism

Rather than representative of apocalyptic expectation, "son of humanity" in pre-Christian Judaism reflected Aramaic usage. The underlying Aramaic is *bar 'enāsh* (Hebrew *' ādām, ben 'ādām*, a human being) and *bar 'enāshā'* (Hebrew *hā-ādām*, the human one).[35] Geza Vermes,

conceived of as an ordination or exaltation to association with or to the office of this Man" (225). Borsch is aware of this lacuna in his hypothesis.

[24]A.J.B. Higgins, *The Son of Man in the Teaching of Jesus* (Cambridge University Press, 1980). Higgins affirms a "son of humanity" figure in Judaism and limits authentic sayings to future sayings. Yet he does this in a novel way.

Higgins writes, "Is it conceivable that Jesus could have used *bar nasha* in an 'apocalyptic' sense in the complete absence of any antecedent?" (53). But is this not the point to be proven: did Jesus use it in an apocalyptic sense? He continues, "Just such an antecedent may be assumed to be behind his employment of it in the glorification sayings" (53). But can we assume such a debatable statement? We have a circle. We assume Jesus used *bar nasha* in an apocalyptic sense. So we then assume that such an apocalyptic antecedent existed in Judaism. So we then have the background needed for Jesus who could have made use of it. Higgins: "It is not the apocalyptic usage that is original to him; what *is* original is his functional reinterpretation of Son of Man to express what he meant by his destiny as the divine agent in judgment and salvation" (53). Higgins' main contribution is that Jesus *neither* used the title "Son of Humanity" as a self-designation *nor* applied it to some figure other than himself. Yet he did use it (36-37). The concept existed. And Jesus used it in a functional way, to refer to *his future function or status*, not his present activity nor his future personal identity. Jesus used it, but not in a titular sense.

Of the kernel sayings which Higgins attributes to Jesus, he writes, "The absence of all these apocalyptic features from the kernel sayings is surely significant; initially the only item of apocalyptic imagery is the Son of Man himself" (125). But if one removes all the apocalyptic aspects from Jesus' use, why does one continue to assume an apocalyptic "son of humanity" in order to explain Jesus' use? If one removes all the apocalyptic aspects, does one not then have a *non-apocalyptic* "son of humanity?" But what is this? No longer the "son of humanity" concept. Could the background not just as easily be Jesus' use of *bar 'enāshā'* as an Aramaic idiom?

The major contribution of Higgins is that he wants to interpret Jesus' use of the "son of humanity" as a future reality in a functional way (121). "On the reasonable assumption (still not disproved) of the existence of a son of man concept in Judaism, Jesus was unique in applying to it a *completely new* and original *non-personal*, functional interpretation, as a means of expressing, in veiled and often misunderstood language, his beliefs about the eschatological judgment" (124). (The italics are mine. The parentheses are Higgins'.)

An interesting fact about both Borsch and Higgins is that, although one has to place them in line with those who accept a Jewish "son of humanity" concept in the background of Jesus, one could almost as easily put them on the other side. One could as readily conclude from Borsch to the non-existence of such a concept. One could conclude from Higgins that it is an assumption for which we have no need.

[25]Borg, *Conflict, Holiness and Politics in the Teachings of Jesus*, 221-27.

Maurice Casey and Barnabas Lindars have all contributed to refining our understanding of the Aramaic expression.[36] There is widespread agreement that the expression in Aramaic was used in a generic (human being, a human being) or an indefinite (someone, anyone) sense.

[26]Casey, *Son of Man*, 35, 90, 112, 122-39.

[27]Dunn, *Christology in the Making*, 65-97.

[28]Barnabas Lindars, "Re-enter the Apocalyptic Son of Man," *New Testament Studies* 22 (1975-76), 52-72. In this article, Lindars accepts that the "son of humanity" was not a title current in Judaism, that the Aramaic *bar 'enāshā'* is idiomatic, and that this idiomatic usage was characteristic of Jesus. In this we can see that he follows Vermes. However, the quasi-titular use in the sayings does not come from the community but from Jesus. Jesus does not inherit but creates the basis for the New Testament usage. Higgins, *The Son of Man in the Teaching of Jesus*, 51, summarizes Lindars by saying that the idiomatic "son of humanity" = I (Jesus), but I (Jesus) = quasi-apocalyptic "son of humanity." Thus, through Jesus, "son of humanity" becomes "Son of Humanity."

Since that article, Lindars has developed his approach and changed his mind on several questions. In his more recent book, *Jesus Son of Man, A Fresh Examination of the Son of Man Sayings in the Gospels in the Light of Recent Research* (Grand Rapids, Mich.: William B. Eerdmans, 1983), Lindars still maintains that there was no pre-Christian "son of humanity" title in Judaism. His position on the Aramaic idiom, however, is now more nuanced than that of Casey and Vermes. *Bar 'enasha'* is still a feature of Jesus' personal style of speech, but not simply a universal statement nor an exclusive self-reference. However, the basis for the quasi-titular New Testament usage is not Jesus (as Lindars earlier maintained) but the Greek translations (as Casey suggested, *Son of Man*, 231).

[29]Geza Vermes' contribution to "the son of humanity debate" can be found in "The Use of Bar Nash/Bar Nasha in Jewish Aramaic," *Post-Biblical Jewish Studies* (Leiden: E.J. Brill, 1975), 147-65, an unaltered reprint of the essay which first appeared as an appendix to Matthew Black's *Aramaic Approach to the Gospels and Acts*, third edition (Oxford: Clarendon Press, 1967), 310-30; *Jesus the Jew, a Historian's Reading of the Gospels* (Philadelphia: Fortress Press, 1973), 160-91; and "The Present State of the 'Son of Man' Debate," *Jesus and the World of Judaism* (Philadelphia: Fortress Press, 1983), 89-99. A significant critical response to Vermes' early seminal article came from Joseph Fitzmyer. For some of Fitzmyer's contributions to the discussion, see "A Review of Matthew Black's *Aramaic Approach to the Gospels and Acts*, 3rd edition," *Catholic Biblical Quarterly* 30 (1968), 417-28, esp. 425-28; "The Study of the Aramaic Background of the NT," in *A Wandering Aramaean, Collected Aramaic Essays* (Missoula, Montana: Scholars Press, 1979), 1-27, a slightly revised form of a lecture first published as "Methodology in the Study of the Aramaic Substratum of Jesus' Sayings in the NT," in *Jésus aux origines de la christologie*, ed. J. Dupont (Gembloux: Duculot, 1975), 73-102; and "The NT Title 'Son of Man' Philologically Considered," *A Wandering Aramaean*, 143-60. Fitzmyer agrees with Vermes about the non-existence of the *bar nāsh/bar nāshā* expression as a title but disagrees with Vermes about its use as a circumlocution for I.

Geza Vermes presented evidence for a third use of the expression as well, as a self-reference or circumlocution for "I." This use has not gone undisputed, yet Vermes' contribution has been to shift weight away from interpreting "the son of humanity" as an apocalyptic messianic title and toward understanding it as an idiomatic Aramaic speech pattern.[37]

[30]John J. Collins, *The Apocalyptic Imagination*, 85, 122. See n. 13 of this chapter.

[31]C.H. Dodd, *The Founder of Christianity* (New York: The Macmillan Co., 1970), 110-13.

[32]R. Leivestad, "Exit the Apocalyptic Son of Man," *New Testament Studies* 18 (1971-72), 243-67. Leivestad, a Scandinavian scholar, maintains that there was no messianic "son of humanity" concept or title in apocalyptic Judaism, that the Similitudes of Enoch are not evidence to the contrary, that the expression "son of humanity" does not have a messianic connotation, and that the apocalyptic "son of humanity" concept and title are a modern invention.

[33]Norman Perrin, *Rediscovering the Teaching of Jesus* (New York: Harper and Row, 1967), 164-99. Perrin limits himself to an analysis of the future "son of humanity" sayings. He rejects the assumption that there existed in pre-Christian Judaism a conception of a transcendent, apocalyptic "son of humanity." Rather, in Jewish apocalypticism there is simply the use of the imagery of Daniel 7:13 by subsequent seers who use it independently of each other (e.g., the Christian use, 1 Enoch, 4 Ezra). These uses are not reflections of a common, underlying "son of humanity" conception, however. In the Christian tradition, the resurrection and ascension of Jesus is interpreted in terms of Dan 7:13, and so Jesus becomes "son of humanity" on the basis of this interpretation of the resurrection. The "coming son of humanity" expectation is thus a product of Christian exegetical traditions without a basis in pre-Christian Jewish apocalypticism or in the teaching of Jesus. It develops from a particular interpretation of the resurrection/ascension. Thus Jesus could not have spoken of the coming of "the son of humanity," either in reference to himself or in reference to a figure other than himself, for no such concept existed to be referred to in this way. The future "son of humanity" sayings are all products of the early Church.

[34]E.Schweizer, "The Son of Man Again," *New Testament Studies* 9 (1962-63), 256-61. As Higgins does not completely fit the category of those who argue for a pre-Christian "son of humanity" concept, so Schweitzer does not completely fit the category of those who do not. Yet he belongs here more than in some other category.

Schweizer holds that the expression was *not yet* a definite title in the time of Jesus, and this is only why Jesus adopted the expression. It became a title through an apocalyptization of Jesus' eschatology by a Jewish apocalyptic group in the early Church.

[35]In Ezekiel the expression *ben 'adam* occurs 93 times and is a situation in which God is addressing Ezekiel. Outside Ezekiel it is found fifteen times where it simply means a human being. See Louis F. Hartmann and Alexander A. Di Lella, *The Book of Daniel*, 85-87.

Vermes' interpretation placed too much weight on the possibility of *bar 'enāsh* being exclusively a self-reference. Maurice Casey's interpretation placed greater emphasis on the undisputed generic meaning of the expression, but with the nuance of "anyone, including myself." The expression contains the capacity for self-reference as part of its generic meaning. An even more precise rendering of the expression has been suggested by Barnabas Lindars for whom the idiomatic expression connotes neither an exclusive self-reference nor universal generic usage, but lies between the two: "someone such as I."

Bar 'enāsh (a human one, a son of humanity) is simply a member of the human species. But *bar 'enāshā'* ("the son of humanity" with the definite article, the Aramaic emphatic state) means "son of humanity" in a special sense. This special sense, for Lindars, is not simply a generic use (humankind in general) nor a simple self-reference (whether that be seen as part of the generic use as in Casey or as a distinct use as in Vermes) but a self-inclusion as a part of a group or class: "someone in my position." Thus, according to Lindars, Jesus, in using *bar 'enāshā'*, was not referring to himself exclusively, yet was doing so intentionally. The Greek translation, as both Casey and Lindars point out, makes the phrase appear to function as an exclusive self-reference, and hence as quasi-titular, but the Aramaic idiom underlying the Greek is not in any sense a messianic title.

---

[36]This perspective goes back as far as Julius Wellhausen, however. Ferdinand Hahn, *The Titles of Jesus*, 16, quotes the following text from Wellhausen, *Skizzen und Vorarbeiten* VI (1900), 194: "In the mouth of Jesus, the expression 'son of man' may have been merely a general expression denoting an individual man; only the primitive community, in connection with its expectation of the parousia, stamped it with titular character."

[37]See n. 29 in this chapter. The shift is now manifested in the recent Spanish translation of the New Testament, *Nueva Biblia Espanõla*, directed by Luis Alonso Schokel and Juan Mateos (Madrid: Ediciones Cristianidad, 1975, Edicion Latino Americana, 1976). *El Hijo del hombre* has become *el hombre* (in Mk 2:10; 2:28) or *este Hombre* (in most of the Synoptic sayings).

Jesus' Prophetic Usage

Some scholars have maintained that none of the "son of humanity" sayings in the New Testament are the authentic words of Jesus himself (Käsemann, Perrin, Teeple, Vielhauer).[38] Even if it were true that none of the sayings *as we have them* are sayings of Jesus himself, this need not imply that Jesus never spoke in this way. It would simply be a question of development within the sayings so that we do not have them in exactly the way Jesus spoke. Our immediate concern is not the authenticity of the sayings but the fact that Jesus used the expression. Any conclusion to the contrary is suspect simply because the evidence is so obvious. More than almost any other expression in the New Testament we find this one on Jesus' lips, and it is Jesus' way of speaking, not the way others speak about him. We find this speech pattern of Jesus over sixty times in the Synoptics alone,[39] a sizable number considering the paucity of many other expressions. The evidence thus supports Jesus' use of *bar 'enāshā'* in his teaching. It was characteristic of his way of speaking.

There are several ways in which the *bar 'enāshā'* sayings have come to be classified. The better known is the threefold classification which goes back to Bultmann and is found in Tödt, Hahn, Fuller and others.[40] A first group comprises sayings in which "the son of humanity" is present and active

---

[38] See E. Käsemann, "The Problem of the Historical Jesus," *Essays on New Testament Themes* (Naperville, Ill.: A.R. Allenson, 1964), 15-47. N. Perrin, "Recent Trends in Research in the Christology of the New Testament," in *Transitions in Biblical Scholarship*, ed. J.C. Rylaarsdam (Chicago: University of Chicago, 1968), 217-33; also *Rediscovering the Teaching of Jesus*, 164-99, 259-60. H.M. Teeple, "The Origin of the Son of Man Christology," *Journal of Biblical Literature* 84 (1965), 213-50. P. Vielhauer, "Gottesreich und Menschensohn in der Verkundigung Jesu," *Festschrift fur Gunther Dehn* (Neukirchen, 1957), 51-79, reprinted in *Aufsatze Zum Neuen Testament* (Munich, 1965), 55-91. For a summary of several of these opinions, see A.J.B. Higgins, *The Son of Man in the Teaching of Jesus* (Cambridge: Cambridge University Press, 1980), 36-40.

[39] See n. 9 in this chapter.

[40] See Rudolf Bultmann, *Theology of the New Testament*, trans. Kendrick Grobel, vol. 2 (New York: Charles Scribner's Sons, 1951), 30; Fuller, *The Mission and Achievement of Jesus*, 95-98.

on earth. A second group are those sayings in which the mission of "the son of humanity" is associated with suffering and death. The third group comprises those sayings which refer to the "the son of humanity" as the one to come in the future. This system of classification is usually but not always associated with an interpretation of "the son of humanity" as an apocalyptic, messianic title.

Those who do not accept a pre-Christian, Jewish *bar 'enāshā'* concept of a quasi-messianic figure classify the sayings differently. Vermes has classified the sayings in terms of their relationship to Daniel 7.[41] Casey's classification separates the sayings into (1) those which are authentic examples of correct Aramaic idiom, (2) the passion predictions, (3) those which were produced by the early Church under the influence of Daniel 7, and (4) miscellaneous sayings.[42]

To indicate the wide diversity of opinion about the authenticity of the sayings we go from those who argue that none of them are authentic (Käsemann, Perrin, Teeple, Vielhauer) to those who argue that the only authentic sayings are among those that refer to the future (Tödt, Hahn, Higgins) to those who maintain that it is the future sayings which are not authentic (Vermes) to those who maintain that there are authentic sayings of Jesus in all three groups (Barrett, Bruce, Marshall, Moule, Schweizer).[43]

Once we move away from *bar 'enāshā'* as an apocalyptic title to recognizing its roots in an Aramaic idiom, progress is possible. Thus, for Casey, those sayings are authentic Jesus material which reflect the underlying Aramaic idiom (his first group). Following this lead, and Barnabas Lindars' interpretation of the underlying Aramaic idiom, Lindars

[41]Vermes, *Jesus the Jew*, 179.

[42]Casey, *Son of Man*, 236-37.

[43]See C.K. Barrett, *Jesus and the Gospel Tradition* (Philadelphia: Fortress Press, 1968); F.F. Bruce, *This is That* (Exeter: Paternoster Press, 1968); I.H. Marshall, "The Synoptic Son of Man Sayings in Recent Discussion," *New Testament Studies* 12 (1965-66), 327-51; C.F.D. Moule, *The New Testament Gospels* (London: B.B.C. Publications, 1965), 46-49; and *The Phenomenon of the New Testament*, 34-36; E. Schweizer, "The Son of Man," *Journal of Biblical Literature* 79 (1960), 119-29, and "The Son of Man Again," *New Testament Studies* 9 (1962-63), 256-61.

identifies nine authentic *bar 'enāshā'* sayings.[44]   All are from Q and Mark: (1) Matthew 8:20 // Luke 9:58; (2) Matthew 11:16-19 // Luke 7:31-35; (3) Matthew 12:32 // Luke 12:10; (4) Luke 11:30; (5) Matthew 9:6 // Mark 2:10 and Luke 5:24; (6) Matthew 10:32 // Luke 12:8; and three sayings underlying the passion predictions, (7) "*bar 'enāshā'* may be delivered up" (Mark 9:31); (8) "*bar 'enāshā'* goes according to his destiny" (Mark 14:21a); and (9) "*bar 'enāshā'* will give his life for many" (Mark 10:45).

Although there may be little agreement on precisely which sayings are authentic Jesus material, it is best to see the *bar 'enāshā'* sayings in their origins as rooted in the teaching of Jesus. In some of the sayings, there is a basic core which comes from Jesus but gets further elaborated and developed (e.g., the passion predictions). Others are perhaps completely the product of the early Church (e.g., those apocalyptic future sayings directly dependent on Daniel 7). But there are still a number of sayings rooted in the life of Jesus and his particular use of an Aramaic idiom.

We can tentatively suggest a direction of development behind the *bar 'enāshā'* sayings. The post-resurrection Christian community preserved Jesus' way of speaking and some of his sayings. However, "the son of humanity" speech pattern was also made to bear more and more the faith and eschatology of the community. The *bar 'enāshā'* expression was eschatologized and came to reflect the expectation of Jesus' return. It was apocalypticized into a way of describing the future hope which was attached to Jesus after his resurrection from the dead. Jesus' way of speaking was made to carry a meaning that was part of the early Christian hope and with which the continued interpretation of Daniel 7 was also associated. Thus there were at least two possible levels of meaning behind "the son of humanity" sayings. The primary level of usage by Jesus was in a non-titular, non-messianic, non-apocalyptic sense, which at times may have been an ordinary way of speaking and at times a way of expressing his own authority. The second level was post-

[44]Lindars, *Jesus, Son of Man*, 27-84.

resurrection development in which the expression and sayings carried more and more meaning in the light of Jesus' life, resurrection, and the early Christian hope.

Casey argues that Daniel 7:13 influenced only a few New Testament sayings.[45] In general, the Gospels' use of "son of humanity" was not derived from Daniel 7. This does not exclude, however, the fact that the Gospel term was so derived in a saying or two, such as in Mark 14:62. But another source or sources lie behind the majority of the occurrences of *bar 'enāshā'* in the Gospels. The term was not a messianic title in Judaism. Yet Jesus knew the expression "ever since he was old enough to find human speech intelligible."[46] He spoke Aramaic, and "son of humanity" was a normal Aramaic expression. Jesus used the expression and his use did not depend upon the influence of Daniel 7. The small group of "son of humanity" sayings in which the influence of Daniel 7 is detectable have their *Sitz im Leben* in the early Church. A group of Christians who had inherited a flexible method of exegesis open to reinterpretation and were in a position similar to the Enoch circle found their expectation of the second coming of Jesus in Daniel 7:13.

The authentic "son of humanity" sayings of Jesus deal with his life on earth, including his death. The majority of inauthentic Synoptic sayings deal with the time of the End, and give Jesus a fundamental role in these last events. It is within this broader framework that the group of sayings influenced by Daniel 7 belong. *Bar'enāshā'* has its *Sitz im Leben* in the life of Jesus, but *as a title* has its *Sitz im Leben* in the work of the early Church.[47]

---

[45]For Casey's survey of the Gospel material, see *Son of Man*, 157-223. For a summary of his results, see 201-19.

[46]Ibid., 157.

[47]James D.G. Dunn (*Christology in the Making*, 65-97) comes to conclusions fairly similar to those of Casey. Jesus used the phrase in a non-titular sense when referring to himself and his mission, and without particular reference to Daniel 7. The interpretation of Daniel 7 as referring to a particular individual can only be traced back to the early Christian movement (or perhaps to Jesus himself for Dunn). In either case, the individualizing exegesis of Daniel 7:13 probably began

Although he approaches Daniel 7 with a different interpretation, John J. Collins supports the thesis that the apocalyptic matrix is the context not for Jesus' use of the *bar 'enāshā'* expression but for the early Christian, post-resurrection, New Testament usage.[48] The belief that Jesus would come again as *bar 'enāshā'* presupposes the resurrection and exaltation of Jesus and manifests a development beyond Jesus' own usage. Given faith in the resurrection and exaltation of Jesus, it was inevitable that he would come to be interpreted within an apocalyptic milieu in light of Daniel 7, which interpretation was then a basis for Jesus' future and imminent second coming as judge.

We can now outline possible stages of development behind the *bar 'enasha'* expression:

A. The usage in Daniel 7 was corporate and symbolic (or perhaps an angelic reference);

B. The usage in pre-Christian Judaism was as an Aramaic way of speaking, an indefinite or a generic use, or a generic use that was inclusive of the self as well;

C. Jesus' usage was along the lines of B above. It was neither an exclusive self-reference, nor simply a universal statement, but a reference to himself and others like himself. It was also able to convey his sense of prophetic authority.

D. The interpretation of the expression within the Synoptic sayings in a quasi-titular and apocalyptic way came after the resurrection and was coupled with an individualizing exegesis of Daniel 7.

---

as a reference to Jesus and not in a pre-Christian milieu. At least the earliest datable interpretation of Daniel's "son of humanity" as an individual figure is the Christian identification of "son of humanity" with Jesus, whether that originated with Jesus or with the community. Dunn refers to the period between the two Jewish revolts (70-132 C.E.) as a period of intense and escalating speculation regarding "the son of humanity" in Daniel's vision, a period of heightened messianic hope and apocalyptic fervor. This was the setting for 4 Ezra and probably the Similitudes of Enoch. Thus the idea of "the son of humanity" as a pre-existent heavenly figure seems not to have emerged until the last decades of the first century.

[48] John J. Collins, *The Apocalyptic Imagination, An Introduction to the Jewish Matrix of Christianity* (New York: Crossroad, 1984), 209-210. For Collins' interpretation of Daniel 7 and of "the son the humanity" as an angel, namely Michael, see pp. 78-85.

The suggestion is not to be dismissed that the meaning underlying the *bar 'enāshā'* expression as used by Jesus is the meaning Jesus put into the expression. The expression remains enigmatic to the degree that the one using it remains an enigma. A particular Aramaic idiom becomes one of Jesus' preferred ways of speaking, especially when speaking in a way that includes or refers to himself. Thus the expression will begin to carry the weight of Jesus' own self-understanding. To the degree that Jesus' own self-understanding remains inaccessible, so does the meaning of *bar 'enāshā'* as used by Jesus. Thus *bar 'enāshā'* will not so much be a key to the consciousness of Jesus as Jesus will be the key to the meaning of *bar 'enāshā'.* It does not express an apocalyptic eschatology on Jesus' part; nor does it express necessarily any messianic self-understanding. It does seem to convey Jesus' sense of prophetic authority and destiny. The expression could well have come to have even more meaning as Jesus' own self-understanding grew and developed. Jesus may well have played a crucial role in the development of this enigmatic expression which he was able to use flexibly to express himself.[49]

Let us look at several texts to see more clearly their possible meaning within the teaching of Jesus.

[49]There are several hints in this direction within "son of humanity" research. A.J.B. Higgins' approach opens the door to thinking of Jesus' use of the expression as new, original, and unique (see n. 24 in this chapter). Also, Lindars, in his early article, is clearly suggestive of this line of approach: *bar 'enāshā*=Jesus; through Jesus "son of humanity" becomes "Son of Humanity" (see n. 28). This need not imply attributing the apocalyptization of the expression to Jesus, but does suggest that the meaning of the expression and the developing self-understanding of Jesus are closely woven together. Dunn is even open to the individualization of the Daniel 7 imagery as having roots in Jesus' usage (*Christology in the Making*, 86-87, 96). Bruce Chilton's assessment seems apt: "While research in this area — which proceeds at a remarkable rate — has laid bare some of the lineaments of meaning which may lie behind Jesus' use of the phrase, a single exact parallel has yet to be found. The conclusion seems reasonable that Jesus applied a somewhat out-of-the-way phrase to himself, and gave it fresh meaning" (*A Galilean Rabbi and His Bible* [Wilmington, Del.: Michael Glazier, 1984], 178-79). In an interesting but debatable fashion, A.E. Harvey proceeds along these lines with respect to the title Messiah: the content of the expression is not pre-determined but to be derived from its application to Jesus (*Jesus and the Constraints of History* [Philadelphia: Westminster Press, 1982], 80-84, 120-53).

> And Jesus said to him, "Foxes have holes, and birds of
> the air have nests; but the son of humanity has nowhere to
> lay his head." (Mt 8:20; // Lk 9:58)

This is a saying from Q not influenced by Daniel 7. The context of the saying is discipleship. Jesus is responding to someone who has just said, "I will follow you wherever you go." Jesus used the occasion to teach something about the cost of discipleship. The saying is a self-reference, but not an exclusive self-reference. Neither is it a universal statement. It doesn't apply to anyone and everyone. It applies to those who intend to follow Jesus and can accept the hardship of that calling. Thus the meaning of the saying is "someone such as I."[50] The contrast is between Jesus with his disciples and others. "I will follow you wherever you go." "But, do you realize, someone such as I has nowhere to lay his head."

> "The son of humanity will be delivered into human
> hands, and they will kill him; and when he is killed, after
> three days he will rise." (Mk 9:31)

Lindars suggests that the Marcan passion predictions can be traced back to three authentic underlying Aramaic sayings. It is commonly acknowledged that the details of the passion predictions came after the fact and are not part of the original Jesus material (e.g., reference to "the elders and the chief priests and the scribes"). Our question is whether the core of the passion predictions functions according to the *bar 'enāshā'* idiom, or what part of the prediction can be taken as authentic because it is in accord with the Aramaic idiom. Lindars argues that the underlying saying is, "Someone may be delivered up."[51]

Lindars argues that the resurrection prediction had an origin separate from that of the passion prediction (which does not deny the possibility of its also being grounded in the teaching of Jesus). The underlying passion prediction

[50]Lindars, *Jesus Son of Man*, 31.
[51]Ibid., 68, 60-74.

was simply an expression of Jesus' premonition of death: "someone may be delivered up." The rest of the saying cannot be reconstructed.

> And then they will see the son of humanity coming in clouds with great power and glory. (Mk 13:26; // Mt 24:30; // Lk 21:27)

This Marcan text refers to the future and manifests a dependence on Daniel 7. The verse is part of the "Marcan apocalypse." The setting is the period shortly before or shortly after the outbreak of the 66-70 C.E. revolt. It is an apocalyptic portrayal of the parousia of Jesus, an event expected to take place soon. The disciples must read the signs right and not follow false prophets, preachers, and messiahs. Then "the son of humanity," Jesus, will come in all his heavenly glory. Casey, Lindars, and Vermes argue that Mark 13:26 and 14:62 are the product of Christianity rather than being authentic Jesus sayings.

Marcan research suggests that Mark as a whole may be a product of an apocalyptic community.[52] Mark 13 manifests both the literary structure and the motifs of an apocalypse (the presentation of a present crisis with historical precedents; pointing toward an eschatological fulfillment, with the primary concern being the present critical moment in which there is required the endurance of the faithful, even to the point of martyrdom; and an apocalyptic philosophy of history, the view that God's purpose for creation has been thwarted by demonic forces which shortly and finally will be defeated when God's reign begins).

The question at this point is how much of this apocalypse is Marcan or even pre-Marcan and how much goes back to Jesus himself.[53] Mark may have compiled it from varied sayings and sources. The composition can be attributed to

---

[52]H.C. Kee, *Community of the New Age, Studies in Mark's Gospel* (Philadelphia: Westminster Press, 1977), 65-66

[53]Ibid., 43-49. Kee refers to the research of Haenchen, Lohmeyer, Lamprecht, and Hartmann. All of these vary in their approach to Mark 13, and yet all speak of

Mark without denying the authenticity of a particular say-ing within it. Yet Casey's conclusion is that Mark 13:26 is not an authentic saying of Jesus but falls within that group of sayings produced by the early Church under the influence of Daniel 7:13.[54] Mark 13:26 is clearly dependent on Daniel 7:13. About this there is no question.

The future sayings directly influenced by Daniel 7:13 reflect a titular use which we have rejected as original with Jesus. The use of *ho huios tou anthrōpou* or *bar 'enāshā'* as an apocalyptic title does not reflect the original Aramaic idiom but results from the expression's having been trans-lated into Greek, and reflects the growing apocalyptization and parousia expectation of the early Church. The use of "the son of humanity" idiom in connection with the parou-sia is not the starting point but the end result of such development. The tradition begins with an Aramaic usage at home in the world of spoken Aramaic.

We have looked at several representative sayings. What we are aware of in Jesus' use of the *bar 'enāshā'* expression is his awareness of his humanity, of his solidarity with us, of his sense of mission and authority. Jesus is not expressing in his usage any identification with a particular messianic or eschatological role. The expression is to some degree enig-matic because the man using it is to some degree an enigma. What is a common enough Aramaic expression becomes a way of speaking for the prophet from Nazareth. *Bar 'enāshā'* is a vehicle for his self-expression. The expression as used by Jesus then is not pre-determined in its content (it is not an apocalyptic title) but receives its content from Jesus' way of using it. It is neither more nor less than what Jesus puts into it. The *bar 'enāshā'* expression is not so much an access to Jesus' self-understanding as his self-understanding is to his

a composite background or sayings tradition behind the Marcan redaction. Even if there are redactional elements in individual verses, this does not exclude a Jesus tradition. Lamprecht sees redactional work in verses 1, 2a, 3f, 5a, 7f, 10, 13, 14, 17, 20, 23, 27. Our concern here is verse 26. Marxsen, *Mark the Evangelist*, sees Mark 13 as the evangelist's own composition, p. 161, a composition with a unity, p. 166, and yet a connection of originally unconnected pieces.

[54]Casey, *Son of Man*, 236-37. See also 165-78.

202 Jesus and Apocalypticism

use of the expression. This partly accounts for the difficulties we have had in understanding the expression. It is not a defined, pre-Christian Jewish concept. It is Jesus' way of speaking.

Jesus and Apocalypticism

We come back to where we were: Jesus' self-awareness was prophetic and social. It is best not to describe it as messianic (which is not to say that it was non-messianic) and best not to describe it as apocalyptic (which is not to say there was not apocalyptic influence at all in his life and message). Messianism and apocalypticism simply do not provide the primary access we need in order to understand him.

Can we say anything more at this point about Jesus' eschatology? We are beginning to see Jesus as a socially and religiously conscious prophet in an eschatologically conscious period of history. Is there any other way of describing Jesus' perspective — one for whom the coming of God's reign was central to his mission and self-understanding? In Jesus of Nazareth we have a (perhaps unparalleled) creative advance within religious history. Yet the language of Judaism is still of help. Jesus' eschatology had its roots in the same place that Jewish eschatology had its — in Jewish hope. *Jesus was a prophet of hope.* And Jesus' hope was rooted in his faith and experience of God, and God's fidelity to God's promises. Jesus' God was a compassionate, generous, and faithful God; no three adjectives could better describe God's love for the people. Jesus knew God personally. Jesus' hope rested upon his faith that God would be true to God's promises. Jesus knew that a new age was close at hand, and in fact for all practical purposes had already begun whether people realized it or not. Jesus also knew that God's fulfillment was not what the people expected. He preached no messianic revolt, no new earthly kingdom of Israel, no cataclysmic disappearance of the world as he knew it, no descent of a new Jerusalem from the heavens. But he did preach that God's reign was close at hand — for those who had the eyes to see. The era of *God's justice* reigning *on earth* had already begun.

Perhaps the most important way to describe Jesus' eschatology is to say that it was *Jesus'* eschatology. And it was an eschatology that did not frame itself in terms of *either* this world *or* another world but rather that God's future for God's people and Israel's future involved *both* this world *and* another world which would co-exist with greater harmony. *God would now reign on earth*, and this reign was about to begin. Jesus' eschatological consciousness was essentially a God-consciousness, that of a prophet to Israel.

Before we proceed to discuss Jesus' teaching, we can bring together a picture toward which our discussion has pointed thus far: Jesus of Nazareth, someone thoroughly human, is also someone called by God. This man was God's man. Although Jesus was truly one of us, the starting point for understanding Jesus must be God. This insight into who Jesus was, that he cannot be understood or interpreted apart from God, neither does disservice to nor compromises our affirmation that Jesus is one of us. Jesus as a human being is God's.

The narrative of the first sequence of events in the public life of Jesus dramatically reveals Jesus' relationship to God. Jesus received the baptism of John, experienced more keenly the action of God in his life, was driven even further into the wilderness where his faith and fidelity were put to the test. With whom are we dealing in these events in the wilderness if not a son of God? The Synoptic accounts of the baptism portray Jesus as one called by God: "Thou art my beloved Son; with thee I am well pleased" (Mt 1:11). Jesus' ordeal in the wilderness allowed God to shape and form a man of faith and prayer, of the *Shema*, whose God was the God of Abraham and Sarah in whom he trusted.

Jesus left the wilderness and eventually returned to Galilee to do his heavenly Father's work; he was an itinerant preacher who healed and drove out demons and proclaimed with all his heart the coming of his Father's reign. Here was one on whose heart it was indeed written that there is but one God whom alone we serve. Who was this Jesus? A prophet, not unlike the prophets of old, one whose entire life was rooted in the Lord, who thirsted for justice, who brought God's word once again to God's people, who was salvation in their midst. Jesus had been anointed with the gift of the Spirit. He knew himself to be and was perceived as a prophet. Although in another age and with a different temperament, he was in some sense another Isaiah (a prophet of faith in God), another Hosea (a prophet of divine love), another Amos (a prophet of justice), one who preached and practiced the message of Micah (who acted justly, loved tenderly, and walked humbly with God). Like Isaiah, upon whom he must often have meditated, this prophet understood himself and ought to be understood in terms of the two bases of faith and justice, or love of God and love of neighbor, or obedience and deeds of loving kindness.

Not only was he a prophet, but a prophet at the dawn of a new period of history. Not a Messiah in accord with popular expectations. Nor some apocalyptic seer. But a God-conscious prophet to the poor of Israel. A man of faith.

And a man of prayer. From the traditional *Shema* of Israel to the innovative *Abba* of his own prayer, it is in his prayer that we are given an appropriate context for understanding and interpreting this first century prophetic figure. For this thoroughly God-conscious prophet, the Lord of the universe was his *abba/imma*. The relationship of Jesus with God was intensely personal; he saw the Lord of Israel as his very own father and he as God's son. What Jesus may well have learned by experience in the wilderness remained with him all his life — his strength was *Abba*.

To understand this man is to penetrate that relationship with his God. Indeed, it is to come to know the Father as well as the son. Prayer, faith, God's word, God's reign form the very being of Jesus of Nazareth, someone like us, but also one of God's chosen ones. Not only someone who was in solidarity with God, but also someone who was in solidarity with the people.

Part Three

Solidarity With The People

7

The Compassionate Sage

One well-attested fact about Jesus is that he taught. All four Gospels, especially the Synoptics, speak of Jesus as a teacher (*didaskalos*).[1] Some have translated the word *didaskalos* as *master*, but *teacher* better conveys the meaning. According to T.W. Manson, "The two most certain facts in the gospel tradition are that Jesus taught and that He was crucified."[2]

[1]Considering only the noun *didaskalos*, its distribution in the NT is as follows: Mk, 12 times; Mt, 12; Lk, 17; Jn, 8; Acts, 1; Paul, 7. Within this distribution, the word refers to Jesus as follows: Mk, 12 times; Mt, 10; Lk, 14; Jn, 7. See Benedict Viviano, *Study as Worship* (Leiden: E.J. Brill, 1978), 161. All the Synoptics refer to Jesus as teacher, and in them Jesus is *addressed* as Teacher, as follows: Mark, 10 times (Mk 4:38; 9:17, 38; 10:17, 20, 35; 12:14, 19, 32; 13:1) Matthew, 6 times (Mt 8:19; 12:38; 19:16; 22:16, 24, 36); Luke, 10 times (Lk 7:40; 8:24; 9:38, 49; 10:25; 18:18; 20:21, 28, 39; 21:7).

[2]T.W. Manson, *The Sayings of Jesus* (Grand Rapids, Mich.: William B. Eerdmans Co., [1937] 1957), 11. Manson remains one of the authorities on the teachings of Jesus. For his discussion of the history of the Jesus tradition, the sources of Jesus' teaching, and the form of that teaching, see ibid., 9-38. Another important study of Jesus' teaching is C.H. Dodd, *The Founder of Christianity* (New York: The Macmillan Co., 1970), 53-79. Also the writings of Norman Perrin, esp. *Rediscovering the Teaching of Jesus* (New York: Harper and Row, 1967), and *Jesus and the Language of the Kingdom, Symbol and Metaphor in New Testament Interpretation* (Philadelphia: Fortress Press, 1976). Also see Hans Conzelmann, *Jesus*, trans. J.R. Lord, ed. John Reumann (Philadelphia: Fortress Press, 1973), 36-81; Joseph Fitzmyer, *A Christological Catechism, New Testament Answers* (New York: Paulist Press, 1982), 19-34.

Although it is recognized that Jesus taught, and that he was acknowledged as a teacher by others, it is no easy task to surface accurately "The Teaching." There is much in the Gospels that one no longer considers the *ipsissima verba* (authentic words) of Jesus: yet there is also much therein that we do consider to be authentic Jesus material. Before the Gospels as we have them were written, there existed collections of sayings of Jesus, such as the collection called Q (from the German *Quelle*, source), one of the sources of the Synoptic tradition, the source which accounts for material that Matthew and Luke have in common but which was not derived from Mark. Q material has been dated around 50 C.E. T.W. Manson's reconstruction of Q included the following material (parentheses indicate some doubt on Manson's part): Luke 3:7-9, 16, 17; 4:1-13; 6:20-49; 7:(1-6a), 6b-9 (10), 18-35; 9:57-62; 10:2, 3, 8-16, 21-24; 11:9-26 (27, 28), 29-36, (37-41), 42-52; 12:(1), 2-12, 22-34, (35-38), 39-46, (47-50), 51-59; 13:18-30, 34, 35; 14:15-24, 26, 27, (34, 35); 16:13, 16-18; 17:1-6, 22-37.[3] This material consists almost entirely of teaching. W.D. Davies describes it as "a kind of Christian book of Proverbs inculcating the good life."[4]

Norman Perrin has provided a listing of a *minimum* that scholarly opinion recognizes as authentic Jesus material.[5]

---

[3]See Manson, *The Sayings of Jesus*, 15-21. A more recent listing of the Q pericopes is that of Richard A. Edwards, *A Concordance to Q* (Missoula, Montana: Society of Biblical Literature and Scholars Press, 1975), i-v. For a discussion of Q, also see W.D. Davies, *The Sermon on the Mount* (Cambridge: Cambridge University Press, 1966), 101-8; Richard A. Edwards, *A Theology of Q: Eschatology, Prophecy, and Wisdom* (Philadelphia: Fortress Press, 1976); Joseph Fitzmyer, *The Gospel According to Luke I-IX*, Anchor Bible 28 (Garden City, N.Y.: Doubleday and Co., 1981), 75-81; Joachim Jeremias, *New Testament Theology, the Proclamation of Jesus*, trans. John Bowden (New York: Charles Scribner's Sons, 1971), 38-39; Howard Clark Kee, *Jesus in History, an Approach to the Study of the Gospels*, second edition (New York: Harcourt Brace Jovanovich, 1977), 76-120.

[4]Davies, *The Sermon on the Mount*, 102.

[5]Perrin, *Jesus and the Language of the Kingdom*, 41. For another listing of authentic core material, see James Breech, *The Silence of Jesus, the Authentic Voice of the Historical Man* (Philadelphia: Fortress Press, 1983), who selects eight sayings and twelve parables, pp. 22, 28, 36, 39, 44, 46, 48, 53 for the eight sayings, p. 66 for the seven photodramatic parables, chaps. 8-12 for the five phonodramatic parables, pp. 225-40 for the reconstructed, original versions of this material.

1. Three kingdom sayings (Luke 11:20; 17:20-21; Matthew 11:12).

2. The Lord's Prayer in a version close to Luke 11:2-4.

3. The proverbial sayings. Mark 3:27; 3:24-26; 8:35; Luke 9:62; Mark 10: 23b, 25; Luke 9:60a; Matthew 7:13-14; Mark 10:31; 7:15; 10:15; Luke 14:11 (cf. 16:15); Matthew 5:39b-41; 5:44-48.

4. The major parables:

> The Hid Treasure and the Pearl, Matthew 13:44-46.
> The Lost Sheep, Lost Coin, Lost (Prodigal) Son, Luke 15:3-32.
> The Great Supper, Matthew 22:1-14; Luke 14:16-24; Gospel of Thomas 92:10-35.
> The Unjust Steward, Luke 16:1-9.
> The Workers in the Vineyard, Matthew 20:1-16.
> The Two Sons, Matthew 21:28-32.
> The Children in the Marketplace, Matthew 11:16-19.
> The Pharisee and the Tax Collector, Luke 18:9-14.
> The Good Samaritan, Luke 10:29-37.
> The Unmerciful Servant, Matthew 18:23-35.
> The Tower Builder and King Going to War, Luke 14:28-32.
> The Friend at Midnight, Luke 11:5-8.
> The Unjust Judge, Luke 18:1-8.
> The Leaven, Luke 13:20-21; Gos. Thom. 97:2-6.
> The Mustard Seed, Mark 4:30-32; Gos. Thom. 84:26-33.
> The Seed Growing by Itself, Mark 4:26-29; Gos. Thom. 85:15-19.
> The Sower, Mark 4:3-8; Gos. Thom. 82:3-13.
> The Wicked Tenants, Mark 12:1-12; Gos. Thom. 93:1-18..

There is no intention here to reduce or limit the teaching of Jesus to these, but such listings do indicate that there is a fairly extensive amount of agreed upon material which allows access to the message of Jesus the Teacher.

Jesus' teaching reflects knowledge of the Hebrew Scriptures, certainly the five books of the Law, the prophetic books, and the Psalms. He taught in many different circumstances to many different kinds of people: in synagogues, outside to crowds who had gathered, in chance encounters when challenged, in arguments with Jewish scribes, within the circle of his disciples. The varied audiences and occasions gave rise to some teaching which was more spontaneous repartee (Mk 2:17), and other teaching which was more considered, elaborate, part of a story (Lk 12:24-48; 17:26-30). Jesus used images when he taught, simile and analogy, which we note especially in his parables. C.H. Dodd speaks of the parables as "the most characteristic element in the teaching of Jesus."[6] Jesus sometimes taught with symbolic actions, as in washing the feet of his disciples, or by calling forth a child, putting his arms around the child, and teaching his disciples to be like children (Mk 9:35-37; Mt 18:1-7; Lk 9:46-48). Jesus' teaching was not hidden or secret. Although he taught the disciples, he taught crowds of people as well. His teaching was simple and frequently addressed to the less educated.

Jesus is specifically called "rabbi" four times in Mark (9:5; 10:51; 11:21; 14:45). The question is how this term was understood at the time of Jesus. It had not yet come to mean what it would later mean in post-70 C.E. Judaism after the triumph of Pharisaism. Originally the title meant "great one," or "my great one." In the time of Jesus it commonly referred to a religious teacher, but suggested nothing more, such as formal study or the later prescribed program of study. This is not to say that Jesus was not "learned" or even "scholarly" but that he was not necessarily formally educated. The expression simply indicates that Jesus was recognized as a teacher and as one having authority.[7]

---

[6]C.H. Dodd, *The Parables of the Kingdom*, revised edition (New York: Charles Scribner's Sons, 1961), 1. Also see T.W. Manson, *The Sayings of Jesus*, 32-35; Perrin, *Rediscovering the Teaching of Jesus*, 78.

[7]There is dispute over the degree to which Jesus, as teacher, was akin to other Jewish teachers, and to what degree *rabbi* indicates a parallel with them. Martin Hengel argues against using the term "rabbi" of Jesus, *The Charismatic Leader and His Followers*, trans. James Greig (New York: Crossroad, 1981), 42-50. "Jesus

In considering the teaching of Jesus, we shall consider (1) the parables, (2) the sayings, (3) Jesus' eschatological teaching, (4) Jesus' ethical teaching, (5) Jesus' teaching about discipleship, (6) Jesus' teaching concerning himself, and (7) the sapiential character of Jesus' teaching.

The Parables

The word parable in biblical scholarship is used in two senses. Within the general category of what are ordinarily considered parables, there are three types or forms: the similitude, the parable proper, and the example story. The similitude and parable proper are both considered metaphors. Both are stories. The similitude, however, narrates or describes typical, everyday occurrences, such as sowing, crops, harvests, a story describing an experience familiar to almost everyone. The parable proper operates with unusual rather than ordinary situations, events which are fictitious but still true to life. The image of a woman searching for a lost coin is a similitude; the story of the prodigal son and the forgiving father is a parable proper. All parables, in the general sense, have fairly standard beginnings, a statement indicating a story is to be told (Luke 10:30; 14:16; 15:11; 16:1; 16:19; 18:2; 18:10), or a question (Luke 15:8-9), or a question asking, "With what shall we compare . . .?" (Mark 4:30-31; Luke 13:20-21). In several instances it is difficult to classify a parable, but for most of the parables there is

was not at all like a scribe of the rabbinical stamp. Consequently to use the term 'rabbi' to give anything like a precise characterization of Jesus is extremely misleading" (42). "For reasons of clarity, therefore, we should desist altogether from the description of Jesus as a 'rabbi'" (50). Yet Hengel may be going too far in his effort to "distinguish" Jesus from the rabbis. Although Jesus was no rabbi in any technical sense, he was still a Palestinian Jewish teacher. For a critique of Hengel, see Viviano, *Study as Worship*, 13, 158-67. The NT references to Jesus as rabbi simply support further the depiction of Jesus as a teacher, one who taught, nothing more, nothing less, nor anything technical, nor anything less. Cf., Ferdinand Hahn, *The Titles of Jesus, Their History in Early Christianity*, trans. Harold Knight and George Ogg (London: Lutterworth Press, 1969), 73-89.

consensus: 12 similitudes, 16 or 17 parables proper, 4 example stories —32 or 33 parables in all in the Synoptic Gospels.[8]

Few topics in biblical research have evoked as much scholarly activity as that on the parables. At the end of the nineteenth century, Adolf Jülicher inaugurated a new era in parable interpretation by discarding the allegorical

[8]Note Perrin's comment in *Jesus and the Language of the Kingdom*, 167. Crossan has convinced Perrin that the story of the good Samaritan is a parable proper and not an example story, whereas in his earlier *Rediscovering the Teaching of Jesus*, 123, Perrin considered it an example story. Madeleine Boucher, *The Parables*, New Testament Message 7 (Wilmington, Del: Michael Glazier, 1981), 154, considers it an example story.

Granted that there will be some differences in classification, Boucher, *The Parables*, 153-57, classifies them as follows (those italicized are those listed among the clearly authentic material of Jesus by Perrin).

Twelve similitudes: *The Growing Seed* (Mk 4:26-29); *The Mustard Seed* (Mk 4:30-32; Mt 13:31-32; Lk 13:18-19); The Two Builders (Mt 7:24-27; Lk 6:47-49); *The Leaven* (Mt 13:33; Lk 13:20-21); The Fishnet (Mt 13:47-50); *The Lost Sheep* (Mt 18:12-14; Lk 15:3-7); The Faithful or Unfaithful Servant (Mt 24:45-51; Lk 12:42-46); *The Friend at Midnight* (Lk 11:5-8); *The Tower Builder* (Lk 14:28-30); *The Warring King* (Lk 14:31-32); The Lost Coin (Lk 15:8-10); The Master and the Servant (Lk 17:7-10).

Sixteen or seventeen parables proper: *The Sower* (Mk 4:3-9, 14-20; Mt 13:3-9, 18-23; Lk 8:5-8, 11-15); *The Wicked Tenants* (Mk 12:1-11; Mt 21:33-43; Lk 20:9-18; The Weeds and the Wheat (Mt 13:24-30, 36-43); *The Treasure* (Mt 13:44); *The Pearl* (Mt 13:45-46); *The Unmerciful Servant* (Mt 18:23-25); *The Laborers in the Vineyard* (Mt 20:1-16); *The Two Sons* (Mt 21:28-32); *The Great Feast / Wedding Garment* (Mt 22:2-10, 11-14; Lk 14:15-24 could be considered as one or two); The Ten Maidens (Mt 25:1-13); The Talents, Pounds (Mt 25:14-30; Lk 19:11-27); The Two Debtors (Lk 7:41-43); The Barren Fig Tree (Lk 13:6-9); *The Prodigal Son* (Lk 15:11-32); *The Unjust Steward* (Lk 16:1-8); The Persistent Widow (Lk 18:1-8).

Four example stories: *The Good Samaritan* (Lk 10:29-37, note Crossan and Perrin consider this a parable proper); The Rich Fool (Lk 12:16-21); the Rich Man and Lazarus (Lk 16:19-31); The Pharisee and Tax Collector (Lk 18:9-14). One can also note that in Mark only four parables are found, two similitudes and two parables proper.

Nine parables are found only in Matthew, one similitude and eight parables proper.

Fourteen parables are found only in Luke, five similitudes, five parables, and four example stories. Only Luke contains example stories.

Six parables can be attributed to Q, four similitudes and two parables.

There are 32 or 33 parables altogether, depending upon whether one counts the Great Feast and Wedding Garment as one or two — 12 similitudes, 16 or 17 parables proper, 4 example stories. Not all of these are necessarily authentic parables of Jesus, but the majority are.

method.[9] Since his time it has become customary to distinguish between parable and allegory, although it is more precise to distinguish not parable from allegory but rather two contrasting methods of interpretation, the historical and allegorical. Since Jülicher parable interpretation has moved away from the allegorical method of interpretation.[10]

The contributions of C.H. Dodd's *Parables of the Kingdom* (1935) included raising awareness of the close relation-

[9]Adolf Julicher, *Die Gleichnisreden Jesu*, 2 vols. (Tubingen: J.C.B. Mohr, 1888-99). For a summary of Julicher's contribution, see Joachim Jeremias, *The Parables of Jesus*, trans. S.H. Hooke, revised edition (New York: Charles Scribner's Sons, 1963), 18-20; Norman Perrin, *Rediscovering the Teaching of Jesus*, 257; and *Jesus and the Language of the Kingdom*, 92-97. Perrin's *Jesus and the Language of the Kingdom*, 89-193, is probably the best introduction to the history of parable research from Julicher to the present.

[10]A word of caution is necessary with respect to the distinction between parable and allegory. Jeremias speaks precisely when he speaks of Julicher's contribution as being a discarding of "the allegorical method" or "allegorical interpretations," and when he himself discusses "allegorization" or the "allegorizing tendency" in the early Church, *The Parables of Jesus*, 18-19, 66-89. Perrin speaks less precisely when he simply uses the word allegory as equivalent of allegorical method of interpretation. Allegory, properly speaking, does not denote a literary form but a way of speaking, a figurative way, or a way of communicating or intending meaning, as he spoke in puns, or metaphors, or allegories. Puns, metaphors, and allegories are not literary forms. Parable does refer to a specific literary form. Thus it is better not to oppose parable and allegory as such, which means opposing a literary form and a way of speaking. A parable may or may not be allegorical; even if it is an allegory, however, this does not mean that one best arrives at its meaning by an allegorical method of interpretation, which is neither a literary form nor a way of speaking but a method of interpretation. Since Julicher we have realized that the "meaning" of a parable, even if it is an allegory, is not best "discovered" or "interpreted" by means of the allegorical method, or the flights of imagination to which that method is open. In other words, the parables (even those one may call allegories from a literary point of view) are better understood when interpreted historically, rather than allegorically.

Madeleine Boucher, *The Parables*, a very readable introduction to the parables, makes this point concerning parable and allegory, 25-31. Also see her *Mysterious Parable: A Literary Study* (Washington, D.C.: Catholic Biblical Association of America, 1977).

Reading both Perrin and Boucher, one ought keep in mind that allegory is being used in two different senses: Allegory = a mode of meaning (Boucher), thus a parable can have an allegorical mode of meaning, non-literal one; and allegory = method of interpretation (Perrin), and thus a parable is better grasped if it is interpreted in its historical setting and not allegorically. Both are correct. Hence it is better to speak of parable interpretation as discarding the allegorical method of interpretation.

ship between parable interpretation and our understanding of the kingdom or reign of God; the insistence that parables had to be interpreted within the historical context of the life of Jesus, the *Sitz im Leben Jesu*; "realized eschatology," the fact that the reign of God is not a future reality but present already in the preaching and ministry of Jesus; and a literary understanding of the parable in relationship to metaphor with the result that two types of metaphor were distinguished, the similitude and parable proper.[11]

Joachim Jeremias' *Parables of Jesus* (1947) was an epoch-making study which is still a starting point for further study of the parables.[12] Jeremias' contribution has been at the textual and historical levels. Jeremias attempted to reconstruct the parables so that we can have them in the form in which Jesus spoke them. The parables, as uttered by Jesus, have been transformed in the history of their transmission. As they have come down to us, they have two historical settings; the original historical setting within some specific situation in the life of Jesus, and subsequently, before they assumed written form, a setting in the primitive Church during which they were transformed. Jeremias gives ten specific principles of transformation in terms of which one can reconstruct or recover the original form and setting.[13]

---

[11]C.H. Dodd, *The Parables of the Kingdom* (New York: Scribner's, [1935, 1936] 1961).

[12]Joachim Jeremias, *The Parables of Jesus*, the second English edition, based upon the sixth German edition of 1962, first published in German in 1947 (New York: Charles Scribner's Sons, 1963). Also see his *Rediscovering the Parables* (New York: Charles Scribner's Sons, 1966), a revision of the earlier work in order to make it less technical and more readable for a wider audience. It meets well the needs of a beginning student.

[13]See *The Parables of Jesus*, 23-114, for these ten principles; also *Rediscovering the Parables*, 16-88. Pp. 113-14 (or 87-88 of the latter) list them as follows:

1. The translation of the parables into Greek involved an inevitable change in their meaning.

2. For the same reason representational material is occasionally "translated."

3. Pleasure in the embellishment of the parables is noticeable at an early date.

4. Occasionally passages of Scripture and folk-story themes have influenced the shaping of the material.

Modern parable interpretation has been conscious not only of historically situating and interpreting the parables, but has also been conscious of their literary character as well. The major contribution or impetus here has come from Amos Wilder.[14] Uniquely competent as both a literary critic and a New Testament scholar, Wilder has influenced a new generation of American scholars.[15] Wilder's contribution to parable research is literary: parable in relationship to metaphor and the nature of language. Wilder distinguishes the different kinds of parables: the example story, the simili-

5. Parables which were originally addressed to opponents or to the crowd have in many cases been applied by the primitive Church to the Christian community.

6. This led to an increasing shift of emphasis to the hortatory aspect, especially from the eschatological to the hortatory.

7. The primitive Church related the parables to its own actual situation, whose chief features were the missionary motive and the delay of the Parousia; it interpreted and expanded them with these factors in view.

8. To an increasing degree the primitive Church interpreted the parables allegorically with a view of the hortatory use.

9. The primitive Church made collections of parables, and fusion of parables took place.

10. The primitive Church provided the parables with a setting, and this often produced a change in the meaning; in particular, by the addition of generalizing conclusions, many parables acquired a universal meaning.

By way of contrast to Jeremias' reconstruction of the original form of the parables, see James Breech, *The Silence of Jesus*, 65-214, 229-40.

[14]Amos N. Wilder, *Early Christian Rhetoric, the Language of the Gospel*, revised edition (Cambridge: Harvard U. Press, [1964] 1971).

[15]E.g., Robert Funk, Dan Otto Via, John Dominic Crossan. See Robert W. Funk, *Language, Hermeneutic, and Word of God* (New York: Harper and Row, 1966); Dan O. Via, *The Parables: Their Literary and Existential Dimension* (Philadelphia: Fortress Press, 1967); John Dominic Crossan, *In Parables: the Challenge of the Historical Jesus* (New York: Harper and Row, 1973). For a summary, see Norman Perrin, *Jesus and the Language of the Kingdom*, 132-168. Funk contributes further to our understanding of parable as metaphor and makes a contribution toward understanding metaphor itself. Both parable and metaphor draw the listener into them as a participant. Via presents four criticisms of an approach to the parables which is overly historical: the nature of the gospel material makes it difficult to pinpoint a *Sitz im Leben Jesu*; a severely historical approach can easily end up speaking to a past historical situation rather than to the present; the historical approach can neglect the aesthetic character of the parables. Via himself concentrates especially on two aspects of the parable, the aesthetic and the existential, two dimensions less emphasized in previous research. Crossan

tude, and the parable proper. Some parables are straight narratives which end with an application. These are example stories: go and do not do likewise, as in the story of the rich man and Lazarus. Other parables are images which reveal rather than exemplify: the similitudes and parables proper. Wilder emphasizes the revelatory character of these parables. They are metaphors, implied comparisons, in contrast to similes. They shock the imagination into realization. The simile can clarify but the metaphor reveals. The similitude is a metaphor, and the parable proper, an extended metaphor.

Jesus' parables speak of the reign of God.[16] The parables as metaphors function in order that the language of the kingdom, the metaphor of the kingdom, can evoke the myth of God acting as King on behalf of the people.[17] Edward Schillebeeckx describes the function of the parable:

> The fact is, a parable turns around a "scandalizing" centre, at any rate a core of paradox and novelty. A parable often stands things on their head; it is meant to break through our conventional thinking and being. A parable is meant to start the listener thinking by means of a

distinguishes between parable and allegory on the basis of a distinction between symbol and allegory, i.e., a distinction between the inexpressible and the expressible. Parables are like symbols in trying to express the inexpressible and thus are not reducible to clear language. The kind of figurative language found in parables does not simply illustrate information but creates a participation that precedes information.

[16]Norman Perrin has contributed three significant works to our understanding of the reign of God, in which he brings the interpretation of the kingdom into conjunction with the history of parable interpretation. *The Kingdom of God in the Teaching of Jesus* (London: SCM Press, 1963), one of the better summaries of the modern discussion on this topic; *Rediscovering the Teaching of Jesus* (New York: Harper and Row, 1957), an exegesis of significant texts pertinent both to the kingdom of God and to the teaching of Jesus; *Jesus and the Language of the Kingdom* (Philadelphia: Fortress Press, 1976), a study of symbol and metaphor in their relationship to Jesus' teaching on the kingdom and Jesus' teaching in parables, containing critique and revision with respect to his earlier studies.

[17]Perrin, *Jesus and the Language of the Kingdom*, 33, speaks about the kingdom as a symbol, not a conception or idea. It is more correct to speak about the kingdom as a metaphor, but Perrin has drawn attention to the symbolic language with which Jesus speaks when he speaks about the reign of God.

built-in element of the "surprising" and the "alienating" in a common, everyday event. It is not every night that one is hauled out of bed to help a needy stranger in dire straits; and you are not continually losing a sheep or a coin. It never happens at all to a good many of us. And yet in the parable I am confronted with it, here and now. The parable obliges me to go on thinking about it. Parables are "teasers." The familiar event is set against an unfamiliar background, and in that way what is commonplace becomes a stimulating challenge. It gives us a jolt.[18]

C.H. Dodd's definition of the parable still remains unsurpassed: "The parable is a metaphor or simile drawn from nature or common life, arresting the hearer by its vividness or strangeness, and leaving the mind in sufficient doubt about its precise application to tease it into active thought."[19] The parables reveal Jesus as a master storyteller, and our study of the content of the parables reveals something to which we concluded earlier in our search for the self-understanding of Jesus: the parables are not about himself, but about God.

One of the most striking characteristics of Jesus' core sayings and parables is that he remained basically silent about himself. Only two of the core sayings make any reference to Jesus, the saying that states he came eating and drinking, and the one that indicates he liberated persons from the demonic. Nor did Jesus tell stories about himself. In that respect, he is the opposite of most contemporary storytellers who say, "An interesting thing *happened to me* on the way to . . . ." Jesus does not organize his experience in the re-active mode, in terms of what happens *to* him. Rather, the perspective that comes

---

[18]Schillebeeckx, *Jesus, an Experiment in Christology*, trans. Hubert Hoskins (New York: Seabury Press, 1979), 156-7.

[19]C.H. Dodd, *The Parables of the Kingdom*, 5. This definition is also the starting point for Robert Funk. See the chapter, "The Parable as Metaphor," in his *Language, Hermeneutic, and Word of God*. For Boucher's definition, see *The Parables*, 14-17.

through in all of his parables is that of someone who is intensely observant of what happens in human life, quite apart from any reference to his own ego.[20]

The word parable in Greek, *parabolē* (Hebrew, *māshāl*) was not restricted historically or biblically as it is today. It referred to various forms of figurative speech. The New Testament uses *parabolē* when speaking of a comparison (Mk 3:23; 13:28-29; Lk 5:36), a proverb (Lk 4:23; 6:39), a wisdom saying (Mk 7:15), a riddle (Mk 7:17), a symbol (Heb 9:9; 11:19), as well as the examples, similitudes, and parables proper to which we apply the expression.

The Sayings of Jesus

In addition to the parables through which we have access to the teaching of the earthly Jesus, we also have a tradition of Jesus' sayings from which the Gospel writers later drew. Individual sayings of Jesus as well as collections were handed down orally but reliably.[21] Some of these may have been isolated sayings or proverbs which were remembered and later found their place in the Gospels. Some may have been gathered together early for catechetical purposes and formed into a collection which the evangelists could take over either in whole or in part. Some are sayings which have not been incorporated into the canonical writings. Luke 11:14-26 is an example of a collection of sayings within his Gospel. Whether or not it existed as a collection before Luke or was formulated by Luke we do not know. Verses 17-20 are a collection which provide a response to the charge that Jesus casts our devils by diabolical power. Verses 21-26 —other sayings concerning possession and exorcism — get "tagged on" by way of association.

---

[20]James Breech, *The Silence of Jesus*, 217. See 213-22.

[21]For some discussion of the Jesus tradition prior to the written Gospels, see T.W. Manson, *The Sayings of Jesus*, 11-15; Joachim Jeremias, *New Testament Theology*, 1-37; and Birger Gerhardsson, *Memory and Manuscript* (Lund: C.W.K. Gleerup, 1964), and *Tradition and Transmission in Early Christianity* (Lund: C.W.K. Gleerup, 1964).

Not all the sayings attributed to Jesus in the Synoptic Gospels are authentic sayings of Jesus (*ipsissima verba Jesu*). The tendency to distinguish between Jesus (in history) and the Christ (Jesus as raised from the dead and proclaimed by the Church) is modern. Early Christian communities did not so distinguish but identified the Risen Lord with Jesus. Nevertheless, scholars have been able to identify some sayings as clearly pre-resurrection utterances of Jesus.

Within the material that scholars ordinarily recognize as authentic Jesus material, even from a minimalist point of view, in addition to the "Our Father" and the majority of the parables, are a number of sayings of Jesus. Perrin includes the three sayings concerning the kingdom (Lk 11:20; 17:20-21; Mt 11:12) as well as fourteen proverbial sayings (Mk 3:24-26; 3:27; 7:15; 8:35; 10:15; 10:23b; 10:31; Lk 9:60a; 9:62; 10:15; 14:11; Mt 5:39b-41; 5:44-48; 7:13-14).[22]

In addition to the authentic sayings of Jesus which we find woven into the Gospels, there are also sayings of Jesus which have not been recorded in the four Gospels, the "agrapha" or so-called unwritten sayings of Jesus.[23] Research into this particular Jesus material dates only from 1889 and was stimulated by the discovery of the Oxyrhynchus papyri and especially the Coptic Gospel of Thomas. The Gospel of Thomas includes the parable of the great fish which is recognized by some as an authentic parable of Jesus and considered by John Dominic Crossan as one of three key parables.[24] The majority of the agrapha are not authentic sayings of Jesus however.

[22]Perrin, *Jesus and the Language of the Kingdom*, 41. Keep in mind that this is a minimum. One ought not quickly identify the teaching of Jesus or even the authentic sayings of Jesus with lists such as these. The sayings simply exemplify the proverbial teaching of Jesus and represent a case for which there is some consensus. I am not suggesting that the *ipsissima verba Jesu* be reduced to these.

[23]Joachim Jeremias, *Unknown Sayings of Jesus* (London: SPCK, 1964), for a discussion of the sources for the agrapha, the varied types of material that they comprise, and the eighteen which Jeremias considers as deserving of attention. Also see *The Gospel According to Thomas, Coptic Text Established and Translated*, by A. Guillaumont, Puech, et al. (New York: Harper and Row, 1959).

[24]John Dominic Crossan, *In Parables: The Challenge of the Historical Jesus* (New York: Harper and Row, 1973), 34.

A good example of the proverbial type sayings of Jesus are the beatitudes.[25] They are found in both Matthew and Luke. Luke includes four beatitudes (6:20-23) and four corresponding woes or curses (6:24-26), which woes are more likely Lucan additions. Matthew has nine beatitudes (5:3-11). The specific verses from Q are Luke 20b-23 (// Mt 5:3, 4, 6, 11-12), four beatitudes which are authentic Jesus material. The other five beatitudes of Matthew are Matthean additions (the meek, the merciful, the pure of heart, the peacemakers, the persecuted for righteousness sake). The four beatitudes which can assuredly be considered as coming from Jesus are:

> Blessed are you poor, for yours is the kingdom of God. Blessed are you that hunger now, for you shall be satisfied. Blessed are you that weep now, for you shall laugh. Blessed are you when people hate you, and when they exclude you or revile you, and cast out your name as evil, on account of the son of humanity! (Lk 6:20-22)

Of these four beatitudes, the first three form one unit, as the parallelism indicates. Manson writes, "The fourth beatitude should almost certainly be assigned to a late date in the ministry. It differs in tone from the other three."[26] Each of the beatitudes may have been uttered at different times and the first three joined together later, but prior to Q. Or the first three may have been uttered as a unit by Jesus and preserved together with the fourth being joined to them later. These are not the only beatitudes of Jesus or at least

[25]For bibliography pertinent to the beatitudes, one can see any major commentary on Matthew 5 or Luke 6, particularly Joseph Fitzmyer, *Luke, I-IX*, 645-46; and F.W. Beare, *The Gospel According to Matthew* (New York: Harper and Row, 1981), 125-38. Also see the bibliography in Fitzmyer, *Luke, I-IX*, 645-46. Helpful material can also be found in Joachim Jeremias, *New Testament Theology*, 109-13, 141-51; T.W. Manson, *The Sayings of Jesus*, 46-49, 150-64; Edward Schillebeeckx, *Jesus*, 172-79. An excellent specialized study is Jacques Dupont, *Les béatitudes*, 3 vols. (Paris: J. Gabalda, 1958, 1969, 1973). For the secondary character of the Lucan woes, see Dupont, vol. 1, 299-342; Fitzmyer, *Luke, I-IX*, 627.

[26]Manson, *The Sayings of Jesus*, 47.

not the only ones attributed to him (see Lk 1:45; 7:23; 10:23; 11:27-28; 12:37, 38, 43; 14:14-15; 23:29).

Since we do not know the actual setting in the life of Jesus when the beatitudes may have been uttered, it is difficult to know the audience to whom they were addressed. Matthew suggests the presence of a crowd but also implies that Jesus may have been speaking more directly to the disciples (Mt 5:1-2). Luke presents Jesus speaking to the disciples (Lk 6:20); yet the crowd is in the background (6:19) and Jesus seems to include them (6:27). There is not sufficient reason to conclude that Jesus was thinking only of his disciples as he spoke. Let us look at the four beatitudes of Jesus which come from Q.

"Blessed are you poor, for yours is the kingdom of God" (6:20). Matthew's version runs, "Blessed are the poor in spirit, for theirs is the kingdom of heaven" (5:3). The Gospel of Thomas also contains the beatitude, "Blessed are the poor, for yours is the kingdom of heaven" (54). There is dispute about whether the Lucan second person or the Matthean third person is more authentic.[27] The Lucan "poor" is more original than the Matthean "poor in spirit" which represents interpretation and generalization. The Gospel of Thomas is closer to Luke, although it reflects the Matthean "kingdom of heaven" in contrast to the Lucan "kingdom of God."

Who are the poor? We cannot be too definitive in responding.[28] The reference is not exclusively to the economically poor, but to the needy, both the socially ostracized and economically disadvantaged. We ought not interpret the expression too spiritually, as Matthew's interpretation may tempt us to do. It was used by Jesus to refer to the actual and concrete poor as well as to social outcasts. Luke's version, the more original, is frank in that respect.

[27]T.W. Manson opts for the second person, *The Sayings of Jesus*, 47.

[28]For particularly good discussions of the poor, see Jeremias, *New Testament Theology*, 108-13; and Schillebeeckx, *Jesus*, 172-78. Also see Bruce J. Molina, *The New Testament World, Insights from Cultural Anthropology* (Atlanta: John Knox Press, 1981), 71-93.

Luke has in mind the poor in contrast to the rich. The corresponding woe makes this clear ("Woe to you that are rich," 6:24). Yet the woe is not original as the beatitude is. So while it helps us to understand Luke's interpretation in contrast to Matthew's, it does not help us understand Jesus. Yet, if we look at the next two beatitudes, those who hunger and those who weep, we do see how Jesus spoke to those who were actually, physically, humanly needy.

It is helpful to imagine the concrete group which Jesus addressed. Both the texts of Matthew and Luke make particular references to the disciples. In the prayer which Jesus taught his disciples, he taught them to pray for bread. Many had left everything to follow him. Poverty, hunger, sadness, and ostracism must have affected his disciples in different ways at different times. Yet, in spite of these conditions and the cost of discipleship, Jesus considered them fortunate. In addition, Jesus spoke to the crowds who so often followed him. They were composed of publicans, sinners, the uneducated and backward, the socially disreputable, the sick, those possessed by demons, children, women. They were living in economic poverty as well as without status in society. To these "poor" Jesus had come to proclaim the good news of the reign of God.

Luke interprets Jesus as having taken as a mandate from the Lord the text of the prophet Isaiah (Lk 4:18-19).

> The Spirit of the Lord God is upon me,
>   because the Lord has anointed me
> to bring good tidings to the afflicted;
>   he has sent me to bind up the brokenhearted,
> to proclaim liberty to the captives,
>   and the opening of the prison to those who are bound;
> to proclaim the year of the Lord's favor,
>   and the day of vengeance of our God;
>   to comfort all who mourn;
> to grant to those who mourn in Zion—
>   to give them a garland instead of ashes,
> the oil of gladness instead of mourning,
>   the mantle of praise instead of a faint spirit;

that they may be called oaks of righteousness,
   the planting of the Lord, that he may be glorified. (Is
   61:1-3)

Commentators generally recognize Isaiah 61:1-3 as lying
behind Luke's first beatitude, and hence as lying behind the
teaching of Jesus as well. Whether or not Jesus actually
inaugurated his mission by reference to the text from Isaiah,
the text is still reflected in the teaching of Jesus. This same
Isaian text is the key text reflecting prophetic/Isaian ampli-
fication of the Jubilee proclamation and thus of a Jubilee
motif in the teaching of Jesus as well.[29] The beatitudes
reflect Jesus' sense of mission. "The poor" is being used in a
sense wider than the economically poor, including existential and social need. Jesus addressed both the outcasts of
society and also his disciples who were more and more being
identified in their solidarity with the poor. Grant the reality,
yet fortunate are these poor. The reign of God is theirs.
What appeared as a paradox was in fact an eschatological
reversal to be expected in the course of history. The closer
God's reign, the less the prevailing set of values would hold.
Jesus emerged again as a prophet of hope and compassion
whose heart and message reached out to the people. Jesus
was for others, for the poor.
   "Blessed are you that hunger now, for you shall be satisfied" (Luke 6:21a). Matthew's version: "Blessed are those
who hunger and thirst for righteousness, for they shall be
satisfied" (5:6). The Gospel of Thomas: "Blessed are the
hungry, for the belly of him who desires shall be filled"(69).
   Again, the beatitude looks toward those immediately and
urgently in need. Satisfaction, a reversal of the course of

---

[29]The most recent, thorough study of this Jubilee motif in the teaching of Jesus is
Sharon Hilda Ringe's *Jubilee Proclamation in the Ministry and Teaching of Jesus:
A Tradition — Critical Study in the Synoptic Gospels and Acts* (Ann Arbor,
Mich.: University Microfilms International, 1981), a doctoral dissertation. Pp.
180-88 for a consideration of the beatitudes. Ringe concludes that Jubilee *themes*
are present in the teaching of Jesus, although there is no evidence that Jesus
consciously presented a Jubilee program as part of his mission. Jesus' message was
in fact but not necessarily *in intent* a Jubilee message.

events, is not far off. The hungry shall not go hungry much longer. The expression "reign of God" is found only in the first beatitude, yet there persists the eschatological character of the blessings. This one is reminiscent of the theme of the eschatological banquet (Is 25:6-8; 49:10-13; Ps 107:1-9; Lk 12:37; 13:29; 14:14-15, 16-24).

"Blessed are you that weep now, for you shall laugh" (Luke 6:21b). Matthew: "Blessed are those who mourn, for they shall be comforted" (5:4). It is difficult to say which version may be more original. The saying carries with it the flavor of those who mourn social oppression — the sadness of the poor and the hungry, as well as the sorrow over the pains of discipleship and the rejection which accompanies it, and grief for whatever cause. As in the second beatitude, the verb is future. Yet the words are "shall laugh shortly." The reversal is close at hand; there is reason for hope. The reversal is not associated with future life but with the coming reign of God here on earth.

The reversal here anticipates days of laughter or comfort. Both are plausible originals and have particular meaning. The weeping and laughter is reminiscent of the captives of Babylon.

> By the waters of Babylon, there we sat down and wept, when we remembered Zion. (Psalm 137:1)

> When the Lord restored the fortunes of Zion, we were like those who dream. Then our mouth was filled with laughter, and our tongue with shouts of joy; then they said among the nations, "The Lord has done great things for them." The Lord has done great things for us; we are glad. Restore our fortunes, O Lord, like the watercourses in the Negeb. (Psalm 126:1-4)

Jewish history knew how the course of events could be reversed, and such a reversal was again anticipated in the teaching of Jesus. Those who are weeping shall soon laugh.

Joy is obviously a sign of the presence of God. We can call to
mind the comfort for the exiles anticipated by Deutero-
Isaiah (61:2). This joy as a sign of the reign of God leads
Schillebeeckx to comment, "Laughter, not crying, is the
deepest purpose that God wills for humanity. That means
therefore that he does not in any case will suffering. On no
account is Jesus prepared to shift suffering and evil on to
God."[30] God wills laughter, and is a God of joy.

As one looks at the three beatitudes that Jesus would have
spoken to the crowd, one finds in them both a reflection of
his image of God and his desire to express a word of consolation to the people. Evidently, when God reigns on earth,
our stomachs will be full and there will be laughter and joy.
Only the first beatitude is expressed as "the reign of God is
yours." Yet the next two imply that same reign, and when
God rules on earth there will be neither hunger nor tears.
Jesus' God is one who will banish both.

The expression *reign of God* is best interpreted as a
Jewish (targumic) circumlocutional way of speaking. The
Greek expressions *hē basileia toū theoū* and *hē basileia toū
ouranoū* (in Hebrew *malkūt shāmayim*) are better translated as reign of God and reign of heaven than as kingdom of
God. The latter connotes more easily a territory ruled
whereas the emphasis is on God, but on God as reigning or
present. In Jesus' usage, the expression does not carry the
apocalyptic sense of a catastrophic cosmic event, but is
rather Jesus' way of speaking, rooted in the metaphor of
God as king. It is a characteristic way of speaking for Jesus
(*ipsissima vox*), a circumlocutional or reverent way of
speaking about God, connoting God as near, present, or
coming. The most direct sense of the expression can sometimes be gained simply by using the word God. "Reign of
God" was not an apocalyptic or eschatological concept; it
was *a way of speaking about God*. The reign of God is God.

[30]Schillebeeckx, *Jesus*, 178. Also see Perrin, *Rediscovering the Teaching*, 87-90.

This usage is not peculiar to Jesus but reflects targumic usage as well.[31]

The targums (Aramaic paraphrases of the Hebrew Bible necessitated by the inability of many Jews to understand the Hebrew) on the prophets show close parallels to Jesus' usage. For example, the Hebrew text of Zechariah 14:9a, "And the Lord will become king over all the earth," is translated or paraphrased in the Zechariah Targum as "and the kingdom of the Lord will be revealed upon all the dwellers of the earth." In the Isaiah Targum, the proclamation "Behold your God!" (Is 40:9) is translated as "the reign of your God is revealed"; and "Your God reigns" (Is 52:7) as "the reign of your God is revealed."[32] As we can see, the kingdom or reign *is* God. Jesus' usage parallels that of the Isaiah Targum, a way of speaking about God.

Understanding Jesus' usage properly makes outmoded many of the discussions about whether the kingdom was present or future in the teaching of Jesus, for God is both here and coming. God cannot be confined within temporal categories.

As to the question whether Jesus himself would have used the expression as we have it in Mark and Luke (the reign of God) or as we have it in Matthew (the reign of heaven), Rudolf Schnackenburg suggests that it was probably Matthew who altered the expression for his Jewish Christian community.[33] On the other hand, Gustav Dalman suggested that Mark and Luke avoided the characteristically Jewish

[31]See especially Bruce David Chilton, "Regnum Dei Deus Est," *Scottish Journal of Theology* 31 (1978), 261-70; *God in Strength: Jesus' Announcement of the Kingdom* (Linz: Plochl, 1979), 277-98. Also Bruce Chilton, ed., *The Kingdom of God in the Teaching of Jesus*, Issues in Religion and Theology, 5 (Philadelphia: Fortress Press, 1984), esp. 22-26, 121-32. Also see Dodd, *The Parables of the Kingdom*, 21-29. Valuable discussions pertinent to the history of the interpretation of the kingdom include G. Lundstrom, *The Kingdom of God in the Teaching of Jesus: A History of Interpretation from the Last Decades of the Nineteenth Century to the Present Day* (Edinburgh: Oliver and Boyd, 1963); Norman Perrin, *The Kingdom of God in the Teaching of Jesus*; and Jacques Schlosser, *Le Regne de Dieu dans les dits de Jesus*, 2 vols. (Paris: J. Gabalda, 1980).

[32]Chilton, "Regnum Dei Deus Est," 264-67.

[33]Rudolf Schnackenburg, *God's Rule and Kingdom*, trans. John Murray (New York: Herder and Herder, 1963), 80.

expression (reign of heaven) out of regard for their Gentile audiences.[34] It may be a difficult question to decide, but again targumic references would suggest reign of God as the expression more likely for Jesus to use.[35]

In the Hebrew Scriptures, it is God's name or glory which dwells with the people, never God Himself. So with respect to Jesus' use of the language of the kingdom, it is God-talk. Jesus is saying: Blessed are you, for God is yours.

We can picture the crowds composed of the poor, the hungry, the sad, the sick, the lame, the outcasts, the uneducated, the unclean. What could Jesus say to them that might have been a word of consolation? Nothing would have taken away their poverty, their sadness; no words were going to feed or clothe them. Yet the heart of the compassionate Jesus reached out to them. What could he have said? He knew how his heavenly Father's love reached out to them as well. And so he said all that he could say: God is yours. The message did not remove the poverty or hunger or pain. And yet it was a word of consolation. And it expressed one of the fundamental religious insights in the teaching of Jesus: GOD BELONGS TO THE PEOPLE. Nothing can separate them from God's love. They may fall outside the realm of the Law or social acceptability but they do not fall outside the realm of God. God belongs to *them*.

The first three beatitudes form a unit. The fourth may well have come from another point in the ministry of Jesus and may reflect a consciousness on the part of Jesus of his own anticipated fate, of the growing divisiveness that his ministry was causing, of the rejection which accompanied the prophets of old, and the ostracization which was "outlawing" his most ardent disciples and leading to their being identified with "the poor." The fourth beatitude seems to have had his disciples particularly in mind.

"Blessed are you when people hate you, and when they exclude you and revile you, and cast out your name as evil, on account of the son of humanity! Rejoice in that day, and

---

[34]Gustaf Dalman, *The Words of Jesus* (Edinburgh: T&T Clark, 1902), 93, also see 189.

[35]Chilton, "Regnum Dei Deus Est," 264.

leap for joy, for behold, your reward is great in heaven; for so their fathers did to the prophets" (Lk 6:22-23). Matthew: "Blessed are you when people revile you and persecute you and utter all kinds of evil against you falsely on my account. Rejoice and be glad, for your reward is great in heaven, for so people persecuted the prophets who were before you" (5:11-12). The Gospel of Thomas: "Blessed are you when you are hated and persecuted, and no place shall be found there where you have been persecuted. . . Blessed are they who have been persecuted in their heart; these are they who have known the Father in truth" (68, 69a).

In the first beatitude, (the reign of) God was present at hand; the verb is present tense. In the second and third beatitudes, the verbs are future. The anticipated reversal was still to come but eagerly anticipated. The fact, however, that the full strength of God was not immediately present was reflected in this fourth beatitude. A time of persecution was still to come before the reversal. The disciples were to be ready for opposition and rejection. Luke mentions four elements of the rejection to come: hatred, ostracization, discrimination, and vilification of one's name. Matthew mentions three: discrimination, persecution, false and evil lies. All this is to be endured for Jesus' sake.

The opposition and rejection were not to be feared, however, but are in fact cause for joy. Manson writes, "It is a proof that those who endure it stand in the succession of the great servants of God in past ages, who received like treatment in their day. Moreover, it is only for a time. The fulfillment of God's purpose is sure, and in that consummation God's servants will find their reward with joy."[36] Obviously, Jesus saw his disciples as also having to play a prophetic role like unto his own.

Having examined these four sayings of Jesus, we can make four observations about the teaching of Jesus as a whole. (1) Jesus' consciousness and teaching reflected an eschatological awareness. This is manifest in the prayer

---

[36]Manson, *The Sayings of Jesus*, 48.

Jesus taught his disciples, in the parables, in the particular kingdom sayings as well as in the eschatological consciousness reflected in the beatitudes. (2) Jesus' love for the poor and the outcast was reflected in the special place they occupy in his ministry. The prophets of old spoke out against injustice. He came to preach good news to the downtrodden. He healed the sick. He was conscious of the hungry even in his prayer. His teaching reflected an ethic of love of neighbor. This ethical concern is reflected in the beatitudes as is Jesus' eschatological awareness. (3) Jesus was also clearly teaching his disciples about discipleship, both its joy and its pain. (4) We must be careful not to read more into these four sayings, but we can note that Jesus said something about himself as well, about his own experience, fear, hunger, rejection, hope, joy, as well as the fate which lay ahead. These four "areas" fairly well represent the concerns of the Teacher.

The Eschatological Teaching of Jesus

The reign of God was central to the consciousness, ministry, preaching and teaching of Jesus. His heavenly Father's closeness formed the horizon within which Jesus lived and preached. There is no denying the centrality of God's reign as the prominent element in the authentic sayings of Jesus, in the parables, in the beatitudes, and in the prayer he taught.

The reign of God was primarily a way of speaking, one of Jesus' ways of speaking about God, about God in relationship to humankind, a circumlocutional, periphrastic way of speaking.[37] In the end, the reign of God *is* God, God as near, or as coming in strength, or as ruling, but still God. Talk about the reign of heaven or reign of God was simply Jesus' way of talking about God, but God in relationship to us, God under the aspect of his power, God as active in our

[37]See n. 31 of this chapter.

history, God as reigning on earth as in heaven — the Israelite notion of the Lord as King. The reign of God does not denote a kingdom of God as much as the sovereignty of a God who is acting in history on our behalf. The earth is subject to the sovereignty of God, the reign of God. Thy kingdom come: may thy reign come even more completely, may Thy power manifest itself and may it rule on earth, may Thy sovereignty be recognized and acknowledged on earth and Thy name held holy. God's reign is his rule, his power, his presence, his glory; it is *God as present* to his people.

In the time of Jesus, however, for many, the activity and power and presence of God was especially associated with the future, with the eschatological times, with the Day of the Lord. Thus (the reign of) God, for Jesus, was still to come. The reign of God not only evoked the image of God acting sovereignly on behalf of the people but that sovereignty as it would soon be established on earth. The reign was envisioned as an eschatological reign, the coming times when God would rule as sovereign on earth.

Three sayings in particular help us understand Jesus' teaching on the reign of God.

> 1. But if it is by the finger of God that I cast out demons, then the kingdom of God has come upon you.
> (Luke 11:20)

This saying comes from Q, has its parallel in Matthew 12:28, and is an authentic saying of Jesus. The Lucan form is the more original. The saying is an interpretation by Jesus of his exorcisms based on Exodus 8:15-19, which discloses Jesus' view that the reign of God, namely, God, was already present and manifest, at least in Jesus and his ministry, and in particular in the exorcisms. It was by the power of God that Jesus cast out demons; the exorcisms were a manifestation of God's power. This power was active and present in the ministry of Jesus; thus (the power and reign of) God had come. Another aspect of this reign is that it was a victory over the power and reign of the Evil One. The exorcisms

show the power of God subduing the forces of evil. Jesus
was the one through whom (the power and reign of) God
was revealed.

2. Being asked by the Pharisees when the kingdom of God
was coming, he answered them, "The kingdom of God is
not coming with signs to be observed; nor will they say
'Lo, here it is!' or 'There!' for behold the kingdom of God
is in the midst of you."(Luke 17:20-21)

This saying of Jesus shows his rejection of a completely or
thoroughly apocalyptic understanding of the reign of God;
it was not to be accompanied by signs (in fact, the only sign
to be given was the sign of Jonah, as stated in Mt 12:39; 16:4;
Lk 11:29-32).[38] This is a clear statement not only of Jesus'
refusal to give signs, but of his own teaching that one will
not detect the coming of (the reign of) God by means of
signs. Other Synoptic passages witness to this refusal on the
part of Jesus: Matthew 12:39; 16:4; Luke 11:29-32; and
Mark 8:11-13.

The Pharisees came and began to argue with him, seeking
from him a sign from heaven, to test him. And he sighed
deeply in his spirit, and said, "Why does this generation
seek a sign? Truly, I say to you, no sign shall be given to
this generation. (Mark 8:11-12)

---

[38]Concerning the authenticity of this saying, see Perrin, *Rediscovering the
Teaching of Jesus*, 68-74; *Jesus and the Language of the Kingdom*, 41. See also
Richard Edwards, *The Sign of Jonah in the Theology of the Evangelists and Q*
(London: SCM Press, 1971). I argued earlier that Jesus was no apocalypticist,
certainly no typical apocalypticist, not denying of course some apocalyptic features. James D.G. Dunn, *Unity and Diversity in the New Testament, an Inquiry
into the Character of Earliest Christianity* (Philadelphia: Westminster Press,
1977), 318-22, suggests that there is an apocalyptic character to Jesus' eschatology,
although in important respects he differs from apocalypticism as well. Jesus'
rejection of historical determinism and accompanying signs is one non-apocalyptic
feature. Also see Robert Jewett, *Jesus Against the Rapture, Seven Unexpected
Prophecies* (Philadelphia: Westminster Press, 1979).

Whatever the full meaning of the signs Jesus refused to give, the sayings indicate that Jesus was not a typical apocalyptic seer.

> The apocalyptic understanding of history is presupposed in searching for signs of the end or calculating its coming, and in rejecting this approach in Luke 17:20f. Jesus is rejecting the understanding of history which it presupposes. The coming of the Kingdom cannot be calculated in advance, nor will it be accompanied by signs such as apocalyptic sought, because the Kingdom is the sovereign power of God breaking into history and human experience in a manner to be determined by God; it is not history moving inevitably to a climax predetermined in accordance with a divine plan to which apocalyptic seers have had access. In effect, we have in this saying a rejection of the apocalyptic understanding of history and a return to the prophetic understanding.[39]

The translation of *entos humōn* in Luke 17:21 has been much discussed, as to whether it is better translated as "within you" or "among you." Most exegetes today accept "among you" as more accurate. The question cannot be decided on linguistic grounds alone. Manson raised two considerations in support of "among you."[40] (1) The Pharisees were being addressed. Would Jesus have referred to the reign of God as being within them? (2) Jesus ordinarily spoke of people entering the reign of God, not the reign entering them. That people enter into it implies that it was in their midst and they could partake of it, participate in it.

> 3. From the days of John the Baptist until now the kingdom of heaven has suffered violence, and the violent take it by force. (Mt 11:12)

---

[39] Perrin, *The Kingdom of God in the Teaching of Jesus* (London: SCM Press, 1963), 177-78, also 174-78; *Rediscovering the Teaching of Jesus*, 72-73; *Jesus and the Language of the Kingdom*, 46.

[40] Manson, *The Sayings of Jesus*, 303-5.

> The law and the prophets were until John; since then the
> good news of the kingdom of God is preached, and every
> one enters it violently. (Lk 16:16)

Matthew's version is accepted by many scholars as closer to the original, although it is difficult to interpret. It suggests the idea that the reign of heaven had begun, indeed began with the ministry and mission of John, but that the reign still endured or suffered violence, and it was evidently not yet fully established. The saying also manifests both present and future aspects of the reign.

The tendency of the early Church was to denigrate the role of John and to consider him a forerunner of Jesus (Mk 9:11-13; Mt 11:14). That tendency does not exist in this saying which reflects a high regard for John and probably reflects the authentic attitude and teaching of Jesus (as do Mt 21:32; Mk 11:27-30). John is seen as present in the new age and is included within it. John marked the shift to a new era in history. Luke's version, which may reflect Lucan editing, makes this point even clearer, but the reality is in the Matthean version as well. From the time of John, (the reign of) God has been with us. Manson comments on the Lucan version thus: "The saying contrasts two periods in history: the period of the Law and prophets and the period of the Kingdom of God. The former is one of promise, the latter of fulfillment; and the ministry of the Baptist is the dividing line between the two."[41] In fact, the Baptist is on this side of the dividing line.

But, although the reign of God has been manifesting itself since the days of John, it still suffers violence (*biazetai*). *Biazetai* can be taken in two senses, as a passive or as a middle voice. As a middle voice, it would mean that it exercises force, shows its power, and thus means that since the time of John the reign of heaven has exercised power, the evidence for which one finds in both John and Jesus. If a passive, *biazetai* has more the sense in the translation

[41]Ibid., 134.

quoted: it suffers, endures violence. This translation would reflect the continuing assault against it by the reign of Satan which has not yet been overcome once and for all. It could well reflect the violent death of John himself, and the violence in store for Jesus and his disciples. This sense goes well with the latter portion of the verse; the violent and violence still snatch at or attack the reign of God which is not yet firmly established on earth in all its sovereignty.

There are eight points to make about Jesus' understanding of (the reign of) God.

1. *(The reign of) God is already here.* Whatever it was that Jesus perceived and which he proclaimed or whatever it was by which he had been grasped, it was already active and present. This aspect of the reign of God is apparent in the authentic sayings of Jesus as well as in many of the parables. C.H. Dodd's *Parables of the Kingdom* (1935) was the major exposition of realized eschatology.

> Whatever we make of them, the sayings which declare the Kingdom of God to have come are explicit and unequivocal. They are moreover the most characteristic and distinctive of the Gospel sayings on the subject. They have no parallel in Jewish teaching or prayers of the period. If therefore we are seeking the *differentia* of the teaching of Jesus upon the Kingdom of God, it is here that it must be found. This declaration that the Kingdom of God has already come necessarily dislocates the whole eschatological scheme in which its expected coming closes the long vista of the future. The *eschaton* has moved from the future to the present, from the sphere of expectation into that of realized experience. It is therefore unsafe to assume that the content of the idea, "The Kingdom of God," as Jesus meant it, may be filled in from the speculations of apocalyptic writers.[42]

However subsequently modified and refined, Dodd's position is still supported. "There is no going back from the recognition that this [the reign of God as present] is an emphasis truly to be found in the the teaching of Jesus concerning the Kingdom of God."[43]

Perrin summarizes the evidence for (the reign of) God as present in the teaching of Jesus as follows: (1) The presence of the reign is part of the message of the parables, in particular the hidden treasure and pearl (Mt 13:44-46), the tower builder and king going to war (Lk 14:28-33), the fig tree (Mk 13:28), and the lamp under the bushel (Mk 4:21). (2) Jesus consistently spoke of himself in eschatological terms (Mk 2:18-22). (3) Jesus applied to himself biblical prophecies which referred to the eschatological age (Mt 11:2-6 refers to Jesus as a fulfillment of Is 35:5; 61:1). (4) Jesus spoke of his ministry in terms which imply that the messianic times have begun (Mt 12:51). (5) The exorcisms manifest the kingdom's presence (Mt 12:28 // Lk 11:20).[44]

2. But, *there is still more to come.* Although (the reign of) God was a reality that was present on earth and in history, it was also a reality the fullness of which had not yet established or manifested itself. Johannes Weiss and Albert Schweitzer called attention to future eschatology in the teaching of Jesus; and, in spite of the work of C.H. Dodd, this futurity in the teaching of Jesus cannot be denied.[45] Today almost all scholars maintain that the reign of God in the teaching of Jesus is both present and future, both already here but not yet consummated. One of the greatest witnesses to Jesus' belief that the reign had not yet been fully established was the centrality of the petition, "Thy kingdom come," in the "Our Father," an authentic saying of Jesus (Lk

[43]Perrin, *The Kingdom of God in the Teaching of Jesus*, 78.

[44]Ibid., 74-78.

[45]For a summary of the emphases of Weiss and Schweitzer, see Perrin, *The Kingdom of God in the Teaching of Jesus*, 16-36. Also see Albert Schweitzer, *The Quest of the Historical Jesus, a Critical Study of Its Progress from Reimarus to Wrede*, trans. W. Montgomery (New York: Macmillan Co.,[1906] 1961), 223-241; Johannes Weiss, *Jesus' Proclamation of the Kingdom of God*, trans. and ed. R.H. Hiers and D.L. Holland (Philadelphia: Fortress Press, 1971). Perrin has summarized the evidence for the kingdom as a future reality in the teaching of Jesus. See *The Kingdom of God in the Teaching of Jesus*, 79-11, esp. 83-90.

11:2 // Mt 6:10), in which he prayed and taught his disciples to pray for *the coming* of the rule of God (also see Mk 1:15; 9:1).

Dodd's interpretation of the parables had established the "presentness" of the heavenly rule; Jeremias' interpretation emphasized (the reign of) God as both present *and* future.[46] According to Jeremias, the future element envisioned by Jesus involved *both an imminent catastrophe and a fulfillment.* Different biblical scholars attempt to identify the bipolarity in varied ways. Jeremias speaks of Jesus' teaching on the reign of God as "eschatology that is in the process of realization."[47] Kummel uses the language of "fulfillment" and "promise"; Jesus' presence in history was a fulfillment that came with the promise that what had begun would be brought to completion.[48] Cullmann speaks about "already" and "not yet"; the decisive battle had already been won, but the final day had not yet arrived.[49]

3. *A climactic event is imminent.* A new day was dawning. (The reign of) God in the teaching of Jesus was experienced both as a present reality and as a hope for the future. In addition to Jesus' hope for the future, there was also the expectation of a course of events that was imminent. A difficulty in this aspect of the teaching of Jesus is that almost all references to it are likely to be influenced by the expectation of the early Church, which not only followed from the teaching of Jesus but also from their experience of the resurrection and the gift of the Spirit. There is no way to excise their sense of imminence from the texts. So is there

[46]For the kingdom as present, see Jeremias, *The Parables of Jesus*, 115-24, on "Now Is the Day of Salvation," and 124-46 on "God's Mercy for Sinners." For the kingdom as future, see 146-60 on "The Great Assurance," and 160-69 on "The Imminence of Catastrophe."

[47]See Jeremias, *The Parables of Jesus*, 230.

[48]Werner Georg Kummel, *Promise and Fulfillment, The Eschatological Message of Jesus*, trans. Dorothea Barton, Studies in Biblical Theology (London: SCM Press, 1969), 141-55.

[49]Oscar Cullmann, *Christ and Time*, trans. Floyd Filson (London: SCM Press, 1962), 71-106; *Salvation in History*, (New York: Harper and Row, 1967).

any basis in the teaching of Jesus that he offered not only a future hope but also an expectation for something close at hand?

Jesus' preaching did have the note of urgency to it (something climactic soon to happen) but he did not teach an imminent parousia in the way that we ordinarily understand that expression (an end of chronological time, a second coming, or the end of history as we know it).[50] Jesus expected *something* to happen soon. As a support for this, one ought not rely upon the so called apocalyptic "son of humanity" sayings based upon Daniel 7:13 (namely, Mk 13:30; 14:62) since these are probably not authentic sayings of Jesus, or sayings in which the teaching of Jesus within them is recoverable. Once one does not rely upon these sayings, it is by no means clear that Jesus taught an imminent eschatology of an apocalyptic sort. Yet the tone of imminence in his authentic words is not absent either.

Jesus' preaching had an urgency to it. To a great degree this urgency reflected not an "imminent" but a "realized" eschatology: now is the time to respond while the word is being proclaimed. It became increasingly clear to Jesus that he would most probably die a violent death. The quality of urgency reflected not only Jesus' present challenge to the hearers but also that which would be even more true after his death. Even more so would people be called upon to be "for him" or "against him." That choice was already here for many, but that choice would soon be decisive, inevitable, and its time was close at hand. One of the climactic eschatological events which Jesus perceived as imminent was probably his own death and the crisis which would follow upon it.[51]

[50]For an excellent summary of the material on Jesus and his teaching about the future and his future expectation, see Perrin, *The Kingdom of God in the Teaching of Jesus*, 131-147, where he discusses the opinions of G.R. Beasley-Murray, O. Cullmann, T.F. Glasson, J.A.T. Robinson, and E. Grasser. For Perrin's own position see *The Kingdom of God in the Teaching of Jesus*, 190-201; *Rediscovering the Teaching of Jesus*, 154-206.

[51]Doubtless, Jesus taught that he would suffer a violent death. We ought not quickly set aside the opinion that what Jesus expected shortly was in fact his death,

But not only did Jesus' preaching carry with it something of the imminent (whether that be the decision for or against discipleship, or his death, or whatever) but the Jewish milieu was full of varied and inconsistent expectations with respect to the future. This does not imply that Jesus could not have or did not transcend them. In fact, I have argued that Jesus was no apocalypticist. Yet even the non-apocalyptic hope of Judaism was filled with eschatological expectation. Jesus' hope may not have been especially messianic (in the more dominant and obvious senses) or apocalyptic (in the more precise sense) but was still an expectation that the history of Israel and Judaism was soon to experience something climactic.

> The time is fulfilled, and the Kingdom of God is at hand; repent, and believe in the gospel. (Mark 1:15)

This saying is not simply expressing a realized eschatology. These present times already experience fulfillment; but the reign is not yet complete but close, at hand. Nor does the saying simply indicate future hope in general; rather it indicates the expectation of something imminent. Thus there are three elements in the teaching of Jesus: present (Mt 12:28), future (Mt 6:10), imminent (Mk 1:15). Even if Mark 1:15 and Matthew 10:7 are "summaries of the message of Jesus" developed in the Jesus tradition, as Perrin suggests, there is no reason to suggest anything less than accurate summaries.[52] They do not imply any developed doctrine of

resurrection, and the coming of the Spirit. See T.F. Glasson, *The Second Advent, the Origin of the New Testament Doctrine*, revised edition (London: Epworth Press, 1947). Dunn, *Unity and Diversity in the New Testament*, suggested that the resurrection of Jesus may have fulfilled his expectation, 211.

[52]See Perrin, *The Kingdom of God in the Teaching of Jesus*, 199-201. Perrin's argument is unconvincing to me here. If it is authentic, why must it be prior to his teaching on the presence and future of the kingdom? It is simply another aspect of the future expectation, and may even be later rather than earlier when Jesus has a more heightened consciousness of impending death. Also, in light of Perrin's later work in *Jesus and the Language*, I am wondering if Perrin himself would not perceive this as treating Jesus' use of the kingdom too much as a steno-symbol rather than a tensive symbol. Cf., A.L. Moore, *The Parousia in the New Testament* Leiden: E.J. Brill, 1966), 90.

parousia as a second coming. They simply reflect Jesus' expectation of something climactic and imminent. Perhaps at this point we ought to introduce the thesis of Marcus Borg: "What faced the hearers of Jesus was not the imminent and inevitable end of the world, but the imminent and yet contingent destruction of Israel."[53]

One of the difficulties in any discussion of Jesus' eschatology is that eschatology in its most precise sense played only a *minor* role in Jesus' teaching! If by eschatology we mean Jesus' teaching about the reign of God, there is no question but that (the reign of) God was the center of Jesus' proclamation and preaching. But if by eschatology we mean more precisely a teaching about the end times,[54] the end of history as we know it, then this *eschaton* is on the periphery of Jesus' teaching, which is not to deny that Jesus believed in resurrection from the dead and judgment. It is simply that Jesus' understanding of (the reign of) God was not apocalyptic, but prophetic in the old sense; *historically conscious*. Like the prophets of old, Jesus was able to read history and God.

The entire discussion on the temporal aspect of Jesus' eschatology (Jesus' doctrine on the reign of God; Jesus' doctrine of God) can be misplaced or over-emphasized.[55] If, as we have maintained, proper understanding of the language of the reign of God as metaphor indicates (as suggested by targumic usage) that the expression is *a way of speaking about God*, the emphasis is not then on a kingdom or reign (with its concomitant concerns about whether it has come or is still to come) but on God. The temporal questions became non-problematic, for God is here, near, and coming. Thus Jesus' teaching about God is not so much eschatological in the strict sense as it is theological, insightful, prophetic. This does not deny our three previous points in

[53]Marcus Borg, *Conflict, Holiness and Politics in the Teachings of Jesus* (New York: Edwin Mellen Press, 1984), 202.

[54]See my discussion of eschatology in chapter two. Also Borg, *Conflict, Holiness and Politics in the Teachings of Jesus*, 4-20.

[55]See in particular Bruce Chilton, *The Kingdom of God*, 1-26, and n. 31 of this chapter. Also Borg, *Conflict, Holiness and Politics in the Teachings of Jesus*, 4-20.

reference to Jesus' eschatology, but rather insists that they are not about some *thing* (a kingdom) but Someone (God). God is present: the one-who-is-with-us. But there is still more to hope for; God is the one-who-is-coming. And a dramatic manifestation of God (the one-who-is-coming-to-be-with-us) is imminent (and this may refer to Jesus' own resurrection and vindication, the outpouring of the Spirit, or the crisis facing Israel).

Thus the word "eschatology," as widely used, is on the verge of losing all meaning. It may be best to abandon it, and use other language to say what we mean. The eschatological teaching of Jesus is Jesus' teaching about the reign of God; that is to say, Jesus' teaching about God — a teaching experientially based and prophetically/biblically grounded.

To turn to a thesis of Marcus Borg and Gerd Theissen: the Jesus movement was essentially a renewal movement within Judaism.[56] Along with the Pharisees, Essenes, and resistance movement, the Jesus movement was one of many renewal movements competing for the loyalty of the people. The Jesus movement, and its program of renewal, were rooted in Jesus' conception and experience of God.

For Borg, other Jewish renewal movements were characterized by their quest for holiness, with holiness being interpreted as separation and purity. This post-exilic quest for holiness explains the emphasis on sabbath observance, proper tithing, racial purity, the emphasis on Torah and Temple. The Essene quest for holiness led to a separation *from* mainline Jewish society. The Pharisees' quest led to a separation *within* Jewish society, although theirs was envisioned as a program for all of Israel. Within the resistance movement, holiness required Judeans to structure their corporate lives unhindered by foreign occupation and oppression. Jesus' program for renewal must be understood within Israel's quest for holiness, but for Jesus renewal did not imply separation but fidelity to the God of Israel as a God of

---

[56]Borg, *Conflict, Holiness and Politics in the Teachings of Jesus*, 17-20, 51-72, 123-43. Gerd Theissen, *Sociology of Early Palestinian Christianity*, trans. John Bowden (Philadelphia: Fortress Press, 1978), esp. 1, 8-23, 77-95.

compassion. Jesus defined holiness as compassion rather than separation,[57] and his definition was rooted in his personal and prophetic understanding of God. For Jesus, God was compassion, forgiveness, and mercy.

Jesus' understanding of God and holiness was not ahistorical, apolitical, or simply a doctrine of the future. As the destiny of the Ninevites was contingently wrapped up with the preaching of Jonah, so the destiny of Israel was at stake in the competing programs for the renewal of Israel. For Borg then "what faced the hearers of Jesus was not the imminent and inevitable end of the world, but the imminent and yet contingent destruction of Israel."[58] Jesus perceived the quest for a holiness understood as separation and racial purity to be an invitation to disaster for Israel. Jesus' concern was for the imminent crisis facing Israel, for the *history* of Israel, not a consciousness derived from a belief that history was coming to an end.

4. With respect to the course of future events and further manifestations of the sovereignty of God, *we cannot speak precisely about what Jesus in fact expected.* Central to his teaching was that even he did not know exactly what to expect. Jesus expected something to happen shortly. But what? When? Shortly, yes, but exactly when: we do not know the day or the hour. And what was about to happen? Jesus' authentic sayings indicate that these were unanswered questions. Jesus was calling forth faith and trust in God, not answering questions in an apocalyptic debate or eschatological catechism. What is clear in the teaching of Jesus is certainty (Jeremias speaks of the great assurance), but at the same time lack of knowledge about specifics. Jesus was a man of faith whose trust in God was his own starting point in life.

Jesus did not provide specific information about what was to come; he avoided and discouraged any type of seek-

[57]Here I prefer to speak differently than Borg. It is not so much that mercy or compassion is an alternative to holiness (Borg,. 123-43) but a new understanding or definition of holiness. For Jesus, holiness *is* compassion.

[58]Same as n. 53.

ing after signs. Norman Perrin in his early work on the teaching of Jesus maintained that Jesus "gave neither specific form to his future expectation . . . nor did he express it in terms of a specific time element."[59] A.L. Moore has described Jesus' perspective on the End as an undelimited nearness.[60]

Although Jesus did not provide specifics, we can say in general that Jesus expected his ministry, teaching and reputation to be vindicated by God. Jesus believed in the doctrine of the resurrection, and there is no reason to think that he did not expect his own resurrection. Martin Rist has written both that "It is understandable that Jesus evidently entertained a belief in the resurrection of the dead, for this was taught both by the Pharisees and in the synagogue," and also that Jesus "did not stress the resurrection belief."[61] Jesus believed in resurrection, yet it was not central in his preaching.

Jesus did not teach a doctrine of the parousia in the sense of one to come who would establish a new age which would be an end to history as we know it. This follows from what we have said about the lack of specifics in the teaching of Jesus as well as the historical and prophetic consciousness of Jesus. Yet the discussion has caused much debate.[62] The

[59]Perrin, *Rediscovering the Teaching of Jesus*, 204; also 57.

[60]Cf. A.L. Moore, *The Parousia in the New Testament* (Leiden: E.J. Brill, 1966). I do not agree with all of Moore's exposition, such as his interpretation of the Parousia hope in the early Church, but I appreciate his articulation and argument that Jesus did not make specific his expectation with regard to the timing of the Parousia. Within the teaching of Jesus, for Moore, there is only an undelimited nearness, namely, no belief that the End *must* come within a specified period. In other words, Jesus' expectation is open with respect to the End. The Parousia for Jesus is near but not delimited. It is the character of the End to be both near and open. A delay as such is not unexpected because there is no delimited, specifying expectation — other than both the nearness and the graciousness (freedom and grace) of God. Thus it is not within our knowledge to specify how much time remains. That Jesus himself was not clear about what would happen, see James D.G. Dunn, *Unity and Diversity in the New Testament*, 211.

[61]Martin Rist, "Jesus and Eschatology," in *Transitions in Biblical Scholarship*, ed. J.C. Rylaarsdam (Chicago: University of Chicago, 1968), 193-215. The quotes are from 198-99.

[62]See Perrin, *The Kingdom of God in the Teaching of Jesus*, 130-147. Among others, Oscar Cullmann maintained that Jesus did have a Parousia doctrine;

opinion that Jesus taught a parousia doctrine is tied up with the New Testament "son of humanity" sayings in which Jesus spoke about "the son of humanity" coming in power on the clouds of heaven, which "son of humanity" may or may not be identified with Jesus himself (Mk 13:26; 14:62). A common opinion is that "son of humanity" referred to an apocalyptic messianic judge and savior but that Jesus did not identify this figure with himself. In other words, Jesus taught the coming of someone other than himself who would vindicate Jesus as well. But we have rejected this interpretation.

There was no messianic "son of humanity" conception in pre-Christian Judaism. The basis in the life of Jesus for the "son of humanity" sayings was his own particular way of speaking. In the language of Jesus "son of humanity" had no particular apocalyptic nor necessarily messianic content. The most appropriate *Sitz im Leben* for the future "son of humanity" sayings was the eschatology of the Church whose expectations had been heightened and influenced by the resurrection of Jesus and the phenomena accompanying the gift of the Spirit. Thus "son of humanity" was a speech pattern characteristic of Jesus which undoubtedly contained within it his own enigmatic self-understanding but does not provide any basis for arguing that Jesus taught the future coming of some such figure. Jesus taught his own future vindication and resurrection, but we have no basis for saying more.

One cannot say that Jesus was mistaken about the parousia since he did not expect one or teach one.[63] Here is an

among others J.A.T. Robinson maintained that Jesus did not. See Cullmann, "The Return of Christ," in *The Early Church* (London: SCM, 1956), 141-72; Robinson, *Jesus and His Coming* (New York: Abingdon, 1957). Also see Borg, *Conflict, Holiness and Politics in the Teachings of Jesus*, 201-27.

[63]Two insightful responses to this difficulty are those of Jeremias, *New Testament Theology*, 139-41; Schillebeeckx, *Jesus*, 152-54, 542-43. I think Jeremias answers "yes" too quickly, although he qualifies this yes. The second qualification is important in that it reflects respect for the freedom of God, a point emphasized by Schillebeeckx. My impression is that there lies underneath Jeremias the tone that we know more about Jesus' imminent expectation than we in fact do. Schillebeeckx, 152, contains the correct emphasis with respect to the question.

244   *The Compassionate Sage*

instance of scholars being mistaken about the eschatology of Jesus, not Jesus being mistaken about an imminent return. This does not imply that the delay of the Parousia was not a problem in the early Church. It was, but they were the ones who expected something which never came in the form they expected it. Jesus resisted such calculations and lived by faith. Although there is much we do not know about Jesus' own hope for the future, we have an insufficient basis for saying that the climactic event he felt to be close at hand was a coming of an apocalyptic "son of humanity" or his own return.

This does not mean that there is no validity to the question of whether Jesus' expectations were fulfilled or not. We simply do not have enough information about what Jesus expected to determine whether he was mistaken. He expected to die, be raised, and be vindicated. He expected his death to be a source of crisis for his disciples. He preached the presentness and nearness of the power of God. He perhaps anticipated a crisis of disastrous proportions facing the nation. But he taught little about the specifics of what he actually expected except that a new era was in the process of beginning. In fact, the life of Jesus leads us to believe that he was willing to live by faith in this regard, to leave the future to God. Jesus' hope was based on his confidence in God, and he needed no more than that. Jesus was aware of the freedom of God and to have said more would be to curtail God's freedom, whereas it was the freedom and power and sovereignty of God that formed the center of his message, and that God was here for those who had the eyes to see.

5. *(The Reign of) God calls forth joy, hope, expectation, trust, faith, and confidence in God.* The response of the individual who hears the proclamation of Jesus varies. The presence of God fills one with joy; the eschatological banquet is about to begin or has already begun; it is a time for feasting and laughter. The "not yetness," however, calls for a hope grounded in confidence that days of fullness will come. The imminence of a new beginning, a new creation, an eschatological and climactic urgency calls forth more

than hope; it stirs up anticipation, expectation. Yet, although God is here, already present as King, God is present only to the one who has eyes to see or ears to hear. The basis for the continuing establishment of God as sovereign on earth is our trust in God. We can be confident. God reigns where there is faith. God's presence is there in response to faith. Without faith one cannot see (the reign of) God. We cannot say, "Here it is." And the fact that the reign of God is "not of this world" does not mean "another world," a supernatural, transcendental world, although that world is not excluded. God already and eternally reigns "there"; the reign of which Jesus spoke is "on earth" as in heaven. It is not of this world in the sense that it is not like the kingdoms of this world. It is not one kingdom alongside others, or over others. It is established on earth, but not *of* this world. The reign is visible and tangible only to those who trust in God — unlike worldly powers which make their power known and felt in other ways. In his preaching and healing Jesus was a man of faith and a prophet of hope. His starting point in his ministry was the trust in God which he learned in the wilderness. God calls forth faith and trust which in turn awaken one to see more clearly the presence of God.

6. Insofar as Jewish hope and eschatology were concerned with God's salvation which some of the people eagerly awaited in the not too distant future, Jesus' eschatology was by contrast an innovation in that he taught that *the moment of salvation is now.* This "eschatology" of Jesus was not strictly speaking an eschatology; its primary reference was not to the future or to the end of history. Its primary reference was to God. Jesus did have a concern for the future, but what was predominate in the parables is that the present was the important moment in the history of salvation.

Jesus did speak of the future; there is even more to come from God. He saw the critical moments ahead in his own mission, the suffering and rejection to come, as well as critical moments for his disciples, after his death and in the face of false teachers and persecution. Momentous times were ahead. Yet, in all of this, Jesus remained a prophet of hope with confidence in God. It was not the future but the present that was urgent. This present moment in the history of salvation, emphasized in Dodd's realized eschatology which has not been dated even if modified, is the proper focus for understanding the preaching of Jesus. Jesus turns our attention from a gaze toward fulfillment in the future to the challenge to respond in faith and action to God now.

This call for an immediate present response is well exemplified in the parable of the supper from which the invited guests excused themselves. The invitation came; the guests had other things to do; they missed the opportune moment and it was too late. The Matthean version (22:1-14) actually contains two parables, the parable of the marriage feast (22:1-10) and the parable of the wedding garment (22:11-14). Originally these were two separate parables. The Lucan version (14:16-24) contains only the story of the banquet and is probably closer to the original. The version in the Gospel of Thomas (64) may be even closer to the original than Luke's. Both Matthew and Luke use the parable to interpret the Gentile mission of the early Church. Those originally invited to the Messianic feast, the Jews, have been passed over and the invitation is to the Gentiles. In Luke's version the servant goes out three times; the first call is to the original guests, or Jews; the second call is to the poor, probably the poor and the outcasts among the Jews; the third is to those on the highways and outside the city, the Gentiles. The original point of the story, however, is the failure of those to respond when they received the invitation. Now is the moment; tomorrow may be too late.

7. Although the reign of God has already begun (God is already here!) and now is the time to decide on its behalf, God's sovereignty has not been fully established. When it is, *God will reign on earth*. The earth will proclaim that it belongs to God. It has become common for some to contrast prophetic eschatology and apocalyptic eschatology as a contrast between a this-worldly hope and an other-worldly hope. Given the exaggerated influence of apocalyptic thought on Jesus, many have come to think of Jesus as

proclaiming a kingdom "not of this world," an other-worldly kingdom whose day is imminent. This is often associated with Jesus' eschatological teaching about a future and apocalyptic Parousia. These emphases, however, are misplaced.

The contrast between prophetic and apocalyptic expectations concerns not where but the way in which God will be established as King on earth. Apocalyptic thought sees an intervention from above and a new creation or new Jerusalem descend; the prophets see the future as the culmination of history as we know it. The prophets spoke of a new Jerusalem and new creation, but with the sense of their being related to the events of history, not transcending those events. Prophetic eschatology became more nationalistic, more political. But both prophetic and apocalyptic eschatology saw God reigning on earth, however it be accomplished. Judaism, and Jewish eschatology as well, remained primarily this-worldly in its hope.

We have rejected an interpretation of Jesus in thorough-going apocalyptic terms. Jesus taught no apocalyptic "son of humanity" eschatology. The reign of God proclaimed by Jesus was a God whose presence could be felt on earth. Granted the reign proclaimed by Jesus was not *of* or *from* this world (Jn 18:36).[64] It was God's reign, not a worldly kingdom. *It was not like the kingdoms of this world*, but it would still be a kingdom on this earth, God sovereign on this earth. Given the propensity of some of the disciples to misinterpret the reign of which Jesus spoke, Jesus emphasized that it was not a kingdom like the kingdoms of old. When God's reign is established on earth, there will be no positions of false dignity and social status; there will simply be God as King and God's people. Although Luke's version of the Lord's Prayer does not contain Matthew's "Thy will be done on earth as it is in heaven," there is no reason to think that the Matthean version is unfaithful to the teaching

---

[64] The textual basis for Jesus' teaching that God's reign was not of this world is John 18:36. This does not imply, however, not on earth. The Greek *ek* in the text is also properly translated as "from" rather than "of."

of Jesus. The future tense in the authentic beatitudes of
Jesus, as we have seen, implies soon, and here. "Blessed are
you that hunger now, for you shall be satisfied. Blessed are
you that weep now, for you shall laugh" (Lk 6:21). There is
no implication of satisfaction and laughter in some other
world, but rather here and now on earth. Jesus' hope was a
Jewish hope, a prophetic hope, a future hope for this earth.
What he exactly envisioned again we cannot say. How it was
all to happen, he himself did not seem to know. His trust was
in God, and his hope was for the "now" and also the "here."
Jesus proclaimed that God had already begun to reign on
earth and would reign even more fully on earth in the times
ahead.

8. God is already reigning. Now is the time to see this for
those who have eyes to see. Yet what God has in store for his
people surpasses even the present blessings; there is more
still to come. When God's reign is fully established on earth,
God will reign over all the nations. Although Jesus saw his
own mission as particularly a mission to the Jews, and
particularly to the poor in Israel, the reign of God he proclaimed would not exclude the Gentiles. Although his mission was primarily to proclaim this inclusive reign of God to
the Jews, Jesus knew God's reign on earth to be "for the
nations." Israel would lose her special place although not
God's special love for her. God's reign would not be nation
conscious, but humanity conscious. We can see how this
teaching of Jesus, especially this eschatological teaching,
and particularly this teaching about the unrestricted character of God's reign would get him in trouble. Jesus' teaching
cuts away at the doctrine of election itself.

Jesus' Ethical Teaching

Jesus' preaching and teaching were essentially God-talk.
Jesus talked to God in prayer, and in his ministry he talked
about God to others.[65] Yet much of Jesus' God-talk was also

---

[65]I take this expression from the life of Dominic who is reported to have said to
his followers that they should speak "only to God or of God." M.H. Vicaire, *St.*

about us. To talk of his heavenly Father was to talk about us
as well. The reign of God not only implies God's outpouring
of love for the people; it also implies the sovereignty of God
as manifest in our love for God and for neighbor. Another
way of saying this is to say that Jesus' teaching was not only
eschatological, in the sense of centered on God's reign, but
also ethical, centered on love as the sign of God's sovereignty on earth. This "ethics" was no mere transitional
ethics, nor only a utopian ideal; it was an "ethics of discipleship," a way of life for his followers, the way those live who
have been grasped already by (the reign of) God.[66] The
eschatological and ethical content in Jesus' preaching are
not in opposition to each other. The ethical pertains to how
those live and respond who have been touched by the
already manifest power of the eschatological reign of God.
God's reign implies both a future hope and a present way of
living.

We can see within the teaching of Jesus two core elements, however we phrase them: consolation and challenge,
or forgiveness and repentance, or the relativization of the
Law and reverence for the the Law, or mercy and judgment,
or God's love and love of neighbor. Jesus' preaching was
"the good news of the reign of God"; it was a word of
consolation enfleshed in the behavior of Jesus as he shared
fellowship with the outcast. Yet God's coming as a consolation to the people did not revoke his word as a word of
challenge. God's love was both compassionate and demanding. It was both a word of forgiveness and a word which
involved repentance. Preaching repentance was as obvious
a part of the teaching of Jesus as was proclaiming forgiveness (Mk 1:15; Mt 4:17).

Jesus' attitude toward the Law is not easy to discern.
Jesus did not annul or repudiate the Law. Although it is
commonplace to describe Jesus as anti-law (anti-Torah),

Dominic and His Times, trans. Kathleen Pond (New York: McGraw Hill Book
Co., 1964), 331. The expression is contained in the Dominican Constitutions.

[66]Hans Bold, "Eschatological or Theocentric Ethics?" in *The Kingdom of God*,
ed. Bruce Chilton (Philadelphia: Fortress Press, 1984), 133-53.

what Jesus opposed was a false understanding of the Law. Jesus opposed rigidification and trivialization of the Law, the gap that the Law was allowed to create between "strict observance" and the *am ha-aretz*, hypocrisy and self-righteousness. Jesus' hostility to the scribes did not flow from his repudiation of the Law but from his understanding of it, an understanding that was quite compatible with the Judaism of his day if one looks at that Judaism at its best rather than in the light of Christian bias. Much of the anti-Jewish and anti-Pharisaic language of the Gospels flows from a post-resurrection Church uneasy about its realtionship to Judaism and from Jewish-Christian conflict after 70 C.E. as Judaism tried to rebuild itself after the fall of Jerusalem. Thus the question of the attitude of the historical Jesus toward the Law is by no means easy to determine. The early Church had come to the decision that the Mosaic Law was not binding, but this decision was not explicit, or even implicit, in the teaching of Jesus, who observed the Law even if his observance was offensive to some interpretations of it.

There is no clear evidence that Jesus taught an abrogation or invalidity to any of the Jewish laws. If he had, it was with respect to eating forbidden, non-kosher, unclean foods. Matthew gives the impression that this was more a question of triviality of some prescriptions, such as washing before eating (15:17-20). Mark's version is more explicit, stating that Jesus actually declared all foods as clean, edible (7:18-19). But the final sentence of Mark 7:19, "Thus he declared all foods clean," is considered by some a gloss, or the work of the evangelist who was making the meaning clear for the Church. Thus it is variously interpreted.[67] Both the Revised Standard Version and the Jerusalem Bible translate it within parentheses. If these were the words of Jesus himself, it would be the only example we have of Jesus teaching that some prescriptions of the Law were no longer intact. Matthew's version may well reflect better the attitude of Jesus toward the Law, that not all law was of equal importance.

[67]See Vermes, *Jesus the Jew,* 28-29. Also see A.E. Harvey, *Jesus and the Constraints of History* (Philadelphia: Westminster, 1982), 39-40).

In his approach to the Sabbath, as in his approach to the Law as a whole, Jesus *understood* the Sabbath.[68] He went to the heart of what the Sabbath was about, and thus what the Law pertaining to it was about. Jesus' disciples plucked ears of grain on the Sabbath (Mk 2:23-28) and Jesus performed a cure on the Sabbath (Mk 2:1-5). According to Jesus, "the Sabbath was made for the people, not people for the Sabbath" (Mk 2:27). This was not new teaching. Since the time of the Maccabees, "the Sabbath is for the people" was an expression that had been in circulation.[69] The Sabbath in Israel was originally an expression of compassion; it gave rest to slaves and cattle. Later, theology supported the practice in the creation story. But the Sabbath had literally been a gift of God to humankind (Dt 5:12-15; Gn 2:2-3; Ex 20:8-11). The Sabbath visibly expressed the compassion of God. Jesus knew God, and understood Sabbath as a gift from God, not a burden. Schillebeeckx writes, "The sabbath rest is interpreted as a 'time for doing good,' not as an action specially suited to the sabbath."[70] Jesus relativized Sabbath law by understanding Sabbath and its radically humanistic character, how God by decreeing Sabbath showed himself to be for us, and hence how being for others on the Sabbath could in no way be a violation of it.

Jesus was not advocating non-observance of the Sabbath. Rather he called into question the attitude, form of observance, or interpretation which had turned God's gift to us into an unbearable burden. Jesus criticized not the Law but a particular interpretation of the Law. For the essence of the Law was love of God and love of neighbor. Jesus' critique of the Pharisaic interpretation was quite Jewish. Jesus was a Jew upholding the Law, critical of a particular Jewish application of the Law as not being faithful to who God was as One-for-Others.

---

[68]Schillebeeckx's interpretation of Jesus and Law is very much to the point. See *Jesus*, 229-56. For his discussion of sabbath see 237-43. Also see A.E. Harvey, *Jesus and the Constraints of History*, 36-65; and Marcus Borg, *Conflict, Holiness and Politics in the Teachings of Jesus*, 145-62.

[69]Schillebeeckx, *Jesus*, 239.

[70]Ibid., 241.

Jesus was not critical of all Pharisees, nor necessarily of Pharisaism itself. Rather, Jesus was critical of a hypocrisy which he found in the lives of many so-called religious people. Rather than allowing the Law to be God's gift, and God to be grace, they imposed all kinds of burdens and restrictions which prevented people from experiencing God as grace and compassion. Jesus preached rather that (the reign of) God was compassion. Jesus' anger with the scribes was with the burden they imposed and the hypocrisy in their own lives (Lk 11:42-47).

Jesus' conflict with the scribes and lawyers did not place him outside Judaism. His was a very Jewish and prophetic critique. Conflictual interpretations of the Law had been part and parcel of Judaism since the beginning of hellenization in Palestine and the emergence of sectarianism.[71] Jesus did not see himself in his Sabbath observance as going against Judaism. Rather he saw himself going to the heart of Judaism. Jesus did not reject the Law but he did not idolize it either. He went to the heart of the Law which was an expression of the will of God. God's will was always determinative for Jesus and he had an uncanny, intuitive awareness of what God would want or do under certain circumstances.

We can learn more about the positive ethical teaching of Jesus by looking at the "sermon on the mount" (Mt 5-7), which is a major collection of the teaching of Jesus. The material in chapters 5-7 is not a unified sermon of Jesus of Nazareth but is rather a collection by Matthew of diverse Jesus material.[72] The collection does provide us with authentic material although some of the material has its

[71]Schillebeeckx discusses the close relationship between Jesus' interpretation of the Law and the Hellenistic Jewish Diaspora interpretation, which was influential in the formation of early Christian efforts to articulate attitudes toward the Law, *Jesus*, 230-33, 248-49.

[72]The best critical treatment in English of the sermon is W.D. Davies, *The Setting of the Sermon on the Mount* (Cambridge: University Press, 1964); it also contains extensive bibliography. A shorter version was later published under the title of *The Sermon on the Mount* (Cambridge: University Press, 1966). Also see F.W. Beare, *The Gospel According to Matthew* (New York: Harper and Row, 1981), 123-201; Marcus Borg, *Conflict, Holiness and Politics in the Teachings of*

origin in the early Church rather than in the teaching of Jesus or at least has undergone development in the course of its history. Our concern here is not the setting of the material in the early Church, nor in the Gospel of Matthew itself, but rather the setting in the life of Jesus insofar as this is ascertainable. We will focus on some of the Q material in the Matthean sermon.

The Beatitudes. The Q material at the very least consists of the four beatitudes, Matthew 5:3, 5, 6, 11-12 // Luke 6:20-23. As we have discussed, the Lucan form is probably more original.

The Image of Salt. The Q material here is Matthew 5:13; Luke 14:34-35 (also see Mark 9:50). In the original setting, the image of salt may have referred to the disciples, or may have been a reference to Israel. It depicts Jesus' way of speaking with images.

The Law Remains. The Q verse is Matthew 5:18 or Luke 16:17. One can see here the difficulty of determining the actual teaching of Jesus on the Law and of even using the Matthean sermon as a source for the teaching of Jesus. We have seen how careful we had to be in order to determine which beatitudes were actually sayings of Jesus. We can say that Jesus used the image of salt, but it is almost impossible to know to whom it originally referred in the teaching of Jesus. This verse considered by itself raises questions. If we take the Lucan version (16:17), Manson suggests that the saying originally referred not to Jesus' teaching on the Law but to the opinion of the scribes which Jesus in fact condemns: "It is easier for heaven and earth to pass away than for the scribes to give up the smallest bit of that tradition by which they make the Law of no effect."[73] Yet Manson is unconvincing. It appears strange that if Jesus had openly rejected the teaching of the scribes about the continuation of

Jesus, 123-34; David Hill, *The Gospel of Matthew* (Greenwood, S.C.: Attic Press, 1972), 108-55; Joachim Jeremias, *The Sermon on the Mount* (Philadelphia: Fortress Press, 1963); and Hans Kung, *On Being a Christian*, trans. Edward Quinn (Garden City, N.Y.: Doubleday and Co., 1976), 244-77; Jan Lambrecht, *The Sermon on the Mount* (Wilmington, Del.: Michael Glazier, 1985).

[73]T.W. Manson, *Sayings of Jesus,* 135.

the Law, his disciples would have taught precisely the opposite, even granting their difficult situation vis-a-vis Judaism. Yet it is difficult to conclude what Jesus did say precisely.

The three verses from Matthew 5:17-19 are probably three separate sayings which were originally transmitted separately. The authenticity of all three can be challenged. Nevertheless, the Q saying in its Lucan form cannot be as easily dismissed, and one must assume that it reflects the attitude if not the exact words of Jesus. F.W. Beare comments on the Matthean verses:

> The question of authenticity is not of primary importance; whether Jesus stated his position in precisely this form of words or not, the saying is a faithful statement of his fundamental attitude. He holds consistently that the Law was given to Israel by God, and that it retains its validity for him and for those who would follow him. If a man would "enter into life" he must "keep the commandments" (Mt 19:17). Only if the principle is applied in the minute way which is demanded in verses 18 and 19 may we feel that he is misrepresented. And Matthew himself brings a broadly different interpretation of how the "fulfillment" of the Law is accomplished, when he sums up the basic teaching of Jesus in the words of the Golden Rule. "Whatever you wish that men would do to you, do so to them; for this is the law and prophets" (7:12).[74]

Although it can be suggested that there is conflict between such a teaching of Jesus and his openness and authority with respect to the Law, it is most likely that Jesus saw his own behavior and interpretation not as a violation but as the fulfillment of the true meaning of the Law. For Jesus it was not a question of doing away with the Law but of properly understanding it.

The Antitheses. The Q material includes Jesus' teaching on divorce (Mt 5:32 // Lk 16:18), and love of enemies (Mt 5:38-48 // Lk 6:27-36). To interpret the antitheses as an

---

[74]F.W. Beare, *The Gospel According to Matthew*, 142.

attack on the Law or Jesus' teaching as opposed to the Law is to misrepresent them. "The fact is that in none of the Antitheses is there an intention to annul the provisions of the Law but only to carry them out to their ultimate meaning."[75] The antitheses do not oppose Jesus and the Law, but rather reflect Jesus going to the heart of the matter, to the spirit, to the full implications, to the true meaning. The "new teaching" of Jesus shows the extent to which a true follower of the Law must go in order to fulfill it. But this is not "new teaching" as much as Jesus' application and interpretation. What is clear is not so much Jesus' opposition to the Law but his own authority with respect to it.

Within the Q material, such as the teaching on divorce and the command to love one's enemies, it appears as if Jesus was changing the Law. Jesus' teaching on divorce, however, was not an abrogation of the Law but an interpretation of it, and an interpretation compatible within Judaism. Varied interpretations of the divorce command existed within Judaism, among the schools of Hillel and Shammai and the Essenes. The interpretation of the "school of Jesus" could be placed along with theirs.[76] Jesus did abandon the principle of an eye for an eye (Mt 5:39-42; Lk 6:29-30). This, however, was also in order to fulfill the Law as Jesus understood it. A proper understanding of the law of love of neighbor in Leviticus requires the breadth to which Jesus gave to it.

---

[75]W.D. Davies, *The Sermon on the Mount*, 29; *The Setting of the Sermon on the Mount*, 102. Also see D. Daube, *The New Testament and Rabbinic Judaism* (New York: Arno Press, [1965] 1973), 55-62.

[76]For a further discussion of divorce in the New Testament teaching, see Jacques Dupont, *Mariage et divorce dans l'Evangile* (Bruges, Belgium: Abbaye de Saint André, 1959); Joseph A. Fitzmyer, "The Matthean Divorce Texts and Some New Palestinian Evidence," *Theological Studies* 37 (1976), 107-226; Thomas Fleming, "Christ and Divorce," *Theological Studies* 24 (1963), 106-120; Wilfrid Harrington, "The New Testament and Divorce," *Irish Theological Quarterly* 39 (1972), 178-87; Quentin Quesnell, "Made Themselves Eunuchs for the Kingdom of Heaven," *Catholic Biblical Quarterly* 30 (1968), 335-58; Bruce Vawter, "Divorce and the New Testament," *Catholic Biblical Quarterly* 39 (1977), 528-42.

Matthew 5:44-48 and Luke 6:27-36 go to the heart of the
ethical teaching of Jesus and his interpretation of the Law.
The Law can be summarized for Jesus by the word "love."
In fact, the whole Law can be contained in the twofold
command "to love God and neighbor" (Mk 12:28-34; Mt
22:34-40; Lk 10:25-28). Both of these commands can be
found in the Torah (Dt 6:4-5; Lv 19:18), but Jesus interpreted them by showing the extent to which true love of
neighbor leads us; it includes love of enemies as well.[77]

The particular structure of the antitheses is Matthean. In
the Q material, this is not a common element. Thus it is
probably Matthew's style. Likewise the content of many of
the antitheses may be Matthean or from the early Church.
But the Q material has claim to authenticity. Jesus probably
spoke about divorce. References can be found in both Q and
Mark (Mk 10:11-12; Mt 19:9; as well as Lk 16:18 // Mt
5:31-32). Likewise the teaching on love has claim to authenticity. Matthew casts it (5:38-48) in the form of two antitheses; the golden rule comes later in Matthew's sermon
(7:12). The Lucan formulation of the love command (6:27-
36) is probably the more original, however.

> But I say to you that hear, love your enemies, do good to
> those who hate you, bless those who curse you, pray for
> those who abuse you. To those who strike you on the
> cheek, offer the other also; and from those who take away
> your coat do not withhold even your shirt. Give to every
> one who begs from you; and of those who take away your
> goods do not ask for them again. And as you wish that
> people would do to you, do so to them.
>
> If you love those who love you, what credit is that to you?
> For even sinners love those who love them. And if you do
> good to those who do good to you, what credit is that to
> you? For even sinners do the same. And if you lend to

---

[77]I have discussed love in the teaching of Jesus in *The Power of Love* (Chicago:
Thomas More Press, 1979), esp. 125-45, 214-33. See Pheme Perkins. *Love Commands in the New Testament* (New York: Paulist Press, 1982).

those from whom you hope to receive, what credit is that
to you? Even sinners lend to sinners, to receive as much
again. But love your enemies, and do good and lend,
expecting nothing in return; and your reward will be
great, and you will be sons of the Most High; for he is
kind to the ungrateful and the selfish. Be merciful, even as
your Father is merciful. (Lk 6:27-36)

Our neighbors include our enemies as well, who are not to
be excluded from our love, as they are not excluded from
God's love. The teaching was bold, frank and radical. Jesus
saw it as the heart of true religion, like the teaching of the
prophets of old. At its core it was Judaism; it was Jesus'
interpretation of Judaism, of the Law. It is what the Law
ultimately is about.

Jesus' teaching on love of enemies was not in contradic-
tion to the Law. Nowhere does the Law explicitly teach not
to love enemies. Yet at times such seems to have been the
attitude which was encouraged (Ps 129:21f; Dt 7:2). Certainly in the time of Jesus this was reflected in the attitude
toward outcasts and Gentiles in the teaching of the Pharisees. The exhortation to hate one's enemies was explicit in
the Qumran sect, whose teaching was not the Law but an
interpretation present in sectarianism.[78] Jesus interpreted
the Law differently because he understood the intent of the
Law differently. One characteristic of Jesus' teaching, as
pointed out by W.D. Davies, was its radical, uncompromising character. If one contrasts the Q material with the
Matthean material as a whole, Matthew has already set
about the task of adapting the teaching of Jesus to the
ongoing life of the Christian community.

Luke 6:36 (Be compassionate as God is compassionate) is
a concise statement of the relationship between Jesus' eschatology or doctrine of God and Jesus' ethics, is a reflection of
the same teaching which we have seen in the beatitudes (God

[78]See F.W. Beare, *The Gospel According to Matthew*, 161; W.D. Davies, *The Sermon on the Mount*, 81-83, 146-47; David Hill, *The Gospel of Matthew*, 129-30.

belongs to the people), and is a programmatic statement of Jesus' understanding of holiness and the renewal of Judaism.[79] It is a succinct statement of Jesus' ethics.

Chapter six of the sermon contains Jesus' instructions on prayer and the "Our Father" which we have considered previously. Chapter six contains further material from Q —about storing up true treasure (Mt 6:19-21 // Lk 12:33-34); the eye as the lamp of the body (Mt 6:22-23 // Lk 11:34-36); no one can serve both God and money (Mt 6:24 // Lk 16:13); and trust and providence (Mt 6:25-34 // Lk 12:22-32).

Chapter seven likewise contains much material from Q: Do not judge (Mt 7:1-5 // Lk 6:37-42); Ask and you shall receive (Mt 7:7-11 // Lk 11:9-13); the golden rule (Mt 7:12 // Lk 6:31); Enter by the narrow gate (Mt 7:13-14 // Lk 13:24); Beware of false prophets (Mt 7:15-20 // Lk 6:43-45); and the one who hears my words and does them is like someone building their house on rock (Mt 7:21, 24-27 // Lk 6:46-49).

Jesus did not preach or teach the annulment of the Law. He himself went to synagogue on the Sabbath, to Jerusalem for feasts and was present in the Temple. He celebrated Passover and respected the practices of fasting and prayer. He was not an iconoclast. In the one point pertaining to clean/unclean food where he may have taught an abrogation of the Law, there is great doubt concerning the Marcan text. In general, Jesus upheld the Law. The antitheses which make Jesus appear as superior to the Law are Matthean, yet the authority with which Jesus ordinarily spoke of the Law does indicate he saw himself as a valid, authoritative, authorized interpreter. And his interpretation both radicalized uncompromisingly the heart of the Law while at the same time relativizing some prescriptions within it. Not all prescriptions were of the same significance. The heart of the

[79]On the point of compassion as Jesus' program of renewal, see Marcus Borg, *Conflict, Holiness and Politics in the Teachings of Jesus,* 73-143. Also see Monika Hellwig, *Jesus, the Compassion of God* (Wilmington, Del.: Michael Glazier, 1983).

Law which is the basis for interpreting the Law is the compassion of God. This "ethics of discipleship" is best summarized as a love of neighbor which includes love of enemy: Be compassionate.

Jesus' Teaching on Discipleship

Sometimes Jesus' teaching pertained to a larger group or crowd, as is probably the case with the first three Lucan beatitudes (6:20-21). At other times Jesus' teaching was directed at a smaller group, those who regularly followed after him and considered themselves his disciples, as is probably the case in the fourth beatitude (Lk 6:22). Jesus not only taught his disciples, however; he also at times taught them *about being disciples.*

The nature of discipleship in the New Testament is a much discussed question. Jesus' closer followers were learners who acknowledged Jesus as rabbi and teacher, which master-disciple relationship had its precedents within the Judaism of Jesus' time.[80] Yet the call to discipleship carried a unique authority and demand. Jesus' disciples were called to a complete break with previous ties in order to be at the service of (the reign of) God. We cannot assume that all of the disciples were called by Jesus. In contrast to the Synoptic tradition in which Jesus takes the initiative, the tradition underlying John 1:35-49 presents Jesus in a more passive role. The disciples came to Jesus.[81] The earliest circle of disciples seems to have had an egalitarian character as well; they were all disciples of Jesus with no rank existing among them.[82] The disciples were not highly organized; they had the character more of a movement than of a communi-

[80]Benedict Viviano, *Study as Worship*, 158-71.

[81]J. Louis Martyn, *The Gospel of John in Christian History* (New York: Paulist Press, 1978), 93-98, 9-54, esp. 29-42.

[82]Elisabeth Schüssler Fiorenza, "The Biblical Roots for the Discipleship of Equals," *Journal of Pastoral Counselling* 14 (1979), 7-15.

ty.[83] But what is it that Jesus taught this group about following after him?

Following after Jesus was a challenging and demanding reality. It required complete commitment. Among the authentic sayings of Jesus are the following:

> No one who puts their hand to the plow and looks back is fit for the kingdom of God. (Lk 9:62)

> How hard it will be for those who have riches to enter the kingdom of God . . . It is easier for a camel to go through the eye of a needle than for a rich person to enter the kingdom of God. (Mk 10:23,25)

> Leave the dead to bury their own dead. (Lk 9:60a)

> Enter by the narrow gate; for the gate is wide and the way is easy that leads to destruction, and those who enter it are many. For the gate is narrow and the way is hard that leads to life, and those who find it are few. (Mt 8:13-14)

> But many that are first will be last, and the last first. (Mk 10:31)

> For those who exalt themselves will be humbled, and those who humble themselves will be exalted. (Lk 14:11)

These six sayings show the radical character of following after Jesus.

Not only was discipleship challenging, requiring complete commitment, entailing a new way of life in which the ordinary values of the world got reversed, it also entailed the clear possibility of suffering and rejection.[84] Jesus not only

[83]Gerd Theissen, *Sociology of Early Palestinian Christianity*, 8-23; James D.G. Dunn, *Unity and Diversity in the New Testament*, 104-6.

[84]A significant modern treatment of the theme of discipleship is that of Dietrich Bonhoeffer, *The Cost of Discipleship* (New York: The Macmillan Co., [1937] 1963). A literary study of the theme of discipleship in Mark's Gospel is Augustine Stock, *Call to Discipleship* (Wilmington, Delaware: Michael Glazier, 1982).

taught about his own suffering and impending death, but in so doing sought to illuminate his disciples about what was in store for them as well, as we saw in the fourth Lucan beatitude. The disciples could expect to be treated in the same fashion as Jesus himself would be treated.

Another saying from Q is open to application to the hardships of discipleship as well.

> A disciple is not above his teacher, but everyone when he is fully taught will be like his teacher. (Lk 6:40)

Matthean editing applies it later as such:

> If they have called the master of the house Beelzebul, how much more will they malign those of his household. (Mt 10:24-25)

Jesus instructed his disciples to be vigilant and unafraid in the face of opposition (Lk 12:4-12, 22-34).

Not only did disciples gather around Jesus, but Jesus sent some of them forth in order to carry his own mission and ministry further. They were not only learners, they became preachers and healers themselves. In the words of T.W. Manson, "The mission of the disciples is one of the best attested facts in the life of Jesus."[85] There is a mission charge in Q (Lk 10:2-3, 8-16) and also in Mark 6:6-13. Matthew 9:37-10:42 is a composite of material from Mark, Q, and special Matthean material. Luke has two mission charges; the first (9:1-6) is based on Mark, and the second (10:1-16) comprises Q as well as special Lucan material. The commissioning of the disciples and accompanying instruction is thus contained in all the sources of the Synoptic tradition.

Jesus' teaching about discipleship indicates its challenging, demanding character. It required a commitment, readiness, and trust. His followers could expect opposition, rejection, and persecution. Those who were ready were sent

---

[85]T.W. Manson, *The Sayings of Jesus*, 73. See 73-78, 179-84.

forth to proclaim (the nearness of) God. They were able to extend the ministry of Jesus further. However, discipleship was not a burden but a joy, for the disciple had been grasped by (the reign of) God and was already living in the midst of God. Discipleship was a privilege.

> Blessed are the eyes which see what you see! For I tell you that many prophets and kings desired to see what you see, and did not see it, and to hear what you hear, and did not hear it. (Lk 10:23-24)

Jesus' Teaching About Himself

Although Jesus did teach some things about himself, he taught very little that was explicit. It was not a part of "The Teaching." He spoke about his fate, but in some ways this was a development of what he had to say about discipleship.

Although I have distinguished four elements in the teaching of Jesus (eschatology, ethics, discipleship, himself), one can readily see how these are so closely related that they are one. Jesus' eschatological teaching pertained to (the reign of) God. This eschatological reign, however, can so engage us that once entered, the disciple is challenged to live a certain way, in accord with the commandment of love. But this "ethics of discipleship" led to further aspects of discipleship and the fate of disciples who lived in accord with the demands of the heavenly reign. This same fate was something that Jesus taught was in store for himself first. All of these elements are aspects of the reign of God which had begun to take over the earth.

The New Testament implies that Jesus taught four things about his future: that he would suffer, die, be raised from the dead, and return again. We have noted that the last element, his return or future and second coming, is not found in the teaching of Jesus himself. Rather it was formulated within the expectations of the early Church as they were increasingly influenced by apocalyptic motifs and prophecies. The other three elements, however, are all present in the teaching of the historical Jesus. The latter, his resurrection from the dead, was not strongly emphasized, however. As we noted previously, the resurrection was not an overly prominent part in his eschatology. Yet it is still something in which he believed (Mk 12:18-27) and he had this in common with the Pharisees. It was not a universally held belief in Judaism but was part of the later tradition. Jesus acknowledged his faith in the resurrection of the dead, and thus there is little reason to think that he did not look toward his own resurrection.

Jesus did not talk much about himself, and when he did, he spoke primarily of the suffering to come. Yet he had firm faith and hope in his own future vindication by God. How this would be accomplished he did not say. There is reason to believe that he himself did not know. This lack of explicit knowledge was the reason for his faith and trust in God. He felt assured that God would vindicate him even if he did not know precisely how. It was quite natural for him to assume that his vindication would involve resurrection.

Jesus' teaching about himself pertained primarily to his suffering and death. His own prophetic intuition, knowledge of Jewish history, the fate of prophets, and an awareness of the Maccabean martyrs told him he could die a martyr's or prophet's death. The untimely death of John the Baptist touched him personally as well. Jesus was well aware that he and his mission had become a source of conflict and tension.[86]

---

[86]This teaching from Luke is at least partially from Q. There is general consensus that Lk 12:51, 53 are Q. Manson considers the entire passage as Q, although he has some reservations about 12:49-50. Richard A. Edwards includes the passage in his concordance of Q. Lk 12:51-53 has a parallel in Mt 10:34-36. Manson suggests a parallel with Jeremiah as a prophet in similar circumstances. See the *Sayings of Jesus*, 119-21. Manson writes, "The natural shrinking from a terrible necessity, and the vision that the task must be carried out. Along with this goes the sense that the fulfillment of the mission means extreme suffering for Himself" (120). The use of "baptism" has a parallel in Mk 10:38-39 and Mt 20:22. For comment on this text, see Virgil Howard, "Did Jesus Speak About His Own Death?" *Catholic Biblical Quarterly* 39 (1977), 515-27; also Reginald Fuller, *The Mission and Achievement of Jesus* (London: SCM, 1954), 59-62.

> I came to cast fire upon the earth; and would that it were already kindled! I have a baptism to be baptized with; and how I am constrained until it is accomplished! Do you think that I have come to give peace on earth? No, I tell you but rather division: for henceforth in one house there will be five divided, three against two and two against three; they will be divided, father against son and son against father, mother against daughter and daughter against mother, mother-in-law against her daughter-in-law and daughter-in-law against her mother-in-law. (Lk 12:49-53)

Jesus was also aware of the fate of John, previous prophets, and of the hostility of Jerusalem in particular.[87]

> At that very hour some Pharisees came, and said to him, "Get away from here, for Herod wants to kill you." And he said to them, "Go and tell that fox, 'Behold, I cast out demons and perform cures today and tomorrow, and the third day I finish my course. Nevertheless I must go on my way today and tomorrow and the day following; for it cannot be that a prophet should perish away from Jerusalem.' O Jerusalem, Jerusalem, killing the prophets and stoning those who are sent to you! How often would I have gathered your children together as a hen gathers her brood under her wings, and you would not! Behold, your house is forsaken. And I tell you, you will not see me until you say, 'Blessed is he who comes in the name of the Lord!'" (Lk 13:31-35)

Jesus was not "taken by surprise," and there is no reason to suspect that he had not so instructed his disciples.

The most explicit references to Jesus' teaching about his fate are the suffering "son of humanity" sayings.[88] There is

---

[87]Luke 13:34-35 is from Q (Mt 23:37-39). See Manson, *Sayings of Jesus*, 126-28. Another reference to Jesus' acute awareness of impending danger is the parable about the man and his vineyard whose son, sent to retrieve his share of the crop, is killed (Mk 12:1-11 // Mt 21:33-43 // Lk 20:9-18).

[88]Mark 8:31; 9:12; 9:31; 10:33; 10:45; 14:21; 14:41; Luke 22:22; Luke 24:7; Matthew 26:2.

no reason to doubt an authenticity at the basis of these sayings, and it is that core which witnesses to Jesus' teaching about his suffering and death. The sayings reflect post-resurrection elements as well. Their core represents authentic teaching of Jesus, but teaching elaborated after the fact. We find in the sayings different levels of elaboration.

> And he said to them, "Elijah does come first to restore all things; and how is it written of the Son of humanity, that he should suffer many things and be treated with contempt? (Mk 9:12)

> But I tell you that Elijah has already come, and they did not know him, but did to him whatever they pleased. So also the Son of humanity will suffer at their hands. (Mt 17:12)

This is a very general reference on the part of Jesus to his suffering, and particularly to the suffering of rejection. There is no reason to doubt that it is based on the teaching of Jesus.

The following sayings are more specific, however. They teach both a *violent* death and the resurrection.

> For he was teaching his disciples, saying to them, "The Son of humanity will be delivered into the hands of men, and they will kill him; and when he is killed, after three days he will rise." (Mk 9:31 // Mt 17:22-23 // Lk 9:44)

> And he began to teach them that the Son of humanity must suffer many things and be rejected by the elders and the chief priests and the scribes, and be killed, and after three days rise again. (Mk 8:31 // Mt 16:21 // Lk 9:22)

We can note the tendency to provide more information. We gradually begin to note details which reflect the after-the-fact character in some of the sayings.

> Behold, we are going up to Jerusalem; and the Son of humanity will be delivered to the chief priests and the

scribes, and they will condemn him to death, and deliver him to the Gentiles; and they will mock him, and spit upon him, and scourge him, and kill him; and after three days he will arise. (Mk 10:33-34 // Mt 20:18-19 // Lk 18:31-33)

The detail in the second verse (10:34) adds detail not known to Jesus but included by the Church after the fact. Notice similar specifics in Mark 14:21 (Mt 26:24; Lk 22:22) with its reference to Judas' betrayal, or in Luke 24:7 and Matthew 26:2 with reference to death by crucifixion in particular. These do not reflect the teaching of Jesus. It is the core of these sayings that Jesus taught. Manson considers Luke 17:25 as an authentic saying of Jesus which is even more basic than the passion predictions of Mark 8:31, 9:31, and 10:33-34.[89]

But first he must suffer many things and be rejected by this generation. (Lk 17:25)

Jeremias considers the *mashal*, "God will deliver up the man to men" (Mk 9:31a) to be the ancient nucleus underlying the passion predictions.[90] Barnabas Lindars considers as authentic three Aramaic sayings lying underneath the formal passion predictions, namely, "the son of humanity may be delivered up," "the son of humanity goes according to his destiny," and "the son of humanity will give his life for many."[91] Many scholars have called the authenticity of these suffering "son of humanity" sayings into question; others have seen insufficient reason to reject them in their entirety.[92] Some accept Jesus' teaching about his death but

[89]T.W. Manson, *Sayings of Jesus*, 141-43.

[90]Jeremias, *New Testament Theology*, 282.

[91]See Barnabas Lindars, *Jesus Son of Man* (Grand Rapids, Mich.: William B. Eerdmans, 1983), 60-84.

[92]For an acceptance of some authenticity within the suffering sayings, see: Fuller, *Mission and Achievement of Jesus*, 55-58; Morna Hooker, *The Son of Man in Mark* (Montreal: McGill University Press, 1967), 103-47; Jeremias, *Parables of Jesus*, 219-21; *New Testament Theology*, 277-86. Casey, *Son of Man* (London:

not about his resurrection. But Jesus believed in resurrection and there is no reason that his vindication would not involve this. Even reference to resurrection after three days could have been the teaching of Jesus.[93]

Jesus and the Sapiential Tradition

Jesus, prophet and sage, is best understood not only in the context of ancient prophecy but also in the context of the sapiential tradition in ancient Israel and Judaism. From the start we must make a distinction between Jesus as a teacher in history influenced by the wisdom tradition, and what is called a wisdom Christology in the New Testament, namely, an interpretation of the person and mission of Christ in terms of Hebrew wisdom or as an incarnation of a pre-existent Wisdom.[94] Wisdom Christology is not our concern here. Neither his disciples nor Jesus himself saw him as an incarnation of such wisdom. Rather, Jesus as a teacher of wisdom is our concern.

Israel's wisdom tradition is not an easily definable or precise tradition.[95] The history of wisdom (*hokmāh*) varies

SPCK, 1979), 232-37, isolates the predictions because of their extensive secondary development and hence resists classification as either authentic *or* inauthentic. He does consider, however, Mark 9:12, 10:45, and 14:21 as authentic (236), and others do have an authentic saying of Jesus in their background but a background which may have been a fairly general statement about how people will die and rise (232-33). But that may be how Jesus in fact did predict his death (233).

[93]See Jeremias, *New Testament Theology*, 285-6. Also see, H.K. McArthur, "On the Third Day," *New Testament Studies* 18 (1971-72), 81-86.

[94]For further discussion of wisdom Christology itself, see James D.G. Dunn, *Christology in the Making* (Philadelphia: Westminster Press, 1980), 163-209. Also *Aspects of Wisdom in Judaism and Early Christianity*, ed. Robert Wilken (Notre Dame: University of Notre Dame Press, 1975). William A. Beardslee, "The Wisdom Tradition and the Synoptic Gospels," *Journal of the American Academy of Religion* 35 (1967), 231-40.

[95]One of the best collections of essays on this topic is *Studies in Ancient Israelite Wisdom*, selected by James L. Crenshaw (New York: KTAV Publishing House, 1976), 46-60 for ample bibliography. For an introduction to the wisdom tradition, see Walter Brueggemann, *In Man We Trust* (Atlanta; John Knox Press, 1972); Dermot Cox, "Introduction to Sapiential Literature," *Proverbs* (Wilmington, Del.: Michael Glazier, 1982); James L. Crenshaw, *Old Testament Wisdom*

in its post-exilic, pre-exilic, and pre-monarchic phases. One must also distinguish between wisdom itself, the wisdom movement, and the wisdom literature.[96] The literature (Proverbs, Qoheleth, Job, Sirach, and Wisdom of Solomon) is post-exilic and includes a variety of forms of wisdom. The movement, however, has a much longer history, going back through the monarchy, with its own distinctive relationship to the prophetic movement, and possibly to the court and king. Solomon and his court may have given a particular impetus to the cultivation of wisdom in Israel, and yet wisdom itself as a way of thinking and mastering the world had its roots not only in days prior to the monarchy but also outside of Israel itself. Thus wisdom pre-dates even Israel, manifests itself as a distinctive movement or tradition within the history of Israel's monarchy, and becomes a written literature after the exile and after the quenching of the prophetic voice.

Israel's wisdom reflected the international character of wisdom and yet was appropriated and particularized; it was not only wisdom technically speaking, it was "Israelite" wisdom.[97] Yet, of all Israel's traditions, none was more under the influence of the nations, more representative of an international movement, less capable of being studied apart from its Near Eastern counterparts in Babylonia and especially Egypt. However, Israel's wisdom did not just manifest an international flavor; it became more and more integrated

(Atlanta: John Knox Press, 1981); or R.B.Y. Scott, *The Way of Wisdom in the Old Testament* (New York: Macmillan Co., 1971). Specialized treatments include Roland Murphy, "The Interpretation of Old Testament Wisdom Literature," *Interpretation* 23 (1969), 289-301; Gerhard von Rad, *Wisdom in Israel*, trans. James D. Masters (Nashville: Abingdon Press, 1978); J.C. Rylaarsdam, *Revelation in Jewish Wisdom Literature* (Chicago: University of Chicago Press, 1946); R.N. Whybray, *The Intellectual Tradition in the Old Testament* (New York: de Gruyter, 1974).

[96]See especially, J.L. Crenshaw, "Method in Determining Wisdom Influence Upon 'Historical' Literature," *Studies in Ancient Israelite Wisdom*, esp. 482-87.

[97]See J.L. Crenshaw, "Prolegomenon," *Studies in Ancient Israelite Wisdom*, 4-9; R.B.Y. Scott, "Solomon and the Beginnings of Wisdom in Israel," *Studies in Ancient Israelite Wisdom*, 84-101.

with Israel's faith and institutions. Late wisdom shows the influence of Hellenism as well, yet wisdom at this period is also seen as God's gift manifested in the Torah.

Both the literature and the tradition manifest different kinds of wisdom: from the knowledge of nature to a popular, practical, proverbial understanding of life; from folk wisdom to the monarchy's juridical, political, pragmatic conduct of affairs of state; from the wisdom of family and court to a more reflective, speculative, academic, intellectual, and even critical or skeptical wisdom; from a purely secular to profoundly religious and even theological wisdom; from home-taught wisdom to the wisdom of the "schools," or a scribal wisdom, a wisdom of the sage.[98] Most wisdom tended to be, however, experiential and existential in character.

A much disputed question is whether "the wise" in Israel's history ever formed something like a recognizable or distinct social group. Whybray has argued that there is no proof for "the existence of any class of persons in Israel whose specific designation was the wise men; or any profession which was distinguished from others by the name *ḥokma*.[99] Although kings maintained a body of advisors and administrators during the time of the monarchy, as a social or professional group they were not identified as the *ḥâkāmîm*. Nor were teachers as a profession so identified. Even evidence for the existence of schools with professional teachers is conclusive only for later post-exilic times. Likewise there is no evidence for a class of writers to whom the

---

[98]On different kinds of Wisdom, see Dermot Cox, *Proverbs*, 30-57; J.L. Crenshaw, "Prolegomenon," 3-5, "Method in Determining Wisdom Influence Upon 'Historical' Literature," *Studies in Ancient Israelite Wisdom*, 482-84; George Fohrer, "Sophia," *Kittel's Theological Dictionary of the New Testament*, vii (Grand Rapids: Wm. B. Eerdmans, 1971), esp. 480-83; Berend Gemser, "The Spiritual Structure of Biblical Aphoristic Wisdom," *Studies in Ancient Israelite Wisdom*, 208-19; Robert Gordis, "Quotations in Wisdom Literature," *Studies in Ancient Israelite Wisdom*, esp. 220-22; von Rad, *Wisdom in Israel*, 3-150, 287-319. Also see Whybray, *The Intellectual Tradition in the Old Testament*.

[99]R.N. Whybray, 13. Crenshaw, however, does speak of the wise as being a professional class. See *Old Testament Wisdom*, 28-42.

expression "the wise" would refer, although there were "scribes" with varying functions throughout Israel's history.[100]

Although the wisdom tradition does not lead one to identify a particular social or professional class, like priests and kings, there were nevertheless "intellectuals" and an "intellectual tradition." The sage was an identifiable person and sages were distinguishable from the prophets, although less identifiable as a group and less institutionalized than the priests and kings. The prophets and sages are distinguishable, but not categorically so. Isaiah and also Amos have been suggested as prophets who exemplify the tradition of wisdom. And although prophecy and its classical expression had ceased, the book of Job manifests a new prophetic spirit in its critical wisdom.[101] The authority of both came from God (Jer 8:8-9; Ex 7:7-26). Yet prophecy and wisdom were distinguishable gifts in Israel's history, and the prophet and sage distinguishable persons.

Prophecy was frequently critical of the political wisdom of the court (Is 31:1-3; Jer 8:8-9). In a classic example, Jeremiah was the enemy of the priest, the sage, and the other prophets. Each had, to some degree, their own sphere of authority.[102]

> Then they said, "Come, let us make plots against Jeremiah, for the law shall not perish from the priest, nor

---

[100]Whybray, 15-54.

[101]For further consideration of the relation between wisdom and prophecy, see Hengel, *The Charismatic Leader*, 47-48. Amos and Isaiah have been studied from the viewpoint of wisdom. Johannes Fichtner, "Isaiah among the Wise," *Studies in Ancient Israelite Wisdom*, 429-438. Samuel Terrien, "Amos and Wisdom," *Studies in Ancient Israelite Wisdom*, 448-455.

[102]Whybray, 24-31, is hesitant to read too much into the text of Jeremiah 18:18. Yet we must maintain a balance between seeing "the wise" as a specific, identifiable, professional class and seeing them as not at all distinguishable. The reality probably lies between; the term has a referent obviously, but not necessarily to a particular class. Likewise we must keep in mind that the referent changes and perhaps dramatically at different periods in Israel's history. In Jeremiah 18:18 and elsewhere Jeremiah is critical of the prophets as well. Thus there is a difference between prophets and prophets, as there are between sage and sage. Cf. Alexander Di Lella, "Conservative and Progressive Theology: Sirach and Wisdom," *Studies in Ancient Israelite Wisdom*, 401-16.

counsel from the wise, nor the word from the prophet.
Come, let us smite him with the tongue, and let us not
heed any of his words." (Jer 18:18)

So there did exist in Israel's history a sapiential or intellectual tradition alongside the prophetic and priestly traditions. All of these traditions were highly affected by the
leap from monarchy to post-exilic Judaism. Wisdom was
characterized by its own way of handing on the tradition,
of instructing the young, educating court advisors, teaching the people, or raising critical questions about the tradition. Like the prophet, the sage could be an establishment
voice or a critical, "prophetic" voice. Not all the prophets
or companies of prophets were prophetic voices in the
sense that Amos, Hosea, Isaiah, and Micah had been. So
likewise the sage could represent the status quo, or political
shrewdness, or reform and the development of tradition.

To what degree was Jesus influenced by this wisdom
tradition? To what degree was he representative of it? A
significant aspect of the ministry of Jesus was his teaching.
He was a prophetic preacher, charismatic healer and exorcist. He was also a teacher, and as a teacher he was concerned with instruction. His teaching had authority and it
was validated by his deeds. In what sense then can we say
that this teacher was a "teacher of wisdom"?

It is well recognized today that the forms within which
Jesus taught were wisdom forms, such as the beatitude, the
parable, the proverb. We have distinguished most of Jesus'
teaching according to form into parables and sayings. The
sayings often have a proverbial character. In that sense the
teachings of Jesus consist primarily of parables and proverbs, the language and teaching forms of Israel's sages.

James Robinson has pointed out that the term *proverb* is
the term used to describe sayings within the wisdom tradition.[103] Sometimes the wisdom literature itself refers to its

[103] James M. Robinson, "Logoi Sophōn: On the Gattung of Q," *Trajectories Through Early Christianity*, ed. Robinson and Koester (Philadelphia: Fortress Press, 1971), 71-113, esp. 103-13.

proverbs as "sayings of the wise" (Eccl 12:11; Prv 22:17). In fact, the literary genre of a "sayings collection" was associated with the sages, the *sophoi,* the *ḥākāmîm.* Is it only coincidence then that the earliest teachings of Jesus have come to us from his disciples as a sayings collection, something of a book of proverbs, of wisdom, of instruction, both eschatological and ethical in character? Robinson suggests that the literary genre to which Q belongs is that of *logoi sophōn,* "sayings of sages," or "words of the wise."[104] Thus it appears that the very form in which Jesus taught would have associated him with the wisdom tradition, an eschatological teacher of truth, wisdom, righteousness.

In our efforts to understand Jesus as one of Judaism's sages, we still have no better guide than the discussion by Bultmann about Jesus as a teacher of wisdom in his *History of the Synoptic Tradition.*[105] Bultmann divides the sayings of Jesus in the Synoptics into three main groups according to the content: wisdom sayings, prophetic sayings, and legal sayings. The first of these three groups concerns us here. Bultmann includes sixty-nine sayings from the Synoptic material in his discussion of the wisdom logia. Using his own critical principles, he concludes that sixteen of these can be ascribed to Jesus.[106] Although some may argue for other sayings as being genuine, we can at least accept Bultmann's suggestion as a minimum. These sayings are Mark 3:24-6; 3:27; 7:15; 8:35; 10:15; 10:23b; 10:25; 10:31; Luke 9:60a; 9:62; 14:11; 16:15; Matthew 5:39b; 5:44-48; 7:13-14; 22:14.

To observe the similarity in form between the teaching of Jesus and the proverbial wisdom of the Hebrew Scriptures, we can contrast the character of Jesus' teaching through exhortation (Lk 9:60a; Mt 7:13-14) and exhortations in the

---

[104]Ibid., 71-75, 103-13.

[105]Rudolf Bultmann, *The History of the Synoptic Tradition,* trans. John Marsh (Oxford: Basil Blackwell, 1963), 69-108.

[106]Ibid., 105. These constitute Perrin's list of proverbial sayings, *Jesus and the Language,* 41. For Perrin's discussion of these sayings, see 48-54. Also see W.A. Beardslee, "Uses of the Proverb in the Synoptic Gospels," *Interpretation* 24 (1970), 61-76.

Hebrew Scriptures (e.g. Prv 1:8; 3:11), which exhortations are in the imperative. Or we can contrast Jesus' teaching using the declarative form (Mk 3:24-26; 7:15; Lk 9:62; 14:11; Mt 22:14 — twelve of Bultmann's sixteen sayings are declarative) and declarations in the Hebrew Scriptures (Sirach 6:15; 13:1; 28:17; Prv 3:13; 15:16; 15:17). Although the history of the tradition usually combined originally separate sayings (such as the three sayings of Mk 8:34-37), or added a new saying to one already in circulation (contrast Mk 9:43-47 with Mt 5:29-30), or changed a saying for some linguistic or dogmatic motive, we still have genuine material which reflects proverbial wisdom. It is even possible that Jesus took a popular proverb and used it for his own purposes. The proverbs and parables of Jesus represent his most genuine teaching. Sayings which come from the period of the early Church simply fit into the teaching style of Jesus himself.

Jesus' wisdom was not only proverbial, it was expressed in a concrete, experiential, figurative, imaginative language. The language of the parables is also the language of wisdom. The general principle in Matthew 5:39-41 is amplified by concrete examples, and we notice this same concreteness in Matthew 5:44-48. This concreteness may sometimes even be hyperbole (Mt 5:39-41). The teaching of Jesus contains paradox (Mk 8:35; 10:25; Lk 9:60a). Jesus' parables (and the parable was a form of instruction developed in the wisdom tradition) contain images, metaphors, and examples.

We ought also mention Jesus' sense of humor or appreciation of the comical.[107] Laughter was to be one of the characteristics of life in the reign of God. Jesus seems to have enjoyed himself — think of the times he is found at a party or someone's house for dinner, or a number of parables which use a wedding celebration as the setting or point of comparison. Heaven is like a feast.

---

[107]For a valuable discussion of the humor of Jesus, see Jakob Jonsson, *Humour and Irony in the New Testament* (Reykjavik: Bokautgafa Menningarsjods, 1965), esp. 90-199 on the Synoptics and on Jesus.

The first thing the father thought of doing for his returning son was throw a feast, almost as if that is what Jesus
would have thought of doing. He must have been a joy to be
with and fun to have around. He could be the utterly serious
prophet of the wilderness but also the master of the art of
teaching with wit.

Think of the "types" of whom Jesus spoke, for example
the Pharisee and publican at prayer (Lk 18:9-14). There is
humor in the story of the "widow who makes life intolerable
for the judge" (Lk 18:1-8). We see not only his love of the
concrete and the use of hyperbole but also his appreciation
of the comic and incongruous as we try to picture the man
with a beam in his eye (Mt 7:3 // Lk 6:41), or people coming
to see an aristocrat in royal dress in the desert (Mt 11:7-8), or
the foolish virgins (Mt 25:1-12).

Jesus even described himself as a groom, and a groom at a
wedding feast or on the wedding night is hardly somber or
serious. Jesus was not "like a mourner at a wedding feast."[108]
His sense of joy could not be contained; now is no time to
fast. His sense of the comic enabled him to teach by using
the ordinary situations of life and making a point from
them. His prayer and ministry were complemented by a
sense of humor which often served an educational purpose.
People enjoyed Jesus' company, and remembered his
stories.

Jesus' teaching and preaching exemplify both prophetic
and sapiential forms and content. Jesus was both preacher
and teacher, both prophet and sage. He respected both
traditions of Israel. We noted early, as we began our discussion of Jesus as a teacher, that there need be no conflict
between being both prophet and teacher. We also noticed in
the traditions the difficulty of clearly delineating prophecy
and wisdom at every point. So in Jesus we see a prophet who
has taken to himself much from the tradition of the wise.
There is nothing incompatible about the blend. "Jesus as a
'teacher' using so-called 'wisdom' forms, and Jesus as an
'eschatological charismatic' or 'messianic' prophet, are in no

[108]Ibid., 144.

sense contraries; the reverse is true: each conditions the other, the unheard-of, revolutionary content of Jesus' message sought the stamp and polish of an established form."[109] Given the challenging and critical character of both prophecy and later wisdom, both are suited to Jesus' charismatic ministry to Judaism. The beginning of wisdom is the fear of the Lord, and the mission of the prophet is the word of the Lord: the Lord was and remained the starting point for Jesus in his prayer, preaching, healing and teaching.

At the same time that we speak about the influence of Israel's wisdom tradition on Jesus and of Jesus as a teacher of wisdom, we must be careful not to subsume him simply under a category. As a prophet Jesus was a late prophet, yet not like the latter day apocalypticists, more like the prophets of old, though not simply a repeat of Isaiah or Jeremiah. Jesus was an individual, a messenger of God who combined in his own way or defined in his own way what it was for him to be a prophet. He was not just "one of the prophets." So likewise with respect to the varied and developing wisdom tradition. Jesus was not just a teacher or sage like others. He individualized wisdom and exemplified it in his own personal way. Thus he was not simply "a teacher of wisdom" as a teacher who may have been associated with a school, nor "one of the scribes" affiliated with the Pharisees, nor yet one of the rabbis, in the sense that the word would have before long in Judaism, nor an apocalyptic seer who relied upon visions and whose authority was associated with one of Israel's ancestors. In the end Jesus was Jesus. Wisdom like prophecy helps us to understand Jesus, but even here he remains enigmatic. For many he was simply "The Teacher," but a prophetic and itinerant teacher. Jesus was known for his wisdom as much as for his mighty deeds.

> And when Jesus had finished these parables, he went away from there, and coming to his own country he taught them in their synagogue, so that they were aston-

---

[109] Hengel, *The Charismatic Leader and His Followers*, 48.

ished, and said, "Where did this man get this wisdom and
these mighty works?" (Mt 13:53-54)

At Caesarea Philippi, when Jesus asked how people perceived him the disciples responded with the fact that Jesus
was seen as a prophet (Mk 8:27-33). The Gospels reflect,
however, that Jesus was also seen in the tradition of Solo-
monic wisdom. Whether historically accurate or not,
Solomon had long been associated with Israel's wisdom
tradition as its chief exemplification.[110]

> And God gave Solomon wisdom and understanding
> beyond measure, and largeness of mind like the sand on
> the seashore, so that Solomon's wisdom surpassed the
> wisdom of all the people of the east, and all the wisdom
> of Egypt. For he was wiser than all other men, wiser
> than Ethan the Ezrahite, and Heman, Calcol, and
> Darda, the sons of Mahol; and his fame was in all the
> nations round about. He also uttered three thousand
> proverbs; and his songs were a thousand and five. He
> spoke of trees, from the cedar that is in Lebanon to the
> hyssop that grows out of the the wall; he spoke also of
> beasts, and of birds, and of reptiles, and of fish. And
> men came from all peoples to hear the wisdom of
> Solomon, and from all the kings of the earth, who had
> heard of his wisdom. (1 Kings 4:29-34)

Yet the assessment of Jesus was that he was not only
greater than the prophets; he was also greater than
Solomon. He was seen by way of contrast to both traditions. Jesus is pictured in the New Testament as greater
than Jonah, greater than Elijah, and even greater than
Moses. Depending upon how one interprets this greater,
there is reason to believe that Jesus may himself have held

[110]See James Crenshaw, *Old Testament Wisdom*, 42-65; R.B.Y. Scott,
"Solomon and the Beginnings of Wisdom in Israel," *Studies in Ancient Israelite
Wisdom*, 84-101.

this view. He may have referred to himself as greater than Jonah. And he spoke with an authority equal to that of Moses in giving the Law. Jesus is also pictured as greater than Solomon.

> The men of Nineveh will arise at the judgment with this generation and condemn it; for they repented at the preaching of Jonah, and behold, something greater than Jonah is here. The queen of the South will arise at the judgment with this generation and condemn it; for she came from the ends of the earth to hear the wisdom of Solomon, and behold, something greater than Solomon is here. (Mt 12:38-42 // Lk 11:29-32)

The understanding of Jesus in the light of the tradition of the wisdom of Solomon is early and shows, if not Jesus' self-understanding, certainly the impression he made on others. Not only was Jesus seen as being like the prophets, but also like *the* sage, Solomon himself. Jesus, the prophet, was also a compassionate sage, the Teacher from Galilee.

8

God Belongs to the People

The inseparability of God and the people is central to an understanding of who Jesus was and what he was about. Underlying Jesus' preaching was his very own experience of God. With a prophetic and sapiential Spirit, Jesus defined the character of true religion and proclaimed his understanding of the God of his ancestors. God is not only YHWH, the One Who Is, but *'immānû'ēl*, the One Who is With Us. What is at stake in the mission and ministry of Jesus is our very definition, image, and understanding of God.

Orthopraxis was also central to who Jesus was and who his disciples were. What is at stake here is the possibility of making Jesus' God incarnate in our world by letting God's love take on flesh. Thus a theology of Jesus underlines the importance both of human reality and orthopraxis, the gospel way of life. Religion is for human beings, and followers of the God of Jesus must witness to the praxis of this in their lives. Edward Schillebeeckx writes; "Jesus' message is passed on only where his life-praxis is followed . . . Jesus made what he spoke about a direct and practical reality in the way he turned toward others. He did not, for example, say to Zacchaeus, 'God loves you,' . . . On the contrary, he went home with him and by praxis made God's love for Zacchaeus a living reality."[1]

The time has come for us to pull together our picture of the mission and ministry of the earthly Jesus. There are some things about which we can be more certain than others, and some things which are more suggestive than definitive. Yet a picture does emerge.

Jesus was a Galilean Jew. The roots of his spirituality and mission lay more amid Mosaic and wilderness motifs than amid Davidic and messianic ones. In the beginning of his ministry, he was associated with John, although his movement became less ascetical, less focused on baptism, less sectarian than John's. Jesus was a prophet in a period of Jewish history when prophecy was no longer prevalent, a prophet somewhat like John and not unlike the prophets of old, radically God-conscious and socially conscious.

The starting point for understanding Jesus was God, his darling *Abba*. Although one cannot historiographically document the following statement, one of the more accurate things to be said about Jesus is that he struggled to love his God with his whole heart, his whole soul, and all his strength: a true and practicing Jew of the *Shema* who had gone to the heart of the *Torah* which ever served as a guide for his life and a source of strength. God was like a father and mother, an *abba* and *imma* to him, and he may have experienced God in this personal fashion and learned to pray in this provocative way during an ordeal in the wilderness, although when and where can only be suggested, not verified.

If the starting point for understanding Jesus is God, as was true of the prophets of old, so likewise is it faith. Perhaps nothing more foundational can be said. He lived by faith and trust in a God whom he personally knew as the one who was with him. He did not seek after signs and wonders;

---

[1]Edward Schillebeeckx, "The Right of Every Christian to Speak in the Light of Evangelical Experience 'In the Midst of Brothers and Sisters,'" in *Preaching and the Non-Ordained*, ed. Nadine Foley (Collegeville, Minn.: The Liturgical Press, 1983), 34.

he did not put God to the test. The foundation of his preaching (and it would seem as if he saw preaching as his primary ministry and responsibility, Mark 1:38) was (the reign of) God.

Jesus was a man of God, a prophet, God's son. But he was also a man for others. Prayer and ministry were like inhaling and exhaling for him. One can not ask the question which was more important. His social conscience was part and parcel of his prophetic consciousness. Messianism was not his concern (he may have seen it as a diabolical distraction for his people!), nor the latter day apocalypticism (which did have a negative effect on a generation that longed to live more for signs than by faith). He healed, but did not seek notoriety for his healings; God's power and compassion simply came out of him.

For Jesus was as much as anything a prophet of compassion, compassionate as *Abba/Imma* was compassionate. If God was the foundation of Jesus' prophetic preaching, God's compassion was the foundation of his experientially based wisdom and teaching. God belongs to the people; God is for the people; God is the one who is with the people. And it is in accord with such an awareness and conviction that Jesus attempted to conform his own life: the compassionate one. This was the hallmark of his vision and his hope for Israel.

Jesus' "eschatology" was not so much a preoccupation with the end times as it was a preoccupation with his times and a preoccupation with his God. His "ethics" was not so much a new Law as it was an understanding of the Law as a gift of his faithful, compassionate, and generous God to the people of Israel. Love of God and love of neighbor, including enemies, were the whole of the Law.

Jesus was not self-preoccupied, and his message had very little to say about himself. His image of God and his interpretations of the Law created opposition as well as gathered crowds and more consciously committed disciples. But Jesus at least gradually anticipated the danger that lay in store for himself, as well as a crisis that lay ahead for his people. How he loved his people! His heart went out to them. Yet their salvation did not lie in separation from the unclean or in racial purity. It lay with being compassionate, in an imitation of *Abba/Imma.*

Jesus was open to Gentile as well as to Jew, to Samaritans, to women, to wealthy and traitorous tax collectors, to the poor, the hungry, the leprous, the Roman, the outcast without social status, to Pharisee as well as the unobservant and uneducated. Where there was faith, he could bring healing. If there was no hope, he would preach God. Where there was goodness and love, he would push his people one step further and teach them from out of the depths of a deeper Source.

Jesus belonged to the people. And he did so because he belonged to God. The only sign he gave us was the sign of Jonah, a sign of the compassion of our God.

Suggested Readings

The following is neither an exhaustive bibliography nor a list of sources cited, but rather what it says — a list of suggestions for further reading, combining some introductory and some specialized works. Additional bibliography on particular questions can readily be found in the notes, and most of the works cited in the notes as well as the references below contain ample bibliography themselves.

I have subdivided this list of readings into five categories which at times overlap, but consider the subdivisions still to be of more help than one lengthy alphabetical listing. All of the references in the fourth division on the teaching of Jesus could have been included in the third division on Jesus research, but I have chosen to separate them. I ordinarily refrain from listing a reference more than once. Within each category, I list the entries alphabetically, but for a particular author I list them chronologically. At times I have included annotations that may be of further help.

I. Geography, History, Literature, and Theology of Ancient Israel and Judah

Ackroyd, Peter R. *Exile and Restoration, a Study of Hebrew Thought of the Sixth Century B.C.* Philadelphia: Westminster Press, 1968.

Aharoni, Yohanan, and Michael Avi-Yonah. *The Macmillan Bible Atlas*. New York: Macmillan Co., 1968.

Anderson, Bernhard. *Understanding the Old Testament*. Third Edition. Englewood Cliffs, N.J.: Prentice Hall, Inc., 1975. An excellent introductory work.

Anderson, Francis, and David Noel Freedman. *Hosea*. The Anchor Bible, Vol. 24. Garden City, N.Y.: Doubleday and Co., 1980.

Anderson, G.W., editor. *Tradition and Interpretation, Essays by Members of the Society for Old Testament Study*. Oxford: Clarendon Press, 1979. A collection of essays by distinguished scholars covering the current state of Old Testament studies.

Baly, Denis. *The Geography of the Bible*. New and Revised Edition. New York: Harper and Row, 1974. A complete revision of the 1957 edition.

Bright, John. *A History of Israel*. Third Edition. Philadelphia: Westminster Press, 1981. The best single history of Israel and Judah during the Old Testament period.

_____ *Jeremiah*. The Anchor Bible, vol. 21. Garden City, N.Y.: Doubleday and Co., 1965.

Brueggemann, Walter. *In Man We Trust*. Atlanta: John Knox Press, 1972. Contains keen insights into the sapiential tradition.

_____ *The Prophetic Imagination*. Philadelphia: Fortress Press, 1978.

Childs, Brevard S. *Introduction to the Old Testament as Scripture*. Philadelphia: Fortress Press, 1979. One of many introductions to the Old Testament. Its contribution is a respect for the canonical and scriptural character of the Bible as religious literature as well as for the need for critical research. Manifests the desire of some to move to a "post-critical era" in biblical research.

Crenshaw, James L. *Old Testament Wisdom*. Atlanta: John Knox Press, 1981. An introduction by a scholar recognized as one of the most competent in the field of Old Testament wisdom.

——————, editor. *Studies in Ancient Israelite Wisdom*. New York: KTAV Pub., 1976. The best single collection of essays by distinguished scholars on the topic of wisdom literature.

Eichrodt, Walter. *Theology of the Old Testament*. Trans. J.A. Baker. The Old Testament Library, 2 vols. Philadelphia: Westminster Press, 1961-67.

Grollenberg, Luc H. *Atlas of the Bible*. New York: Thomas Nelson and Sons, 1957.

Hayes, John H., and J. Maxwell Miller, editors. *Israelite and Judaean History*. Philadelphia: Westminster Press, 1977.

Heschel, Abraham. *The Prophets*. New York: Harper and Row, 1962. Reprint (2 vols.). New York: Harper Torchbooks, 1971.

Kaiser, Otto. *Isaiah 1-12*. Second edition. Old Testament Library. Philadelphia: Westminster Press, 1983. And *Isaiah 13-19*. Westminster Press, 1974.

Knight, Douglas A., and Gene M. Tucker, editors. *The Hebrew Bible and Its Modern Interpreters*. Philadelphia: Fortress Press, and Chico, Calif.: Scholars Press, 1985. A collection of excellent essays by fifteen distinguished scholars covering the field of Hebrew Bible studies. The first volume in the triology, The Bible and Its Modern Interpreters. Initiated by the Society of Biblical Literature, the essays are reviews of the current state of scholarship in the varied subdisciplines.

May, Herbert G., editor. *Oxford Bible Atlas*. Second edition. New York: Oxford University Press, 1974.

Murphy-O'Connor, Jerome. *The Holy Land, An Archaeological Guide from Earliest Times to 1700*. New York: Oxford University Press, 1980. The best currently available scholarly guide for Jerusalem and the Holy Land. A revised edition to appear soon.

Noth, Martin. *The History of Israel.* Trans. Stanley Godman. New York: Harper and Brothers, 1958.

von Rad, Gerhard. *Old Testament Theology.* Trans. D.M. G. Stalker. 2 vols. New York: Harper and Row, 1962-1965.

──────────. *The Message of the Prophets.* Trans. D.M.G. Stalker. New York: Harper and Row, 1968. A revised version of material from the second volume of *Old Testament Theology.*

──────────. *Wisdom in Israel.* Trans. James D. Martin. Nashville: Abingdon Press, 1978.

Rylaarsdam, C. *Revelation in Jewish Wisdom Literature.* Chicago: University of Chicago Press, 1946.

Scott, R.B.Y. *The Relevance of the Prophets.* Revised Edition. New York: Macmillan Co., 1971.

──────────. *The Way of Wisdom in the Old Testament.* New York: Macmillan Co., 1971.

Spriggs, D.G. *Two Old Testament Theologies.* Studies in Biblical Theology, second series. Naperville, Ill.: A.R. Allenson, 1974.

Whybray, R.N. *The Intellectual Tradition in the Old Testament.* New York: de Gruyter, 1974.

Wright, G.E., and F.W. Filson, editors. *The Westminster Historical Atlas to the Bible.* Philadelphia: Westminster Press, 1956.

II. Early Judaism and Christian Origins

Barr, James. "Jewish Apocalyptic in Recent Scholarly Study." *Bulletin of the John Rylands Library* 58 (1975): 9-35.

Becker, Joachim. *Messianic Expectation in the Old Testament*. Trans. David E. Green. Philadelphia: Fortress Press, 1980.

Charles, Robert Henry. *Eschatology, The Doctrine of a Future Life in Israel, Judaism and Christianity*. New York: Schocken Books, 1970. First published in 1899, with a second edition in 1913 which has been reprinted. Charles has been a noted master of Jewish apocalyptic literature. Given developments in this field as well as the discoveries in the Judean Desert since Charles' death, the work is now dated in particular areas, yet still an excellent introduction to the study of Jewish eschatology, especially as it pertains to the teaching on resurrection and future life.

Collins, John J. "Towards the Morphology of a Genre." *Semeia* 14 (1979): 1-20. A study of apocalyptic.

_____ *The Apocalyptic Imagination: An Introduction to the Jewish Matrix of Christianity*. New York: Crossroad, 1984.

Derrett, J. Duncan M. *Jesus' Audience, the Social and Psychological Environment in Which He Worked*. London: Darton, Longman and Todd, 1973. An introductory work with an excellent annotated bibliography.

Fitzmyer, J.A. "The Languages of Palestine in the First Century A.D." *Catholic Biblical Quarterly* 32 (1970): 501-31. Reprinted in *A Wandering Aramean, Collected Aramaic Essays*, 29-56. Missoula, Montana: Scholars Press, 1979.

Foerster, Werner. *From the Exile to Christ — A Historical Introduction to Palestinian Judaism*. Philadelphia: Fortress Press, 1964.

Freyne, Sean. *The World of the New Testament*. The New Testament Message. Wilmington, Del.: Michael Glazier, 1980. A good introductory survey.

_____ *Galilee from Alexander the Great to Hadrian, 323 B.C.E. to 135 C.E., a Study of Second Temple Judaism*. Wilmington, Del. and Notre Dame, Ind.: Michael Glazier and University of Notre Dame, co-publishers, 1980. A more advanced and specialized study, significant because there is less available in the area of Galilean studies.

Grant, Frederick C. *The Economic Background of the Gospels.* London: Oxford University Press, 1926.

_____. *Ancient Judaism and the New Testament.* New York: Macmillan Co., 1959.

Grant, Michael. *Herod the Great.* London: Weidenfield and Nicholson, 1971.

Hanson, Paul D. *The Dawn of Apocalyptic.* Phildelphia: Fortress Press, 1979. A consideration of the historical and sociological roots of apocalypticism.

Hengel, Martin. *Judaism and Hellenism, Studies in their Encounter in Palestine during the Early Hellenistic Period.* Trans. John Bowden. 2 vols. Philadelphia: Fortress Press, 1974. A detailed study of the hellenization of Judaism.

_____. *Jews, Greeks and Barbarians.* Trans. John Bowden. Philadelphia: Fortress Press, 1980. An introductory and more recent study of the hellenization of pre-Christian Judaism by an expert in the field.

Hoehner, Harold W. *Herod Antipas.* Cambridge: University Press, 1972.

Jeremias, Joachim. *Jerusalem in the Time of Jesus, An Investigation into Economic and Social Conditions during the New Testament Period.* Trans. F.H. and C.H. Cane. London: SCM Press, 1969. Recognized as an authoritative study of the socio-economic situation in Jerusalem.

Jones, Arnold H.M. *The Herods of Judaea.* Oxford: Clarendon Press, 1938.

Josephus, Flavius. *Complete Works.* Trans. William Whiston. New Edition. Grand Rapids: Kregel Publications, 1960. One of the major historical sources for Early Judaism. Flavius Josephus was born in Judea c. 37-38 C.E. His first major work, completed c. 80 C.E., *The Wars of the Jews,* covers the Maccabean period, Herod the Great, Archelaus, the Roman procurators, and the great revolt of 66-70 C.E. His second major work, *The Antiquities of the Jews*, completed c. 93 C.E., gives an account of Jewish history until 66 C.E.

Kraft, Robert A., and George W.E. Nickelsburg, editors. *Early Judaism and Its Modern Interpreters.* Philadelphia: Fortress Press, and Chico, Calif.: Scholars Press, forthcoming. A significant collection of excellent essays covering the field of Early Judaism. The second volume in the trilogy, The Bible and Its Modern Interpreters. Initiated by the Society of Biblical Literature.

McNamara, Martin. *Targum and Testament, Aramaic Paraphrases of the Hebrew Bible: A Light on the New Testament.* Shannon, Ireland: Irish University Press, 1972.

_____. *Intertestamental Literature.* Old Testament Message, vol. 23. Wilmington, Del.: Michael Glazier, Inc., 1983. A good introduction with a helpful annotated bibliography.

_____. *Palestinian Judaism and the New Testament.* Wilmington, Del.: Michael Glazier, 1983. An excellent introductory study.

Miller, Merrill P. "Targum, Midrash, and the Use of the Old Testament in the New Testament." *Journal for the Study of Judaism* 2 (1971): 29-82.

Moore, George Foot. *Judaism in the First Centuries of the Christian Era, The Age of the Tannaim.* 2 vols. New York: Schocken Books, (1927) 1971. Still one of the better studies on Judaism.

Mowinckel, Sigmund. *He That Cometh, The Messiah Concept in the Old Testament and Later Judaism.* Trans. G.W. Anderson. Nashville: Abingdon Press, 1954. Perhaps the best single volume on the development of the messiah concept.

Neusner, Jacob. *From Politics to Piety, the Emergence of Pharisaic Judaism.* Englewood Cliffs, N.J.: Prentice-Hall, 1973.

_____. *First Century Judaism in Crisis.* Nashville: Abingdon Press, 1975. The story of Rabbi Johanan ben Zakkai and Jamnia.

Nickelsburg, George W.E. *Jewish Literature Between the Bible and the Mishnah.* Philadelphia: Fortress Press, 1981. Excellent introduction to intertestamental or post-biblical Jewish literature.

Perowne, Stewart. *The Life and Times of Herod the Great.* Nashville: Abingdon Press, 1959.

Plöger, Otto. *Theocracy and Eschatology.* Trans. S. Rudman. Richmond: John Knox Press, 1968.

Rowley, H.H. *The Relevance of Apocalyptic.* New York: Harper and Row, 1955.

Russell, David Syme. *The Method and Message of Jewish Apocalyptic, 200 B.C. - A.D. 100.* Philadelphia: Westminster Press, 1964.

_____. *Between the Testaments.* Revised Edition. Philadelphia: Fortress Press, 1965.

_____. *Apocalyptic, Ancient and Modern.* Philadelphia: Fortress Press, 1978.

Sandmel, Samuel. *Herod, Profile of a Tyrant.* New York: J.B. Lippincott, 1967.

_____. *Judaism and Christian Beginnings.* New York: Oxford University Press, 1978.

Schurer, Emil. *The History of the Jewish People in the Age of Jesus Christ, (175 B.C. - A.D. 135).* 2 vols. A new English version revised and edited by Geza Vermes, Fergus Millar, Matthew Black, and Pamela Vermes. Edinburgh: T. and T. Clark, 1973-1979. A monumental resource for the history and institutions of Early Judaism. *A History of the Jewish People in the Time of Jesus*, ed. Nahum Glatzer (New York: Schocken Books, 1961) is an abridged edition of vol. 1 of Schurer's work, based on an earlier edition.

Sherwin-White, A.N. *Roman Society and Roman Law in the New Testament*. Oxford: Clarendon Press, 1963.

Tarn, W.W. *Hellenistic Civilization*. Third Edition. New York: The New American Library (1952) 1975. Provides an historical outline in chapter one and a consideration of the relationship between Hellenism and the Jews in chapter six.

Tcherikover, Victor. *Hellenistic Civilization and the Jews*. Trans. S. Applebaum. Philadelphia: The Jewish Publication Society of America, 1959.

de Vaux, Roland. *Ancient Israel*. 2 vols. New York: McGraw Hill, 1961. Remains a significant source for the study of the social and religious institutions of Israel.

Vermes, Geza, *The Dead Sea Scrolls, Qumran in Perspective*. Cleveland: World Pub. Co., 1978. A highly recommended introduction by a recognized Jewish scholar.

Viviano, Benedict T. *Study as Worship, Aboth and the New Testament*. Leiden: E.J. Brill, 1978.

Wilkinson, John. *Jerusalem as Jesus Knew It, Archaeology as Evidence*. London: Thames and Hudson, 1978.

Yadin, Yigael. *Masada, Herod's Fortress and the Zealots' Last Stand*. Trans. Moshe Pearlman. New York: Random House, 1966. An excellent study of how archaeology works.

III. Jesus Research and New Testament Studies

Aulen, Gustaf. *Jesus in Contemporary Historical Research*. Trans. Ingalill H. Hjelm. Philadelphia: Fortress Press, 1976.

Ben-Chorin, Shalom. "The Image of Jesus in Modern Judaism." Trans. Arlene Swidler. *Journal of Ecumenical Studies* 11 (1974): 401-30. An excellent and thorough survey of Jesus research within Jewish studies through 1974.

Borsch, Frederick Houk. *The Son of Man in Myth and History.* New Testament Library. London: SCM Press, 1967. See note 23, chapter six.

Buber, Martin. *Two Types of Faith.* Trans. Norman P. Goldhawk. New York: Harper and Row, 1951. An interpretation of Jesus by a great modern interpreter of Judaism.

Bultmann, Rudolf. *The History of the Synoptic Tradition.* Revised Edition. Trans. John Marsh. New York: Harper and Row, (1921/1958) 1963.

_____. "New Testament and Mythology." *In Kerygma and Myth, A Theological Debate*, ed. Hans Werner Bartsch, rev. trans. Reginald Fuller, 1-44. New York: Harper and Row, (1941/1953) 1961. Bultmann's initial statement on demythologizing.

_____. *Jesus Christ and Mythology.* New York: Charles Scribner's Sons, 1958. A later discussion of demythologizing. Lectures given in 1951 in the United States.

_____. "The Primitive Christian Kerygma and the Historical Jesus." In *The Historical Jesus and the Kerygmatic Christ*, ed. and trans. C.E. Braaten and R.A. Harrisville, 15-42. Nashville: Abingdon Press, (1960, 1962) 1964. A definitive statement of Bultmann's position on the relationship between the historical Jesus and the Christ of faith.

Casey, Maurice. *Son of Man, the Interpretation and Influence of Daniel 7.* London: SPCK, 1979. Highly recommended as a discussion of the non-apocalyptic, Aramaic character of the "son of humanity" expression.

Collins, Raymond F. *Introduction to the New Testament.* Garden City, N.Y.: Doubleday and Co., 1983. An excellent, recent introduction, which gives attention to critical exegesis as well as some specifically Catholic questions. Contains a significant bibliography.

Conzelmann, Hans. *Jesus.* Trans. J. Raymond Lord. Ed. John Reumann. Philadelphia: Fortress Press, 1973. A translation of the classic article, "Jesus Christus," from *Die Religion in Geschichte und Gegenwart.*

Cullman, Oscar. *The Christology of the New Testament.* Revised Edition. Trans. Shirley C. Guthrie and Charles A. M. Hall. Philadelphia: Westminster Press, 1963. A pioneering and still significant study.

Davies, W.D., and D. Daube, editors. *The Background of the New Testament and Its Eschatology.* Cambridge: University Press, 1956.

Daube, David. *The New Testament and Rabbinic Judaism.* New York: Arno Press, (1956) 1973.

Dibelius, Martin. *Jesus.* Trans. C.B. Hedrick and F.C. Grant. Philadelphia: Westminster, 1949.

Dodd, C.H. "Jesus as Teacher and Prophet," in *Mysterium Christi*, eds. G.K.A. Bell and D. Adolf Deissmann, 53-66. London: Longmans, Green and Co., 1970.

_____ *The Founder of Christianity.* New York: Macmillan Co., 1970. Dodd still provides balanced and perceptive insights.

Dunn, James D.G. *Christology in the Making, A New Testament Inquiry into the Origins of the Doctrine of the Incarnation.* Philadelphia: Westminster Press, 1980. For a brief summary of the history of the quest for Jesus' self-understanding, see 22-26. For a qualification on Jeremias' research on Jesus' use of *abba*, see 26-29.

Dupont, Jacques. *Les tentations de Jésus au désert.* Studia Neotestamentica 4. Bruges: Desclee de Brouwer, 1968.

Edwards, Richard A. *A Theology of Q: Eschatology, Prophecy, and Wisdom.* Philadelphia: Fortress Press, 1976.

Epp, Eldon Jay, and George W. MacRae. *The New Testament and Its Modern Interpreters*. Philadelphia: Fortress Press, and Chico, Calif.: Scholars Press, forthcoming. A collection of essays covering the field of New Testament Studies. The third volume in the trilogy, The Bible and Its Modern Interpreters. Initiated by the Society of Biblical Literature.

Fitzmyer, Joseph. *A Christological Catechism, New Testament Answers*. New York: Paulist Press, 1981.

——————. *An Introductory Bibliography for the Study of Scripture*. Revised edition. Rome: Biblical Institute Press, 1981.

Flusser, David. *Jesus*. Trans. Ronald Walls. New York: Herder and Herder, 1969.

Fuchs, Ernst. "The Quest of the Historical Jesus." In his *Studies of the Historical Jesus*. Trans. A. Scobie, 11-31. London: SCM, 1964.

Fuller, Reginald. *The Mission and Achievement of Jesus*. Studies in Biblical Theology, 12. London: SCM, 1954.

——————. *The Foundations of New Testament Christology*. New York: Charles Scribner's Sons, 1965. A very readable exposition of the issues involved in New Testament Christology.

Gerhardsson, Birger. *The Testing of God's Son: An Analysis of an Early Christian Midrash*. Trans. John Toy Lund. Sweden: CWK Gleerup, 1966.

Hahn, Ferdinand. *The Titles of Jesus in Christology, Their History in Early Christianity*. Trans. Harold Knight and George Ogg. London: Lutterworth Press, 1969. A post-Bultmannian exposition.

Hengel, Martin. *The Charismatic Leader and His Followers*. Trans. James Greig. New York: Crossroad, 1981.

——————. *The Son of God*. Trans. John Bowden. Philadelphia: Fortress Press, 1976.

294   *Suggested Readings*

Higgins, A.J.B. *The Son of Man in the Teaching of Jesus.* London: Cambridge University Press, 1980. Part one contains a good summary of recent discussion. See note 24, chapter six.

Hooker, Morna. *The Son of Man in Mark.* Montreal: McGill University Press, 1967.

Hull, John M. *Hellenistic Magic and the Synoptic Tradition.* Naperville, Ill.: Alec R. Allenson, 1974. A good survey of the relationship between Jesus, the Gospels,and the magical traditions.

Kahler, Martin. *The So-Called Historical Jesus and the Historic Biblical Christ.* Trans. and ed. Carl Braaten. Philadelphia: Fortress Press, (1896) 1964.

Kasemann, Ernst. "The Problem of the Historical Jesus."In his *Essays on New Testament Themes*, trans. W.J. Montague, 15-47. London: SCM, 1964.

Leivestad, Ragnar. "Exit the Apocalyptic Son of Man." *New Testament Studies 18 (1971-72): 243-67.* A succinct statement of the perspective that "son of humanity" is not an apocalyptic title.

Lindars, Barnabas. "Re-enter the Apocalyptic Son of Man." *New Testament Studies* 22 (1975): 52-72.

_____ *Jesus Son of Man, a Fresh Examination of the Son of Man Sayings in the Gospels in the Light of Recent Research.* Grand Rapids, Mich.: William B. Eerdmans Pub. Co., 1983. See note 28, chapter six.

Mauser, Ulrich W. *Christ in the Wilderness.* London: SCM Press, 1936.

Nolan, Albert. *Jesus Before Christianity.* Maryknoll: Orbis Press, 1978.

Reumann, John. *Jesus in the Church's Gospels.* Philadelphia: Fortress Press, 1968.

Robinson, James. *A New Quest of the Historical Jesus.* London: SCM, 1968. A clear statement of the issues and principles involved in the twentieth century quest.

Sandmel, Samuel. *A Jewish Understanding of the New Testament.* Cincinnati: Hebrew Union College Press, 1957.

Schillebeeckx, Edward. *Jesus, An Experiment in Christology.* Trans. Hubert Hoskins. New York: Seabury, 1979. A monumental survey and creative interpretation of New Testament scholarship. Also see his *Christ, The Experience of Jesus as Lord,* trans. John Bowden (New York: Seabury, 1980), 826-32, for a discussion on the process of identifying Jesus.

Schottroff, Willy, and Wolfgang Stegeman, editors. *God of the Lowly: Socio-Historical Interpretation of the Bible.* Trans. M.J. O'Connell. Maryknoll, N.Y.: Orbis Books, 1984.

Schweitzer, Albert. *The Quest of the Historical Jesus.* Trans. W. Montgomery, with a preface by F.C. Burkitt. New York: Macmillan Co., (1906) 1961. The classic survey of the nineteenth century quest along with Schweitzer's conclusions following upon the survey. A turning point in Life of Jesus research.

Segundo, Juan Luis. *The Historical Jesus of the Synoptics.* Trans. John Drury. Maryknoll, N.Y.: Orbis Books, 1985.

Smith, Morton. *Jesus the Magician.* New York: Harper and Row, 1978.

Strauss, David Friedrich. *The Life of Jesus Critically Examined.* Trans. George Eliot, and ed. P.C. Hodgson. Lives of Jesus Series. Philadelphia: Fortress Press, (1835) 1972.

Taylor, Vincent. *The Names of Jesus.* New York: St. Martin's Press, 1953.

Theissen, Gerd. *Sociology of Early Palestinian Christianity.* Trans. John Bowden. Philadelphia: Fortress Press, 1978.

Earliest Christianity, the Jesus movement, is best understood as a renewal movement within Judaism that was distinct from the renewal programs of the Essenes, Pharisees, and the resistance movement.

Thompson, William M. *The Jesus Debate, A Survey and Synthesis.* New York: Paulist Press, 1985.

Tidball, Derek. *The Social Context of the New Testament, A Sociological Analysis.* Grand Rapids, Mich.: Zondervan Pub., 1984.

Tödt, H.E. *The Son of Man in the Synoptic Tradition.* Trans. Dorothea Barton. Philadelphia: Westminster Press, 1965. See note 21, chapter six.

Vermes, Geza. "The Use of *Bar Nāsh/Bar Nāsha* in Jewish Aramaic." In *Post-Biblical Jewish Studies,* 147-65. Leiden: E.J. Brill, 1975. First published as an appendix to Matthew Black's *Aramaic Approach to the Gospels and Acts,* Third edition, 310-30. Oxford: Clarendon Press, 1967. A significant step in the new direction of interpretation of the "son of humanity."

_____. *Jesus the Jew, A Historian's Reading of the Gospels.* Philadelphia: Fortress Press, 1973. A valuable Jewish contribution to the study of Jesus.

Weiss, Johannes. *Jesus' Proclamation of the Kingdom of God.* Trans. R.H. Hiers and D.L. Holland. Lives of Jesus Series. Philadelphia: Fortress Press, (1892) 1971.

Wink, Walter. *John the Baptist in the Gospel Tradition.* Cambridge: University Press, 1968.

Wrede, William. *The Messianic Secret.* Trans. J. Greig. Greenwood, S.C.: Attic Press, (1901) 1971.

IV. The Teaching of Jesus

Boff, Leonardo. *The Lord's Prayer, The Prayer of Integral Liberation.* Trans. Theodore Morrow. New York: Orbis Books, 1983.

Borg, Marcus J. *Conflict, Holiness and Politics in the Teachings of Jesus.* New York: Edwin Mellen Press, 1984. Conflict is the context for understanding the teaching of Jesus, a conflict precipitated by Jesus' opposition to Israel's quest for holiness and the substitution of an alternative program for the renewal of Judaism based on mercy.

Boucher, Madeleine. *The Mysterious Parable: A Literary Study.* Washington, D.C.: Catholic Biblical Association of America, 1977.

_____. *The Parables.* New Testament Message, 7. Wilmington, Del.: Michael Glazier, 1981. An introductory exposition.

Breech, James. *The Silence of Jesus, the Authentic Voice of the Historical Man.* Philadelphia: Fortress Press, 1983.

Brown, Raymond. "The Pater Noster as an Eschatological Prayer." In *New Testament Essays*, 217-253. Milwaukee: Bruce Publishing Co., 1965.

Bultmann, Rudolf. *Jesus and the Word.* Trans. Louise Pettibone Smith and Erminie Huntress Lantero. New York: Charles Scribner's Sons, (1926/1934) 1958. Bultmann's interpretation of the teaching of Jesus in historical context.

Chilton, Bruce D. *A Galilean Rabbi and his Bible, Jesus' Use of the Intrepreted Scripture of his Time.* Wilmington, Del.: Michael Glazier, 1984. Even more important than rabbinic Judaism or sectarian and pseudepigraphical writings for understanding the early Judaism as well as teaching and preaching of Jesus is that of targum research.

Crossan, John Dominic. *In Parables: The Challenge of the Historical Jesus.* New York: Harper and Row, 1973.

_____. *In Fragments: The Aphorisms of Jesus*. New York: Harper and Row, 1984.

Dalman, Gustaf. *The Words of Jesus*. Edinburgh: T. and T. Clark, 1902.

Davies, W.D. *The Setting of the Sermon on the Mount*. Cambridge: University Press, 1964. Also available in an abridged form as *The Sermon on the Mount*, Cambridge University Press, 1966.

Dodd, C.H. *The Parables of the Kingdom*. Revised edition. New York: Charles Scribner's Sons, (1935) 1961. A pioneering work in parable research.

Funk, Robert W. *Language, Hermeneutic, and Word of God*. New York: Harper and Row, 1966.

Jeremias, Joachim. *The Parables of Jesus*. Revised edition. Trans. S.H. Hooke. New York: Charles Scribner's Sons, 1963. A starting point for contemporary parable research, available in an abridged version as *Rediscovering the Parables* (New York: Charles Scribner's Sons, 1966).

_____. *The Prayers of Jesus*. Studies in Biblical Theology, Second Series, 6. Naperville, Ill.: Alec R. Allenson, 1967.

_____. *New Testament Theology, The Proclamation of Jesus*. Trans. John Bowden. New York: Charles Scribner's Sons, 1971. A very balanced approach to the teaching of Jesus by a consummate scholar.

Jewett, Robert. *Jesus Against the Rapture, Seven Unexpected Prophecies*. Philadelphia: Westminster Press, 1979. The authentic teaching of Jesus is a contrast to apocalypticism, old and new.

Lambrecht, Jan. *Once More Astonished, The Parables of Jesus*. New York: Crossroad, 1981.

La Verdiere, Eugene. *When We Pray, Meditation on the Lord's Prayer.* Notre Dame: Ave Marie Press, 1983. Both exegetical and meditative.

Linnemann, Eta. *Jesus of the Parables.* Trans. John Sturdy. New York: Harper and Row, 1966. Published in England under the title *The Parables of Jesus.*

Lohmeyer, Ernst. *Our Father, an Introduction to the Lord's Prayer.* Trans. John Bowden. New York: Harper and Row, 1965.

Manson, T.W. *The Sayings of Jesus.* Grand Rapids, Mich.: William B. Eerdmans Publishing Co., 1979. First published as Part 2 of *The Mission and Message of Jesus,* 1937, and then re-issued as a separate volume, 1949.

Montefiore, Claude G. *Some Elements of the Religious Teaching of Jesus.* London: Macmillan and Co., 1910. A reconstruction of Jesus' teaching by an eminent Jewish theologian representative of liberal Judaism.

Perkins, Pheme. *Love Commands in the New Testament.* New York: Paulist Press, 1982.

Perrin, Norman. *The Kingdom of God in the Teaching of Jesus.* London: SCM, 1963. An excellent and concise survey of the modern discussion.

—————— *Rediscovering the Teaching of Jesus.* New York: Harper and Row, 1967. Contains an excellent annotated bibiography, 209-15.

—————— *Jesus and the Language of the Kingdom.* Philadelphia: Fortress Press, 1976. The best available summary of the history of modern parable interpretation. Also helpful for its annotated bibliography, 209-15.

Petuchowski, Jakob J., and Michael Brocke, editors. *The Lord's Prayer and Jewish Liturgy.* New York: Seabury Press, 1978.

Rist, Martin. "Jesus and Eschatology." In *Transitions in Biblical Scholarship,* ed. J.C. Rylaarsdam, 193-215. Chicago: University of Chicago Press, 1968.

Robinson, John A.T. *Jesus and His Coming.* Nashville: Abingdon, 1957.

Via, Dan Otto, Jr. *The Parables: Their Literary and Existential Dimensions.* Philadelphia: Fortress Press, 1967.

Wilder, Amos N. *Early Christian Rhetoric, The Language of the Gospel.* Cambridge, Mass: Harvard University Press, 1971. A literary study of the parable.

V. On the Dialogue between Judaism and Christianity, as Pertinent to Jesus Research

Ben-Chorin, Shalom. See entry above under *Jesus Research and New Testament Studies.*

Borowitz, Eugene B. *Contemporary Christologies, A Jewish Response.* New York: Paulist Press, 1980.

Cargas, Harry James, editor. *When God and Man Failed, Non-Jewish Views of the Holocaust.* New York: Macmillan Pub. Co., 1981. A significant anthology of non-Jewish Holocaust literature, containing a valuable bibliography.

Hagner, Donald A. *The Jewish Reclamation of Jesus, an Analysis and Critique of Modern Jewish Study of Jesus.* Grand Rapids, Mich.: Zondervan Pub. House, 1984.

McGarry, Michael B. *Christology after Auschwitz.* New York: Paulist Press, 1977. A survey of formal church statements and theological opinions by a Catholic theologian.

Mussner, Franz. *Tractate on the Jews, The Significance of Judaism for Christian Faith.* Trans. Leonard Swindler. Philadelphia: Fortress Press, 1984. A challenging Catholic theological reflection on Judaism.

Pawlikowski. John T. *Christ in the Light of the Christian-Jewish Dialogue.* Studies on Judaism and Christianity. New York: Paulist Press, 1982.

Sandmel, Samuel. *We Jews and Jesus.* New York: Oxford University Press, (1965) 1973. A Jewish author who has made many contributions to the study of Judaism and Christianity.

Thoma, Clemens. *A Christian Theology of Judaism.* Trans. Helga Crones. Studies in Judaism and Christianity. New York: Paulist Press, 1980. Another important contemporary Catholic theology of Judaism.

Index of Selected Topics

Index of Authors

Index of Biblical Citations